YOUR TRAVELLING COMPANION

ETOWAH VALLEY GOLF CLUB • HENDERSONVILLE, NC ▲

Golf
Vacations
1993-94 Northeast Edition

(FROM THE PUBLISHERS

BOB & KATHY THORPE

Welcome to the 93/94 Golf Vacations" Directory - NorthEast Edition !

From its first publication as a sixty page appendix at the back of one of our earlier "Ontario Golf Courses" Directory, the Golf Vacations Directory has grown larger than we had ever thought possible. It has grown so large in fact, that it has become two editions . . . a NorthEast edition for summertime golf holidays and a SouthEast (and Islands) edition for wintertime destinations . . . due out later this year. Some of the mid-eastern U.S. states (swing states) are active in promoting golf (and golf packages) year round and could very well be in both editions.

We have been fortunate to visit many of the facilities highlighted in this book and have met key people in accommodations, golf courses, Departments of Tourism, Convention & Visitors Bureaus, Golf Promotion Associations, etc. all of whom are most anxious to have you visit and experience the golf holidays and hospitality of their areas.

So many excellent, enticing courses . . . so little time to play!

Our writer, Jeff Rosenplot (not a golfer) has spent countless hours researching material we gathered in our travels and we hope that you enjoy reading his text which threads its way through the book outlining history, places of interest, and side trips that could make your next golfing holiday even more meaningful for you and your friends / family.

Thank you for purchasing this edition, please "mention Golf Connections when contacting our advertisers" and drive carefully on the highways and . . . on the course.

Bob & Kathy Thorpe

ENJOY GOLF PACKAGES FROM $155* IN COLONIAL WILLIAMSBURG.

For as little as $155*per day, you can enjoy another century <u>and</u> take on the challenge of our award winning championship golf courses.

The Golden Horseshoe Gold Course has been selected as one of the top thirty resort courses by Golf Digest. The par 3's here are "Best in the South" according to Southern Links.

The new Golden Horseshoe Green Course has been named one of the five best new resort courses. All of which has helped Colonial Williamsburg win three Gold

Medals from Golf magazine.

Each package includes:
- **Accomodations**
- **Breakfast and dinner daily.**
- **Golf for the length of your stay.**
- **Golf cart for two, 18 holes daily.**
- **Unlimited practice balls each day.**
- **Golf clinic (for eight or more persons).**
- **Unlimited tennis for length of stay.**
- **Meal gratuities.**

For a free brochure detailing our current golf packages and our two championship courses, just call us at 1-800-HISTORY.

Colonial Williamsburg

* Per golfer, per day, double occupancy, 2 night minimum. Does not include state or local taxes. Offer expires June 30, 1993.

RIVER RUN GOLF CLUB • BERLIN, MARYLAND ▲

▼ EAGLES LANDING GOLF COURSE • OCEAN CITY, MARYLAND

TALAMORE GOLF COURSE • PINEHURST, NORTH CAROLINA ▲

▼ THE GAUNTLET GOLF & COUNTRY CLUB • SOUTHPORT NORTH CAROLINA

HENRY HORTON STATE PARK GOLF COURSE • CHAPEL HILL, TENNESSEE ▲

▼ HYLAND HILLS GOLF CLUB • SOUTHERN PINES, NORTH CAROLINA

HERITAGE HILLS GOLF RESORT • YORK COUNTY, PENNSYLVANIA ▲

▼ QUAIL HOLLOW RESORT • CONCORD, OHIO

FORD'S COLONY COUNTRY CLUB • WILLIAMSBURG, VIRGINIA ▲

▼ COLONIAL WILLIAMSBURG GOLDEN HORSESHOE G.C. • WILLIAMSBURG, VIRGINIA

LIONHEAD
THE MOST 'PRIVATE' PUBLIC
GOLF FACILITY IN CANADA

DEERHURST HIGHLANDS • HUNTSVILLE, ONTARIO ▲

▼ THE ROCK • DRUMMOND ISLAND, MICHIGAN

BRISTOL HARBOUR GOLF CLUB • CANANDAIGUA, NEW YORK ▲

▼ TICONDEROGA COUNTRY CLUB • LAKE PLACID, NEW YORK

LE CHATEAU MONTEBELLO GOLF COURSE • MONTEBELLO, QUEBEC ▲

▼ GOLF BROMONT • BROMONT, QUEBEC

RUSTICO RESORT GOLF & COUNTRY CLUB • SOUTH RUSTICO, PRINCE EDWARD ISLAND ▲

▼ WHITE POINT BEACH LODGE & COUNTRY CLUB • WHITE POINT BEACH, NOVA SCOTIA

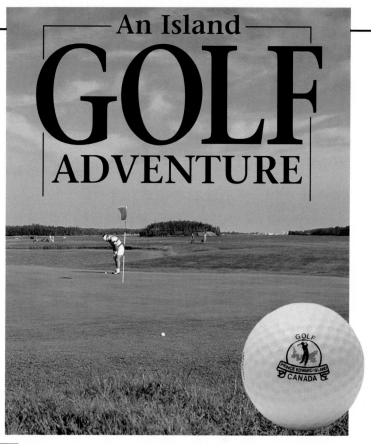

An Island
GOLF
ADVENTURE

The adventure begins when you arrive... maybe it's the gently rolling landscape and the clean fresh ocean air or a feeling of pure relaxation... whatever it is, when you get on the course you'll soon realize that we take our Golf very seriously. And we've been serious about it since 1906. Through beautiful tree-lined fairways and along side the ocean our 11 courses offer a special adventure and some great challenges. Each course is unique and each will have you wishing you had more time to stay with us.

For complete details on your golf adventure on Prince Edward Island call for our free 1993 Golf Directory...

TOLL FREE SERVICE • 1-800-463-4PEI(4734) *Operator #74*

GOLF Prince Edward Island
P.O. Box 2653, Charlottetown
Prince Edward Island, Canada
C1A 8C3

New Brunswick, Canada

DREAM GREENS

New Friends. *New Values. New Adventures.*
New Brunswick

TABLE OF CONTENTS

PUBLISHERS
Bob & Kathy Thorpe

MANAGING EDITOR
Jeff Rosenplot

ASSISTANT EDITOR
Darlene Benny

CREATIVE ARTIST
Janet Thorpe

PRESIDENT
Robert Thorpe

VP SALES & ADVERTISING
Kathy Thorpe

SR. ACCOUNT EXECUTIVE
Mary Lou Totty

ACCOUNT EXECUTIVES
Mike Ellis   Craig Russell
Lillian Stone

RESEARCH
Judy Pauker Michelle Semeniuk

CIRCULATION
Patricia Thorpe

Copyright GOLF CONNECTIONS
3455 Harvester Rd. Unit #2, Burlington, Ontario L7N 3P2
Tel: (416) 333-0019 • Fax: (416) 333-6883

© Canada: 393149 © USA: TX2686456

GOLF ETIQUETTE GUIDE

The main intent of any golf holiday is to relax and enjoy not only the challenge of various golf courses but to savour the beautiful surroundings.

Although you have paid for the privilege to play, it is still good to remember that you are a guest of the course and should abide by any rules established by each facility. Some facilities have rules that are a little more lax than at others.

Nonetheless we have listed some basic guidelines that will help you to enjoy your day on the course even more. Don't leave home without them. . .

• Every player should have (or should rent) a set of golf clubs

• No more than four players in any group

• Alcoholic beverages should not be taken on the course

• Always remember the three R's . .
Replace divots / Repair ball marks / Rake sand traps after use

• Never start anywhere except No. 1 tee, unless instructed to do otherwise by the pro shop or starter

• Slow play is a definite no-no. Always make an effort to keep up to the group in front of you, or let faster players through. A normal 18 hole round of golf should take no more than 4-1/2 hours (even on holiday)

• Singles and twosomes should expect to be joined with others particularly during peak times

• Only two riders and two golf bags are normally permitted on power carts. Juniors should not be permitted to operate the power cart.

• Power carts should be kept at least thirty feet from the greens and tees and on cart paths whenever possible

• Power carts/pull carts should be returned to the clubhouse or pro shop after use.

• The rules of golf are governed by the United States Golf Assoc. (in U.S.A) and the Royal Canadian Golf Assoc. (in Canada) except where ammended by local club rules. These usually appear on the back of a scorecard.

KEY TO SYMBOLS

You may call ahead to reserve a starting tee time. Each course has its own reservation policy and it is a good idea to call ahead to be sure you can be accommodated.

There is a practice driving area available on site.

There is a practice putting green available on site.

GREEN FEE RANGE	
up to $20.00	$
$21. to $30.	$$
$31. to $45.	$$$
$46. to $60.	$$$$
over $60.00	$$$$$

We record the highest rates charged by the course . . . usually for peak-season play.

Prices may be lower during off-season.

DRESS CODE

Although on holiday, it should be remembered that many golf courses have dress codes in effect. Again the following is but a guideline, but should be considered. It would be a shame to be refused play because of how you are dressed.

- No tank tops, abbreviated shorts, jogging shorts, cut-off jeans, bathing suits, track suits, or shirts without sleeves.

- Shirts and shoes should be worn at all times. No spiked heel shoes or boots.

A note concerning children on the golf course . . .

It would be wise to call the facility in advance as to their policy on caddies or spectators. Some facilities, not all, do not allow either.

It takes thousands of hours of nurture and care to maintain a golf course in excellent playing shape. Please do your part to preserve it. Don't litter.

GENERAL INFORMATION

Crossing the friendly border between Canada and the U.S.A. for a golf vacation can be difficult or smooth depending upon your knowledge of what is permissable to be brought into the country and what documents are required.

Since Golf Connections' Head Office is in Ontario, we have listed below what you should know when crossing the border into Ontario. We hope it will be of help.

CUSTOMS & IMMIGRATION

American visitors are required to carry citizenship, birth, baptisimal or naturalization certificates or alien registration receipt card. Citizens of all other countries must have a valid passport. Some also require a visitor's visa. Travellers under the age of 18 and unaccompanied by an adult need a letter of permission from a parent or guardian to travel to Canada.

DUTY FREE INFORMATION

Visitors to Ontario are allowed to bring in a reasonable amount of personal effects, a 2 day supply of food and a full tank of gas. You may bring golf clubs, fishing tackle and gear, and some kinds of bait, but some restrictions may apply to other kinds. Gifts valued up to forty dollars each (Cdn. funds) are duty free provided they do not contain alcohol, tobacco or advertising material.

Visitors 19 years of age or over may import 1.1 litres (40 ounces) of liquor or wine or 8.2 litres (288 ounces) of beer. Those 16 or over can bring 200 cigarettes, 50 cigars, and 1 kg (2.2 pounds) of tobacco. Visitors must be sixteen or older in order to bring in a hunting rifle or shot gun and 200 rounds of ammunition.

Fully automatic weapons and guns less than 66cm (26 inches) in length are prohibited. For detailed information contact: Revenue Canada, Customs & Excise, Public Relations Branch, Ottawa, Ontario, Canada K1A 0l5.

Americans returning to the U.S. after 48 hours may take back $400.00 (U.S.) worth of merchandise duty free every 30 days. After less than 48 hours, $25.00 is allowed.

CURRENCY / CREDIT CARDS

It is recommended that visitors to Canada use Canadian funds. A good rate of exchange is offered at the currency exchanges at international airports, banks, trust companies and currency exchanges located at many centres located on the U.S. / Canada border.

All major credit cards, including Visa, Mastercard and American Express are welcome at most Canadian Establishments.

If fishing, hunting, boating and/or camping is also scheduled as part of your golf holiday, here is information of importance from Ontario.

No doubt each State and Province that are part of this GOLF VACATIONS Directory have their own list of regulations. Unfortunately space does not permit us to provide data from all areas. When in doubt though . . . contact the Department of Tourism of the area in which you intend to holiday.

FISHING & HUNTING IN ONTARIO

All persons must have a current licence to fish and/or hunt in Ontario. These licences are available at most tourist operators, bait and tackle shops, sporting goods stores, marinas, information booths and Ministry of Natural Resources offices.

Resident fishing licences are required for anyone over 17 years of age and under 65. Non-residents are required to have a fishing licence if over 16 years. Four day, twenty-one day, seasonal and spousal licences are available. If fishing for muskie or lake trout an additional tag is required. Limit size and season regulations vary throughout Ontario and are available from the Ministry of Natural Resources, 99 Wellesley St. W., Whitney Block, Toronto, Ontario, Canada M7A 1W3

When transporting fish, they should be packaged one fish per package with skin left on for easy identification.

All hunters must also be licenced. Seasons vary for different areas and species. Licence fees are set by the Ministry of Natural Resources.

BOATING

Pleasure craft may enter Canada by trailer or under their own power. The required entry permit is issued by Customs at the point of entry and returned at the point of departure. All boats powered by motors 10 hp or over must be licenced and the licence number clearly marked on both sides of the vessel. Boat licences from outside Ontario are acceptable. Overboard discharge of garbage or untreated sewage is forbidden.

CROWN LAND CAMPING

Non residents of Canada 18 years or older are required to obtain a permit to camp on crown land. A daily fee of $3.50 per individual ($6.00 per family) will be charged. Non residents who are guests of Ontario tourist establishments or Provincial or National Parks do not need special crown land camping permits.

DRIVING IN ONTARIO

A valid drivers licence from any country is good in Canada for three months. If driving from the U.S. be sure to bring the vehicle registration forms and a free Canadian Non-Resident Insurance Card from your insurance agent, or the policy itself.

Ontario law requires that adults and children over 18 kg (40 lbs.) in weight wear seat belts. Windshields and sidefront windows must allow a clear view of the vehicles interior. Studded tires are forbidden on Ontario highways.

LIQUOR

Anyone 19 or older may buy and consume liquor, wine or beer. These are available from government agencies located throughout Ontario. Licenced premises may serve alcohol from 11:00 am to 1:00 am except on Sundays when the time permitted is from noon to 1:00 am.

In Ontario it is an offence to consume alcohol in other than a residence or licenced premise. Driving motorized vehicles, including boats, while impaired is illegal.

HOSPITAL AND MEDICAL SERVICES

Visitors are urged to obtain health insurance before leaving their home country. It is possible that your health insurance does not extend coverage outside your country of residence. If you are taking medicine prescribed by your doctor, bring an adequate supply and a copy of the prescription in case it needs to be renewed by a doctor in Ontario.

TAX EXEMPTIONS

When you buy goods for export, you can claim exemption from the 8% Ontario Retail Sales Tax on your accumulated purchases in excess of $100.00 exclusive of tax. For full details and an application form, ask for the Provincial Sales Tax Refunds for Visitors to Ontario brochure available at Ontario merchants.

Visitors to Canada may apply for a rebate of the 7% Goods and Services Tax if the amount paid for goods and/or short term accommodation in Canada is $100.00 Canadian funds or more. Rebates may be issued by taking the completed form to a participating Duty Free Shop for cash rebate or by mailing the form to Revenue Canada, Customs & Excise, Visitors Rebate Program, Ottawa, Ontario, Canada K1A 1J5. For further G.S.T. information for visitors from outside Canada you are invited to call (613) 991-3346, or write Revenue Canada at the preceding address.

ATLANTIC CANADA

PRINCE EDWARD ISLAND

STANHOPE GOLF COURSE • STANHOPE, PRINCE EDWARD ISLAND ▲

Golf
Vacations

Micmac Indian legend says that the Great Spirit first created the universe and the Micmac people, then noticed that a large amount of dark red clay was left over. He took the clay and fashioned it into a crescent shape, and it became the most beautiful jewel in the universe. The Micmacs named it Abegweit, *the "land cradled by the waves"; today, it is known as Prince Edward Island*

In 1534, the Island was discovered by Jacques Cartier, who was fascinated by its colour and its beauty. In 1720, the first white settlers, the French Acadians, established themselves at **Port La Joye**, across the harbour from Charlottetown. Later, the Island changed hands, and by 1758, Britain occupied Prince Edward Island and deported most of the Acadian settlers back to Europe, (many would later arrive in Louisiana, and become known as "Cajuns"). The few remaining Acadians escaped expulsion by fleeing into the woods.

In 1764, Captain Samuel Holland was sent from England to survey the Island. He divided it into 67 townships of 20,000 acres each, and, through a lottery held in London, influential Britons drew lots for land grants for the colony. This launched a century-long struggle between Island farmers and absentee landowners and tyrannical rent collectors, and finally in 1853, the Land Purchase Act authorized the Island Government to buy back most of the lots for resale to tenants. The remaining land was purchased and resold by the Government after 1873, the year Prince Edward Island joined Confederaton.

The province's golden age in the mid-19th century was tied to the shipbuilding industry. Between 1840 and 1890, over 3100 wooden vessels were constructed at 176 locations. During the 18th and 19th centuries, British settlers arrived, mostly Scots fleeing hard times in their homeland, and thousands of Irish seeking opportunity in the New World. As well, the American Revolutionary War forced the United Empire Loyalists to move northward, many settling on the Island.

Today, Prince Edward Island is a vacationer's dream, with a rich variety of landscapes, from grassy hills and lush farmland, to rocky shorelines and sparkling white beaches, picturesque fishing and farming communities, beautiful churches and one-of-a-kind attractions. Stretching from **North Cape** to **Egmont Bay**, the "North by Northwest" region is the sort of rural P.E.I. you've always hoped to find. In **Tignish**, visit the St. Simon and St. Jude Church, where a magnificent pipe organ is still used during services. Heading south, **O'Leary's** "Potato Museum" displays exhibits about potatoes. In a province whose principle export is the spud, this place is a must-see.

RODD CHIP-INN GOLF VACATIONS

FROM

$ **151**⁵⁰

*per person
double occupancy*

THE ISLAND'S LEADER IN GOLF PACKAGES

The most flexible golf packages available on Prince Edward Island! Enjoy glorious golf on your choice of five championship golf courses and relaxing nights at your choice of six Rodd Hotels and Resorts.

FEATURES:
- Three nights accommodations*
- Three rounds of golf at your choice of five 18-hole courses
- $10 dining voucher per golfer

Ask about our 2-, 4-, 5-, 6-, and 7-day golf vacations

DATES:
Off Season: May, June, Sept., Oct.
High Season: July, August

CONDITIONS:
Reservations subject to room availability at booking time. Taxes extra. Credit card guarantee or cash deposit required upon booking. Buyers responsible for booking tee-off times.

Toll Free Service
1-800-565-RODD
Operator #33

Price from: (per person, double occupancy)*	Off	High
Rodd Brudenell River Resort	$165.00	$187.50
Rodd Mill River Resort	$171.00	$193.50
Loyalist Country Inn - *Affiliated with Rodd Hotels and Resorts*	$157.50	$181.50
The Charlottetown - *A Rodd Classic Hotel*	$151.50	$187.50
Rodd Royalty Inn	$154.50	$187.50
Rodd Confederation Inn and Suites	$151.50	$178.50

*Single, triple and quad rates also available

RODD HOTELS & RESORTS
*P.O. Box 432, Charlottetown
Prince Edward Island C1A 7K7*
(902)892-7448

PROVINCIAL
PARKS
PRINCE EDWARD ISLAND, CANADA
Naturally Entertaining!

MILL RIVER PROVINCIAL GOLF COURSE

MILL RIVER, P.E.I. (Route 2 to Mill River)
Telephone: (902)859-2238   Fax: (902)859-8765   Office: (902)859-8790

Manager: Greg McKee   Head Pro: Steve Dowling - CPGA
Course Supt.: Blair Duggan - CGSA   Architect: C.E. "Robbie" Robinson

18 Holes   Par 72   6830 yds.
"Set among hills of spruce this course features one of the most
unusual water holes anywhere. The 8th hole is split in two by a chain of
small ponds running the entire length of the fairway." *Golf Illustrated 1991*
Home of the N.H.L Philadelphia Flyers training camp 1992.

$	Resort	Golf Pkgs.	Public	Power Carts	Lessons	Lounge	Snack Bar	Meals	Open All Year

*Some little known areas are the provincial park beaches at **Kildare** and **West Point**, where you can find stretches of solitude that seem neverending. At the southern tip of the region is the West Point Lighthouse, overlooking the Northumberland Strait across from New Brunswick. If you climb to the top and are lucky enough, you might just catch a glimpse of the sea monster or the phantom ship reportedly sighted from there.*

*Following the southeast curve of the Island, you'll find the town of **Summerside**. A leading shipbuilding community in the 1800s, it has developed rapidly and become a popular resort area. Many of the elegant homes in the region were dubbed "fox houses", due to the fortunes made and lost in the silver fox industry. The area has today established quite a reputation as a host of international sports tournaments, including the International Hydro-Plane Regatta at the end of July, and the 1994 World Senior Softball Festival. Remaining true to its heritage, however, the town crier still proclaims high noon in front of Town Hall daily.*

*Fans of seafood will probably already know about the famous Malpeque oysters, harvested fresh from **Malpeque Bay** off the region's north shore. Secluded coves and miles upon miles of warm beaches line the shore of this relaxing tract.*

SUMMERSIDE GOLF CLUB

SUMMERSIDE, P.E.I. (On Water Street in Summerside.)
Telephone: (902)436-2505   Office: (902)436-2246

General Manager: Jerry Eman
Director of Golf: Terry Hamilton - CPGA

18 Holes   Par 72   6239 yds.

Home of the Lobster Carnival Open and the Atlantic Senior Open.
This challenging layout has hosted regional and national championships
and provides experienced and novice golfers a true test of golf.

$			Public	Power Carts	Lessons	Lounge	Snack Bar	Meals	

GREEN GABLES GOLF COURSE
CAVENDISH, P.E.I. (Located on Route #6)
Telephone: (902)963-2488

Owner: Prince Edward Island National Park
Head Pro: Errol Nicholson - CPGA

18 Holes   Par 72   6331 yds.
Rating: Men's - 70.5, Ladies' - 73

Each hole at this course has been named for a person or place
written of by Lucy Maude Montgomery in her tales of "Anne of Green Gables".

$$		Golf Pkgs.	Public	Power Carts	Lessons	Lounge	Snack Bar	Meals		

Continuing a path around the curve, on the northwestern shore of the Island, lies an area called "The Land of Anne". Named for the famous "Anne of Green Gables", by L.M. Montgomery, the region is ripe with real-life settings from this heart-warming tale. From the Green Gables House, to the Haunted Wood and Lovers Lane, you're invited to come visit all these immortal places where you will definitely feel the presence of Anne Shirley.

*The first annual Lucy Maud Montgomery Festival, celebrating the author of this Maritime classic, is scheduled to be held in the **Cavendish** area August 19-22, 1993, with highlights including ice cream socials and dramatized scenes from Montgomery's books. A barn dance is also on the calender.*

FOREST HILLS GOLF COURSE

FOREST HILLS GOLF COURSE
CAVENDISH, P.E.I. (On Route 6, the north shore, across from Rainbow Valley)
Telephone: (902)963-2887

Owner: Eleanor Rowledge

9 Holes   Par 36   2800 yds.

These are among the most challenging
9 holes of golf on Prince Edward Island.

$			Public	Power Carts	Lessons		Snack Bar			

- GREEN GABLES -
The Lucy Maude
Montgomery Legacy

Mention the name "Anne" or talk about a place called Avonlea, and chances are most people will know you're talking about "Anne of Green Gables". Now nearly a century old, this timeless story has held a special place in the hearts of millions, and made its author, Lucy Maud Montgomery, and its setting in Cavendish, Prince Edward Island, quite famous. This book, and it's subsequent series of tales, follows the life of fiery red-head Anne Shirley. Orphaned when she is very young, Anne is taken in by an elderly couple to help on their farm. Anne's spirited approach to everything she encounters continues to inspire and entertain new generations of young readers, who keep coming back to this celebrated Maritime writer.

Lucy Maud Montgomery was born in New London, P.E.I. on November 30, 1874. When she was almost two, her mother died and she went to live with her maternal grandparents in Cavendish. It was in their house that she wrote "Anne of Green Gables", writing in the evenings after completing the days chores. What remains today of her grandparents' farmhouse is a stone cellar on property that has been passed down from father to son for four generations. The current owner is a direct descendant of Lucy's grandfather, Alexander Macneill.

After receiving her teacher's qualifications, Montgomery accepted teaching positions in Bideford and Belmont, where she boarded in a drafty, cold farmhouse. She was routinely too tired to write after a day's teaching, so she rose an hour early each morning, put on a heavy coat and wrote what she could.

Green Gables House, which was the inspiration for her famed story, still survives and was the home of her grandfather Macneill's cousins. In 1937, Parks Canada restored the house and furnished it as it would have been in Anne's day, and it remains open to the public, admission-free.

In March of 1898, her grandfather died and she returned to Cavendish to attend her aging grandmother. Lucy would spent the next 13 years there.

The one place she loved best was her Uncle John Campbell's house at Park Corner. Lucy spent summer holidays there as a girl, moved there when her grandmother died, and was even married in the parlour. Many parts of the house and grounds were inspiration for her later work. The house is still owned by descendants, and is open to the public. Valuable Montgomery artifacts, including rare first editions of her books, are on display.

Lucy Maud Montgomery died in 1942. She lay in state at Green Gables and was buried in the Cavendish Cemetery in a plot on the crest of a hill she had selected herself because it overlooked all the places she loved in life.

Montgomery's "Avonlea" stories have gained new life thanks to a popular young-adult television series called "The Road To Avonlea". With this new wave of celebrity, and her books constantly in demand, it would not be surprising if Anne Shirley remained a strong figure in Canadian literature for another hundred years.

You will be pleasantly surprised by the seemingly limitless flow of beaches on which to stroll in the warm Atlantic summer sun, as well as the quaint and picturesque scenery of small-town P.E.I. For the most adventurous, there are amusement parks and attractions such as Rainbow Valley, the Great Island Amusement Park, Ripley's Believe it or Not, and the Sandspit. Camp sites and hiking and nature trails are abundant, with Prince Edward Island National Park encompassing the shore along the Gulf of St. Lawrence.

Golf and
Country Club

RUSTICO RESORT GOLF & COUNTRY CLUB

SOUTH RUSTICO, P.E.I. (At Rte. 242, off Rte. 6, 12 Mi. from Charlottetown.)
Telephone: (902)963-2357   Fax: (902)963-3205

Manager: John Langdale
Course Supt.: Mark Sheridan

Head Pro: David Bowlan
Architects: J. Proud/J. Langdale

18 Holes Par 72 5900 yds.

All holes have a view of the ocean. This course is
moderately wooded, adding to the challenge for the
experienced golfer but not intimidating for the recreational golfer.

$	Resort	Golf Pkgs.	Public	Power Carts	Lessons	Lounge	Snack Bar	Meals	
$	Resort	Golf Pkgs.	Public	Power Carts	Lessons	Lounge	Snack Bar	Meals	

CLYDE RIVER GOLF CLUB

CLYDE RIVER, P.E.I. (8 Mi. from Charlottetown, 1 Mi. off the Trans-Canada Hwy.)
Telephone: (902)675-2585   Off Season: (902)675-4602

Manager: Oswald MacEachern
Course Supt.: Roger Cassey

9 Holes Par 36 3156 yds.

A gently rolling course set amidst a rural agricultural area.

$			Public	Power Carts			Snack Bar		

*Rolling along the southwest shore, on the Northumberland Strait across from Nova Scotia, is an area called "Charlotte's Shore", so named because this region is home to P.E.I.'s capital city, **Charlottetown**. The city was named after Charlotte, a consort of England's King George III, and, in 1864, hosted the "Charlottetown Conference", a 5-day discussion with members of Upper and Lower Canada and the Maritimes, which led to the Canada of today. Known as the "Cradle of Confederation", Charlottetown has become a major metropolitan city while retaining its rural origins. The city is also home to the Charlottetown Festival, a world-renowned theatrical celebration, most noted for its musical version of "Anne", which has drawn sell-out crowds for 27 years. The Festival also produces childrens' theatre and cabaret-style shows. The Off-Stage Theatre presents "Annekenstein", a parody of the "Anne of Green Gables" phenomenon.*

West of Charlottetown, you'll find Island scenery at its best, with rolling hills, red cliffs, winding rivers, beaches and gentle waves, and you'll discover shallow sea water that really reaches bathtub temperatures. Clam digging is a popular pastime, and a tasty one, too!

PROVINCIAL

PARKS

PRINCE EDWARD ISLAND, CANADA

Naturally Entertaining!

THE LINKS AT CROWBUSH COVE

MORELL, P.E.I. (18 miles East of Charlottetown on Route #350)
Telephone: (902)652-2356

Owner: Department of Tourism & Parks
Course Supt.: Nancy Pierce - CGSA

Manager: Harry Simmonds
Architect: Thomas McBroom

18 Holes   Par 72   6475 yds.

A links style course surrounded by sand dunes and featuring nine water holes, undulating fairways, pot bunkers, challenging greens and panoramic views of P.E.I.'s beautiful north shore.

$$$		Golf Pkgs.	Public	Power Carts	Lessons	Lounge	Snack Bar	Meals	

Along the southern shore is an area called "Hills and Harbours", and it is just that; there is a point in the centre of the region called Selkirk Road, where you can stand and see over the hills to Northumberland Strait miles to the south. This is a part of the province where you can experience the real Prince Edward Island, a land of hearty sea air and warm, friendly faces. There are countless opportunities for hiking, touring, taking boat trips and photographing the rugged, beautiful landscape. "Hills and Harbours" has miles of unpaved back roads just begging to be explored. Seal-watching is a popular pastime for visitors, and you can take boat tours into the Murray River, outside of Montague, to view the wildlife up close. Montague itself is often called "Montague the Beautiful", and is home to the Garden of the Gulf Museum.

For history buffs, the **Orwell Corner Historic Village** is a heritage site that recreates this rural cross-roads community much as it was in the last century. The Village also hosts a ceilidh, or musical concert, every Wednesday evening during the summer and fall, with fiddle music and step-dancing. Jutting into the Northumberland Strait is Point Prim, with a 60-foot lighthouse that is the oldest on the Island, and is Canada's only round brick lighthouse.

Following the Island to its eastern tip, you'll come to an aptly named "Bays and Dunes" region. There you'll find a host of quiet, isolated beaches and sculted sand dunes, while inland lies heavily wooded areas and abundant nature trails. Deep-sea fishing charters are available, and very fresh seafood is for sale everywhere. **St. Peters**, on St. Peters Bay, is a prime area for blueberries, while the St. Peters Bay itself is a major producer of succulent Island Blue Mussels.

PROVINCIAL

PARKS

PRINCE EDWARD ISLAND, CANADA

Naturally Entertaining!

BRUDENELL RIVER PROVINCIAL GOLF COURSE

MONTAGUE, P.E.I. (On Route #3, 32 Mi. E. of Charlottetown)
Telephone: (902)652-2356

Manager: Jack Kane   Head Pro: Ron Giggey
Course Supt.: Dale Murchison   Architect: C.E. "Robbie" Robinson

18 Holes   Par 72   6000 yds.

Rated #19 in Canada by Score Magazine this course is the site of
four National Amateur Golf Championship and four Canadian Tour stops.

$		Golf Pkgs.	Public	Power Carts	Lessons	Lounge	Snack Bar	Meals	

The beaches in the region are considered by some to be the best on the Island. Be sure to visit the "singing sand" shores, which really do sing as you walk along them, due to the high silicone content in the sand.

The town of Souris is the main service centre for the area, with a ferry to the nearby Magdelen Islands and some tremendous fishing. The town is also host to the Souris Regatta, held in July, as well as the Rollo Bay Fiddle Festival, which features talent from around North America and is held at the same time.

It's common knowledge that you can't get permanently lost on Prince Edward Island, so don't worry if you happen to lose your way; on the Island, the worst that can happen to you is that, sooner or later, you'll come to the edge. Besides, friendly Islanders are always glad to help with directions.

GLEN AFTON GOLF COURSE

NINE MILE CREEK, P.E.I. (Follow Route 19 from Cornwall to Nine Mile Creek.)
Telephone: (902)675-3000

Owner: Delmar Currie
Course Supt.: Harley Currie

Pro Shop Mgr.: Karen Currie
Architect: Bill Robinson

18 Holes   Par 70   5736 yds.

A warm and friendly 18 hole golf course featuring
gently rolling hills, sand traps, water hazards and woods,
with many holes overlooking the beautiful Northumberland Strait.

$			Public	Power Carts			Snack Bar		

ATLANTIC CANADA

NOVA SCOTIA

HIGHLAND LINKS GOLF COURSE • CAPE BRETON, NOVA SCOTIA ▲

Golf
Vacations

Home to singer Anne Murray and water that flows backwards, Nova Scotia has been a land sought by travellers since the days of the French pioneers in the early 17th century. Today, the province beckons vacationers with a warm Atlantic coast and a variety of locations and accommodations unavailable anywhere else. Micmac Indian legend says that the land once belonged to the mighty god Glooscap, who created the landscape of Nova Scotia by scattering the five island out from his home at **Cape Blomidon**.

Settled in the 1600s by French Acadians, then taken by the British and the American United Empire Loyalists in the late 1700s, Nova Scotia drew immigrants by its promise of a New World. Many of the original families are still represented by descendents who share their ancestors' love of the freedom of Maritime life. Some recommended historic sites include the reconstructed French Habitation at **Port Royal**, as well as the British Fort Anne at **Annapolis Royal**, and the Acadian sites at **Grande Pre'**.

The "Evangeline Trail", across the Bay of Fundy from New Brunswick, was immortalized in Longfellow's epic poem, Evangeline, about the Expulsion of the Acadians by the British and the Loyalists. The trail runs from Yarmouth to Halifax, a 200-mile, six-hour drive that goes through the lush Annapolis Valley, and along the Acadian region of St. Mary's Bay. Here you'll find apple orchards and strawberry fields that seem to run on forever, and great viewing points from cliffs overlooking Fundy where you can catch a glimpse of massive, majestic whales heading back out to sea.

Yarmouth, at the western tip of the province, was settled in 1761, and is situated on Yarmouth Harbour. It is Nova Scotia's second-largest seaport, after Halifax, and it has a great shipping tradition. Ferries operate between Yarmouth and Bar Harbor and Portland, Maine. Annapolis Royal, northwest along the Evangeline Trail, is Canada's oldest European settlement, dating back to 1605. Known as "the town of many firsts", it was the site of the first drama written and performed in North America, as well as the first Common Law Court in Canada, and first tidal power plant in North America.

At the far end of the trail lies **Windsor**, known by Nova Scotians as the "Gateway to the Annapolis Valley". It is located halfway between the North Pole and the Equator, and is home to the Fort Edward National Historic Site, the oldest blockhouse in Canada. Constructed in 1750, it was used as one of the main assembly points in the Deportation of the Acadians in 1755.

The "Glooscap Trail", named after the Micmac Indian legend, follows the Bay of Fundy shoreline to Windsor, where it meets the Evangeline Trail. The Bay of Fundy, due to its proximity to the Atlantic Ocean, has the world's highest tides. Twice daily, 115 billion tons of water move in and out of the 160-mile Bay. The swell of the tide can be up to 40 feet, with the record being 54 feet. The power of the incoming tide is so great that it often causes "tidal bores", which is a wave of water that moves upstream and collides with the feeding river's current, making it seem as if the river is flowing backwards. The phenomenon is found nowhere else in North America.

ANNAPOLIS ROYAL GOLF & COUNTRY CLUB

ANNAPOLIS ROYAL, NS

Telephone: (902)532-2064

Owner: William Esslinger   Manager: David Anderson

18 Holes   Par 70   5264

A scenic course overlooking the historic town of Annapolis Royal.
Just a few minutes away from the Upper Clements Theme Park.

$$		Golf Pkgs.	Public	Power Carts	Lessons	Lounge	Snack Bar	Meals		

A popular destination is **Springhill**, birthplace of singer Anne Murray and a former coal mining town. Museums offer insight into both Anne Murray's life, with momentos from her successful career, and the mining disasters that plagued this community in the late 1950s.

Parrsboro, south of Springhill on Minas Bay, is the site of a recent fossil discovery which is shedding light on the emergence of mammals following the Age of Dinosaurs. Fossil cliffs can be found at Joggins, on Chignecto Bay, and specimens can be picked up along the beach.

Truro is a scenic city overlooking Cobequid Bay that was settled by New Englanders and Scot-Irish immigrants after the Expulsion of the Acadians in 1755. It is now home to the provincial teacher's college and agricultural university, and the "tidal bores" can be seen from town. Truro is a popular destination because of it's central location, as well as it's great golf and harness racing, and beautiful Victoria Park, a 1,000-acre forest with two waterfalls, in the centre of town.

The "Sunrise Trail" is what summer in the Maritimes is all about. Stretching from the boundary with New Brunswick, through to the Canso Causeway and Cape Breton Island, this is a land of warm-water beaches and sun-filled summer days. Overlooking the balmy Northumberland Strait, this area is a sun-worshippers' dream.

Golf Package
at the
BEST WESTERN

Claymore Inn
Antigonish
Conference Centre

**Two nights deluxe accommodations
Eighteen hole green fees**

$96 per person . . . . . . August & September
$86 per person . . . . October, May, June
Based on double occupancy

**One night deluxe accommodations
Eighteen hole green fees**

$48 per person . . . . . . August & September
$43 per person . . . . October, May, June
Based on double occupancy

Antigonish has a reputation as a beautiful
area for holiday fun and now with its
newly expanded 18-hole golf course,
it is quickly becoming a golfer's
paradise. The Antigonish Golf
& Country Club is a well designed,
professionally developed course and
has over 6600 yards of some of the most
challenging golfing in Nova Scotia.
For more details on the course see page 26.

*Ask about our other special packages: Ski , Honeymoon,
Renew the Romance, Family Get-Away*

TO BOOK YOUR GOLF GETAWAY CONTACT:

Best Western Claymore Inn / Antigonish Conference Centre

(902)863-1050

Check Inns: **1-800-565-0000** Reservations: **1-800-528-1234**

P.O. Box #1720, Church Street, Antigonish, N.S. B2G 2M5

*This region was settled by Scottish immigrants, a legacy evident in the family and town names along the shore. **Antigonish** is the "Highland Heart" of Nova Scotia, and is the site of the annual Highland Games which feature traditional Scottish contests. It is also home of St. Francis Xavier University and Festival Antigonish, a summer-long theatre festival. **Pugwash** is the site of the "Gathering of the Clans" held each July 1 and begun by Cyrus Eaton, who was head of the Chesapeake and Ohio Railway in the United States.*

***Pictou**, one of the largest communities on the Northumberland coast, is called the "Birthplace of New Scotland", and was settled in 1773 by Scottish Highlanders who came on board the ship Hector, representing the beginning of the Scottish wave of migration that was to have a major impact on the development of the province.*

ANTIGONISH GOLF & COUNTRY CLUB

ANTIGONISH, N.S. (Off Cloverville Rd., off College St., minutes from downtown)
Telephone: (902)863-4797

Head Pro: Edwin Ryan   Course Supt.: Mike MacLellan
Architect: Robert Moote

18 Holes   Par 72   6190 yds.

Home of the Annual *"Kilted Golf Tournament"*.
This course offers a scenic view of the entire town.
The 2nd hole is a par-3 with the tee 120 feet above the green.

$$		Golf Pkgs.	Public	Power Carts	Lessons	Lounge	Snack Bar	Meals	

NORTHUMBERLAND SEASHORE GOLF LINKS

PUGWASH, N.S. (On Gulf Shore Rd., in Pugwash, off Rte. #6 from Amherst)
Telephone: (902)243-3389   Fax: (902)243-3213

Manager: R.A. (Ron) Mackenzie   Course Supt.: John W. Mills
Architects: Jeffrey Cornish/ C.E. "Robbie" Robinson

18 Holes   Par 72   6192 yds.

This course features open and tree lined fairways with some "links" style holes right on the ocean. Fast and true greens present a real challenge.

$$			Public	Power Carts		Lounge	Snack Bar	Meals	

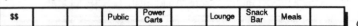

Dundee
R E S O R T

Dundee is Dundee. A beautiful and friendly place - a holiday resort conveniently located between Port Hawksbury and Sydney on the Bras d'Or Lakes, Cape Breton Island.

Dundee Resort offers an 18-hole professionally designed golf course, 39 fully equipped housekeeping cottages set in the hillside, overlooking the lakes, a marina with 28 seasonal and 4 daily berths, tennis, swimming pool, children's playground, and boat rentals.

The licensed dining room offers an appetizing selection of fresh seafood and home style meals each evening as well as a daily luncheon menu. Relax before and after dinner in the lounge.

GOLF PACKAGES AVAILABLE

from **$91.00** (per person / quad occ.)

Includes:
- 2 nights accommodation (two bedroom cottage)
- 3 days unlimited golf
- unlimited use of 1 golf cart
- unlimited use of resort facilities

FOR MORE INFORMATION AND RESERVATIONS CONTACT:

Dundee Resort
(902)345-2649 Toll Free: 1-800-565-5660

R.R. #2 West Bay, Cape Breton, N.S. Canada B0E 3K0

DUNDEE RESORT

WEST BAY, N.S. (Take Route #4 to Cape Breton Island and follow the signs)
Reservations: (902)345-2649   Golf Course: (902)345-2639
Toll Free: 1-800-565-5660

Manager: Graham Hudson   Head Pro: Bobby Hussey
Architect: Robert Moote

18 Holes   Par 72   6100 yds.

This course is well known for its
steep elevations and beautiful views of Bras d'Or Lake.

$$	Resort	Golf Pkgs.	Public	Power Carts	Lessons	Lounge	Snack Bar	Meals	

THE PERFECT DECISION

The Silver Dart Lodge represents the ideal base for your Cape Breton vacation - with your choice of where to stay. Nestled in 94 rolling acres, the Lodge and historic MacNeil House offer superb views of the magnificent Bras d'Or Lakes. Located in the beautiful village of Baddeck, you are at the start and finish of the world-famous Cabot Trail, and within easy driving distance of Cape Breton's major attractions.

The Silver Dart Lodge offers a choice of newly refurbished, high-quality accommodations to meet every taste and budget; comfortable motel units with balconies, spacious housekeeping suites, cottages/chalets with kitchenettes, hardwood floors and fireplaces.

The historic MacNeil House is an exquisitely renovated, 19th-century country mansion. You have a choice of one- or two-bedroom suites, with a jacuzzi, fireplace in the living room and a complete kitchen.

The Lodge provides a wealth of experiences: the memorable McCurdy's Restaurant, heated swimming pool, golf driving and chipping area, lawn games, walking trails, waterfront area, rowboats, bicycles, children's play area, birdlife and terrific photo opportunities.

During your stay, Lodge staff would be pleased to arrange for an afternoon or evening sail on the majestic schooner or ketch, golf at the nearby course, a horse and carriage tour of the village or an escorted bus tour to experience the renowned splendor of the world-famous Cabot Trail.

When all things are considered choosing the Silver Dart Lodge is...
the Perfect Decision!

Tel: (902) 295-2340
Fax: (902) 295-2484

P.O. Box #399, Baddeck, N. S., Canada B0E 1B0

Oxford is the "Blueberry Capital of Canada", and is the processing centre of the berry for Cumberland County, which is the world's largest producer. A roadside park at the edge of town has a lake even saltier than the ocean. Lobster is another delicacy native to the Northumberland coast, and it is plentiful and inexpensive in fishing towns all up and down the coast.

The Canso Causeway, linking mainland Nova Scotia to **Cape Breton Island**, was built in 1955 and is the deepest causeway of its kind in the world, at 217 feet. Cape Breton Island itself is known for its scenic drives, spectacular wilderness areas and lively Maritime folk festivals. Its heritage is a mix of French, English, Scottish and Micmac Indian, and is home to one of the oldest Micmac settlements in the province at Chapel Island Reserve, as well as the annual St. Anne's Mission, a spiritual and cultural event for the tribe.

Guglielmo Marconi built the first of his three transatlantic communications stations at **Table Head, Glace Bay** in 1902; a second was built at **Marconi Towers** in 1907, and the third in **Louisburg** in 1913 as a receiving station. Known as the "wireless", this heralded the beginning of a new age in worldwide telecommunications. However, all that remains today of Marconi's achievements are the giant concrete blocks upon which rested the wooden towers housing the copper wire transmitters and receivers.

Sydney is Nova Scotia's third-largest centre, and is known as "The Steel City". Founded in 1785 by Loyalists from New York State, and followed two decades later by Scottish Highlanders, the city boomed in the early 20th century with the building of the Dominion Steel and Coal Company, which was then the largest self-contained steel plant in North America. The company still survives, and remains the city's major industry. Nearby **New Waterford**, located at the edge of the Atlantic Ocean, is the largest coal-producing town in eastern Canada.

HIGHLANDS LINKS

HIGHLANDS LINKS

INGONISH BEACH, N.S. (Drive the internationally famous Cabot Trail to Ingonish)
Pro Shop: (902)285-2600   Park Office: (902)285-2866

Owner: Cape Breton Highlands National Park   Head Pro: Joe Robinson - CPGA
Course Supt.: Martin Walsh   Architect: Stanley Thompson

18 Holes   Par 71   6198 yds.

Unforgiving rough, wee undulating Scottish greens and changeable swirling ocean weather offer strategic challenges reminiscent of some of Scotland's historic courses. This course is designed to be played, enjoyed and experienced on foot.

$$	Resort	Golf Pkgs.	Public		Lessons	Lounge	Snack Bar			

In vibrant contrast, tiny towns are scattered throughout Cape Breton, places like Jersey, with a population of 38; North River Bridge, with a population of 53; and South Gut St. Ann's, population 64, are proof positive that rural Nova Scotia and its proud heritage of living free are alive and well.

Along the northern point of the island is the Cape Breton Highlands National Park, with mountains that have a top height of 1,745 feet. There's no better place in the province to get a look at everything around you than from the peak of one of the Highlands mountains. As well, you can find Cabot Landing, a provincial park marking the landing point of John Cabot in 1497, which staked Britain's claim to the island.

Following the Atlantic coastline back onto the mainland, you can pick up the "Marine Trail", running from Chedabucto Bay to the Halifax-Dartmouth area. Here you can find some of the best salmon streams in the province, as well as the freshest seafood available.

On the levee separating Chedabucto Bay from the Atlantic is the city of Canso, founded in 1605 and named after the Micmac kamsok, meaning "opposite of the lofty cliffs". Grassy Island, Nova Scotia's newest national historic site, shelters Canso from the Atlantic Ocean, and we part of a tug-of-war between the British and French in early North American history.

Sherbrooke Village, inland on St. Mary's River, is the site of an authentic recreation of a community's boom days in the 1860s, with costumed guides and restored buildings. Nearby, Jeddore Oyster Pond offers an illustration of life in a typical fishing family at the turn of the century.

BELMONT RESORT & GOLF COURSE
GUYSBOROUGH, N.S. (Travel the scenic Marine Drive)
Telephone: (902)533-3904   Pro Shop: (902)533-2255

Owner: Belmont Resort   Manager: Lloyd P. Hines
Head Pro: Ken White   Course Supt.: David Andrews

9 Holes (Dble. T's) Par 70 5199 yds.

A waterfront golf course set in beautiful Guysborough Harbour.

$$	Resort	Golf Pkgs.	Public	Power Carts	Lessons	Lounge	Snack Bar	Meals	

The Eastern Shore Beaches, a collection of sandy tracts outside Dartmouth, offer Provincial beach parks with day-use beaches. Ship Harbour East is the site of North America's largest cultivated mussel farm.

The twin cities of **Halifax** and **Dartmouth** are the cultural, business and education centres of Maritime Canada. Halifax is Nova Scotia's capital city, it's largest city, and the world's second-largest natural harbour. Halifax Harbour is 10 miles in length, and during it's history has been a haven for explorers, sea traders, navy ships, oceangoing passenger liners, freighters and cargo container ships. The city was founded in 1749 by the British to replace Annapolis Royal as capital and to balance the French presence at Louisbourg, on Cape Breton Island. Part of the city was destroyed by an explosion in 1917 resulting from a ship collision, which was the largest man-made disaster prior to Hiroshima. The architecture is dominated by the Citadel in the heart of the city, and offers a blend between historic buildings and a modern skyline.

Called the "City of Trees", Halifax has eight major parks within its boundaries, as well as museums, art galleries and live theatre. Both Halifax and Dartmouth are strategically placed on opposite sides of a spoon-shaped harbour, with the wide bowl of the Bedford Basin at its end. The Basin offers sailing and boating, and was used as a marshalling area for convoys in both World Wars. It is today a popular spot for regattas and races throughout the summer.

Dartmouth is Nova Scotia's second-largest city, and is a residential, commercial and industrial centre. Founded in 1750 by the British, it is the site of many historic buildings and museums, and is the southern terminus of the Shubenacadie Canal, which links Halifax Harbour with Cobequid Bay, and the Bay of Fundy. Two toll bridges span the harbour, and a regular passenger ferry service connects the two downtown areas.

Along the southern shore of Nova Scotia is a picturesque and romantic area called the "Lighthouse Route". Following the coastline from Halifax to Yarmouth, the route takes you through active fishing villages, seaports and stretches of wilderness shoreline. The romance of the southern shore includes stories of rum-running, pirate raids and ghostly galleons that blaze on moonlit nights. Coastal towns are steeped in Maritime tradition, and have countless stories to tell.

Lunenburg has a long and proud history as a port and fishing town, and is the birthplace of the famous "Bluenose" tall ship, pictured on the Canadian dime. Built on a stunning peninsula with a front and back harbour, the town has become a major tourist destination. Lunenburg was first settled by German, Swiss and Montebeliardian Protestants in 1753, with German being spoken well into the 1800s. The architecutre, traditions and local surnames still reflect a strong European heritage.

Peggy's Cove, perched on the rocks at the edge of the sea, has become Canada's best-known example of an East-coast fishing village. The Cove is dominated by a famous lighthouse high on a wave-smoothed granite rock shelf. The light is no longer operational , but now serves as Canada's only post office in a lighthouse.

Birchtown was named in honour of General Birch, the New York commandant who gave protection to African-American Loyalists who supported the British during the Revolutionary War. The village was first settled by a thousand Blacks who came to Shelburne with the Loyalist migration in 1783. At the time, it was the largest free Black settlement in North America.

Nova Scotia is a province firmly rooted in its Maritime past, while pressing eagerly towards the next century. From the shore of the Northumberland Strait, to the "tidal bores" in the Bay of Fundy; from the Atlantic Coast to the coast of Cape Breton Island, you would be hard pressed to find a more rewarding, relaxing vacation destination.

R • E • S • O • R • T

"A POINT TO REMEMBER"

You won't soon forget. The ocean. The constant rollers breaking on a long, long sandy beach. Golf, tennis, swimming and hiking by day. A fine meal with a fine wine by night. A cozy crackling fire in your beachfront cottage that ends the perfect Nova Scotia day.

Enjoy our CPGA rated, nine hole, seaside golf course (par 70). Eleven other courses within easy driving distance offer variety and challenge. For the non-golfers in your party, and the rest days, there is a lot to do. The private, one kilometre, white sand ocean beach, tennis courts, canoes, paddleboats, bicycles and island picnics, rainy day programs, indoor sports, day trips for history buffs, touring and deep sea fishing. Full on-site recreation, social and youth programs, will make this holiday worth remembering for everyone.

Nestled amidst 350 acres of sheltering spruce & pines, our cozy log cabins are equipped with one, two or three bedrooms, Franklin fireplaces and covered verandas overlooking our beach. Our lodge offers more traditional rooms with outside decks to enjoy the sun and the views.

Guests have been coming here since 1928, so remember us when you make your vacation plans this summer. For more information or reservations call:

1-800-665-4863
(Nova Scotia & P.E.I.)

1-800-565-5068
(Canada & U.S.A.)

White Point Beach Lodge, White Point, Queens County, Nova Scotia B0T 1G0

WHITE POINT BEACH LODGE & COUNTRY CLUB

WHITE POINT BEACH, N.S. (Just off hwy. #103)
Clubhouse: (902)683-2069   Pro Shop: (902)683-2485   Fax: (902)354-7278

Manager: Cy Cruikshank   Head Pro: Richard Dumeah - CPGA
Course Supt.: Ed Jollimore   Architect: Donald Ross

9 Holes (Dbl. Tees) Par 70 5860 yds.

A gently rolling seaside course that inspires, challenges and entertains. The Atlantic Ocean adds dramatically to the play and the pleasure.

$$	Resort	Golf Pkgs.	Public	Power Carts	Lessons	Lounge	Snack Bar	Meals	Open All Year

ATLANTIC CANADA

NEW BRUNSWICK

MACTAQUAC PARK GOLF COURSE • MACTAQUAC, NEW BRUNSWICK ▲

Golf
Vacations

Settled by Micmac and Malecites Indians as they travelled down the oa-lus-tuk, (the "goodly river"), New Brunswick has become a land of opportunity and year-round entertainment.

The province is a paradox almost, because although it is part of the Maritimes, it is also firmly a part of the mainland. This makes New Brunswick accessible and open to travellers from all over Canada and the United States.

The Saint John River Valley is roughly the dividing line between the two countries. New Brunswick shares a border and a friendly relationship with Maine, its American neighbour, and thousands of visitors travel both ways each year.

European discovery of the area came in 1604, when Samuel de Champlain landed at the mouth of the Saint John River and named it for France. Often called the "Rhine of North America", the river and lake system run through lush green fields for over 450 miles. The river and it's tributaries are beautiful, however; they are historically important transportation lifelines and are now a source of hydroelectric power to the region.

Kings County, near the mouth of the Saint John, is called the "Covered Bridge Capital of Atlantic Canada", with seventeen covered bridges in the county, and a total of seventy throughout the province.

The Provincial Capital of Fredericton is often called the "Gateway to the Maritimes", and is a city of dignified old homes and bustling markets. Visit the Legislative Assembly and the Christ Church Cathedral for a taste of European architecture, and stop at the Beaverbrook Art Gallery for an outstanding collection of British paintings that date back to Elizabethan times. Fredericton is host to many celebrations throughout the summer, including the Festival Francophone, the Fredericton River Jubilee, the Harvest Blues and Jazz Festival and an open-air concert series in Officers' Square.

In the westernmost tip of the province lie Edmunston and the Madawaska area, between Maine and Quebec. The area is rich in diverse European culture, with a hearty French influence due to its proximity to it's provincial neighbour. Here you can enjoy exciting nightlife, fascinating church architecture and the annual Foire Brayonne Festival.

EDMUNDSTON GOLF CLUB

EDMUNDSTON, N.B. (On Victoria St., 2.5 Km from City Bridge, off Church St.)
Telephone: (506)735-5667   Other: (506)735-3086   Fax: (506)739-6960

Manager: Ed Dunn   Head Pro: Ed Dunn - CPGA
Course Supt.: Ed Dunn   Architect: Arthur Murray

18 Holes   Par 73   6514 yds.

Approximately 65 new sand traps, new clubhouse and outdoor swimming pool. A scenic course set upon rolling hills, it features three par 5's in a row.

$$		Golf Pkgs.	Public	Power Carts	Lessons	Lounge	Snack Bar	Meals		
$$		Golf Pkgs.	Public	Power Carts	Lessons	Lounge	Snack Bar	Meals		

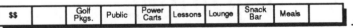

Kingsclear Hotel & Resort
Offers You
a Hole in 1

Kingsclear Hotel & Resort offers you an all-in-one golfing holiday – all in one superb location. Overlooking the scenic Saint John River and just minutes away from the spectacular Mactaquac championship golf course, Kingsclear is a golf lover's delight.

Tee off to a challenging round of golf at the 6,950-yard, 18-hole course at Mactaquac Provincial Park. Then swing into our luxuriously appointed rooms, relax in the hot tub or watch the sun set as you dine on world-class cuisine in our restaurant. Book a golf package at Kingsclear Hotel & Resort – where everything's above par for a pamper-perfect golfing holiday.

We're located off the Trans-Canada Highway at Exit 274, 12 kilometres west of Fredericton. Call 1-800-561-5111 today for reservations.

HOTEL & RESORT

R.R. #6, Fredericton
New Brunswick, E3B 4X7
Reservations Toll Free • 1-800-561-5111
Telephone 506-363-5111
Fax 506-363-3000

G⬤LF *at*

MACTAQUAC PARK GOLF COURSE, *Mactaquac, N.B.*
Championship 18 hole course ■ One of Canada's premier
courses ■ Featured in "The Great Courses of Canada" by
J. Gordon ■ Host of 1992 Atlantic Classic ■ Golf Professional
and Pro Shop ■ Licenced Restaurant and Lounge ■ Provincial
Park and Campground ■ Marina and supervised swimming
■ Self-guided Hiking Trails
Pro Shop (506) 363-4139   Park (506) 363-3011
Fax. (506) 363 3690
On Highway 105, 18 miles west of Fredericton, N.B.

New 🚢 Nouveau
Brunswick
Provincial Parks

Along the southern shore of New Brunswick is the Fundy Tidal Coast, running from the southern Maine border to Chignecto Bay and looking across to Nova Scotia. Here you will also find the world's highest tides as seen in Nova Scotia, where 115 billion tons of water swirls its way up the shores of the Bay of Fundy twice every day. The continual tide has sculpted great echoing caverns and jagged cliffs along the tidal basin. In 1604, Champlain and Sieur de Monts came upon the tides, and it was only with the help of the native population that they were able to survive the first harsh winter.

*In 1783, the United Empire Loyalists found safe harbour in the Bay of Fundy, and the history of these people is thoroughly documented and preserved in the New Brunswick Museum and Archives in **Saint John**.*

Saint John is Canada's oldest incorporated city, and is home to the oldest city market in the country. The city survived a major fire in 1877, and many areas of the city have preserved their historic homes.

Moosehead Breweries, Canada's oldest and last major independent brewery, dates back to 1867, when Susannah Oland brewed a single vat of beer from family recipes in her backyard in Dartmouth, Nova Scotia.

***Partridge Island**, off shore from Saint John, was North America's first quarantine station for new immigrants. Celebrations like Loyalist Days, Buskers on the Boardwalk and Festival-By-The-Sea are popular attractions in the Saint John area.*

*The world's first chocolate bar is reputed to have been created at the Ganong family candy factory in **St. Stephen** in 1910. Today, the company thrives, and was the first factory to make lollipops, (1895), and to sell chocolates in Valentine heart packaging, (1932). The shop is open to the public.*

***St. Martins**, along the coast, consists of a large stretch of beach and caves popular for exploring and ideal for birdwatching. Twin covered bridges at the harbour are favorites of photographers and painters. The Quaco Museum depicts the shipbuilding era, where in the early days as many as 126 ships were under construction here at one time.*

MACTAQUAC PROVINCIAL PARK GOLF CLUB

MACTAQUAC, N.B. (On Rte #105, from Hwy. 2, at exit #274)
Telephone: (506)363-4139   Fax: (506)363-3690

Owner: Province of New Brunswick   Head Pro: Alan Howie
Course Supt.: Ken Creighton   Architect: William F. Mitchell

18 Holes   Par 72   6423 yds.

Recognized as one of the great golf courses in Canada, it will be host to the Priority Courier Classic, an Atlantic C.P.G.A. event. Long, wide fairways with deer crossings on most holes. For more information see our ad on opposite page.

$$	Golf Pkgs.	Public	Power Carts	Lessons	Lounge	Snack Bar	Meals	

G⬤LF *at*

HERRING COVE GOLF COURSE, *Campobello Island, N.B.*
Scenic 9 hole course overlooking Bay of Fundy ■ Golf
Professional and Pro Shop ■ Licenced Restaurant ■ Provincial
Park and Campground ■ Beautiful salt water beach ■ Hiking
Trails and Whale Watching Tours ■ Historic Roosevelt
International Park

Pro Shop (506) 752-2449   Campground (506) 752-2396
Off U.S. Route 1, 60 miles from St. Stephen, N.B.

New ⛵ Nouveau
Brunswick
Provincial Parks

*Hugging the Fundy Tidal Coast are several islands worth a visit. First is **Deer Island**, renowned for its fishing innovations, then **Campbello Island**, which was the summer retreat of former U.S. President Franklin Roosevelt, and **Grand Manan** in the Grand Manan Channel, which is a naturalist's paradise, offering glimpses or rare species such as the puffin.*

*Marking the boundary between New Brunswick and Nova Scotia, the area known as the Southeast Shores is book-ended by two national parks. The coastline is a diverse mix of jagged cliffs, spreading marshes and warm, sandy beaches. The Flowerpot Rocks, enormous rock sculptures fashioned by eons of water erosion, guard the cliffs at **Hopewell Cape**, where tide-worn caverns entice explorers to walk on the ocean floor at low tide. This is also one of the best places to view the Fundy Tides.*

The area is a cross-section of French and English cultures, both dating back to the turbulent time of the Acadians. Both sides now live comfortably together near some of the warmest salt water beaches north of Florida.

*The coastal town of **Shediac** offers some of the balmiest waters in the province at Parlee Beach Provincial Park. Noted for it's annual Lobster Festival, Shediac is called the "Lobster Capital of the World". The town is also home to Oasis Park, a theme park with bungee jumping and water slides.*

HERRING COVE PROVINCIAL PARK GOLF COURSE

CAMPOBELLO ISLAND, N.B. (Cross international bridge from Lubec Maine)
Park Office: (506)752-2369   Pro Shop: (506)752-2449   Toll Free: 1-800-442-4442

Owner: Province of New Brunswick   Head Pro: Bruce Vantassel - CPGA
Course Supt.: Clinton Calder - CGSA   Architect: Jeffrey Cornish

9 Holes   Par 36   2901 yds.

Scenic views of the Bay of Fundy with a campground adjacent
for accommodations. Historic Roosevelt Campobello International
Park nearby. For more information see our full page ad opposite.

$$			Public	Power Carts	Lessons	Lounge	Snack Bar	Meals		

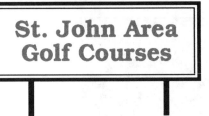

ALGONQUIN GOLF CLUB

ST. ANDREWS, N.B. (On Reed Ave., three blocks from The Algonquin Resort)
Telephone: (506)529-8823   N.B. Toll Free: 1-800-268-9411
Fax: (506)529-4194

Manager: J.W. Frise   Head Pro: Lindon Garron
Course Supt.: Leon Harvey   Architect: Donald Ross

18 Holes   Par 72   6546 yds.

This course offers a variety of scenic views, The Town of St. Andrews, the
Harbour and the Bay. Accommodations available on site at The Algonquin Resort.

$$	Resort	Golf Pkgs.	Public	Power Carts	Lessons	Lounge	Snack Bar	Meals	

HAMPTON COUNTRY CLUB

HAMPTON, N.B. (On Smithtown Rd., off Rte. #1, toward the town of Hampton.)
Telephone: (506)832-3407

President: Ivan Henry   Head Pro: Duncan Mayberry
Course Supt.: Darren Holt   Architect: Cecil Manuge

18 Holes   Par 72   6193 yds.

This course has a 236 yard par 3 on #10, a 666 yard par 6 on #6,
and a long carry over water on #5. The entire course is quite hilly.

$$		Golf Pkgs.	Public	Power Carts	Lessons	Lounge	Snack Bar		

WESTFIELD GOLF & COUNTRY CLUB

WESTFIELD, N.B. (Westfield exit off Rte. #7 to Rte #102, turn R. at intersection)
Telephone: (506)757-2250

Manager: Christine Rogers   Head Pro: Bobby Barr
Course Supt.: Paul Marr   Architects: Donald Ross/C.E. "Robbie" Robinson

18 Holes   Par 69   5699 yds.

Located on a hill overlooking the
Saint John River, the "Rhine of North America".

$$		Golf Pkgs.	Public	Power Carts	Lessons	Lounge	Snack Bar	Meals	

Moncton, the largest city in the northern region, is perhaps most famous for Magnetic Hill, which is the 3rd-most visited Canadian natural phenomenon. First observed in horse-and-buggy days, vehicles appear to coast uphill, and water seems to flow upwards.

Downtown Moncton is a vibrant blend of stately older houses and a clean, modern city. Walk brick pathways under period lampposts to pedestrian malls, or stroll along the waterfront Promenade, or gaze out from Bore Park to see the "tidal bores" in the Bay of Fundy.

Other amusements in the area include Crystal Palace, Atlantic Canada's largest indoor amusement park, as well as Magic Mountain Water Park, Wharf Village Shoppes and restaurants, and a zoo.

The Miramichi Basin, named for the Miramichi River which flows through, is located on the Atlantic Ocean, and follows the river's path into the heart of the province. This area is a fisherman's paradise, specializing in Atlantic Salmon. They grow them big here -- even royalty has come to fish these waters. "Running the river" is a favorite pastime, and there are countless spots to "put in" with a canoe along the river system. Canoe rentals are available, as are guided trips.

MAGNETIC HILL GOLF & COUNTRY CLUB

MONCTON, N.B. (Off Hwy 2 at exits 488 A or B, at world famous Magnetic Hill)
Telephone: (506)858-1611   Fax: (506)858-8901

Manager: Kent Clarke   Head Pro: Jamie Van Wart
Course Supt.: Len Killam   Architect: Jimmy Johnstone

18 Holes Par 69 5670 yds.

This course is a mixture of flat and hilly terrain.
Located next to Magnetic Hill it offers picturesque views.

$$		Golf Pkgs.	Public	Power Carts	Lessons	Lounge	Snack Bar		

HOWARD JOHNSON®

For the footloose traveller, with golf clubs in the trunk of the car and a few days to explore, there is a sweeping tour of New Brunswick that will relax and rejuvinate.

The tour takes in four cities around the province and in each the Howard Johnson provides executive accommodation with indoor pools and saunas, friendly restaurants and the excellent service that Howard Johnson guests expect and enjoy.

Starting in the northwest corner of Canada's gateway to the Atlantic provinces, Edmundston is the first stop. The capital of the mythical Republic of Madawaska, Edmundston is a small, cosmopolitan city whose French inhabitants appreciate good food and good times.

The Edmundston Golf Club is a scenic 18 hole championship course over rolling hills.

It features a restaurant, a bar and an outdoor swimming pool.

After Edmundston, visit one of the province's most curious phenomena, Magnetic Hill, where vehicles appear to coast uphill without power. Located just next to the hill is the Magnetic Hill Golf & Country Club. A mixture of flat and hilly terrain, the course is challenging but golf balls only roll uphill with the assistance of a golf club.

The course is just minutes from downtown Moncton with its outstanding shopping and eclectic mix of tempting restaurants.

Throughout this New Brunswick tour, Howard Johnson pamper their guests with special golfing arrangements and evening relaxation in their welcoming lounges and restaurants.

GOLF PACKAGES INCLUDE:
• Executive Accommodations • Full Breakfast
• Green Fees • Power Cart • All Taxes

Howard Johnson - **Edmundston**
Play at Edmundston Golf Club, a beautiful, challenging course where over sixty five sand traps (with new sand) await you.

Reservations: 100 Rice Street, Edmundston, N.B. E3V 1T4
Telephone: *(506)739-7321* • Facsimile: *(506)735-9101*

Howard Johnson - **Moncton**
Play at Magnetic Hill Golf & Country Club, a very picturesque course located next to World Famous Magnetic Hill.

Reservations: Trans-Canada Hwy. at Magnetic Hill
P.O. Box 5005, Moncton, N.B. E1C 8R7
Telephone: *(506)384-1050* • Facsimile: *(506)859-6070*

*The Miramichi Folksong Festival is held in the **Chatham/Newscastle** area, with traditional fiddle music and step-dancing. As well, the Irish Celebration in Chatham pays tribute to the broad Irish heritage in this region.*

*The Maritimer's love of weaving a good tale is alive in the Miramichi Basin. The Great Fire of 1825 is a favorite with locals, as well as famous Maritime ghost stories. When you're in **Boiestown**, step into the Woodmen's Museum and ask them to tell you about the legend of the eerie Dungarvon Whooper.*

Native son Lord Beaverbrook, a newspaperman from Britain and one of Churchill's cabinet members during the War, is part of New Brunswick's proud patriotism, and many of Beaverbrook's former homes and artifacts are on view throughout the area.

The northeast part of New Brunswick, jutting out with a family of islands into the North Atlantic, is called the Acadian Coast. Named for the original Acadian settlers who moved to the area after their expulsion from Nova Scotia in 1755, it remains a very unique part of Canada, as locals, who are descendents of the original Acadians, carry on the language and culture of their ancestors.

"Lands End" Island is unspoiled, with long stretches of sandy beaches and a lighthouse built in 1856. The Miscou Islands extend into the Baie des Chaleurs as the province's northernmost point. Pokeshaw Island, known as "Bird Island", is stark and surrounded by steep cliffs. However, it is home to hundreds of seabirds and is a favorite spot for artists and photographers.

***Caraquet** is located on the Baie des Chaleurs, and boasts New Brunswick's largest fishing fleet. Caraquet is a progressive town, offering visitors fresh shellfish from the ocean at its colourful wharf. Nearby, the Acadian Historical Village is a showcase of early Acadian life. As well, the Tracadie Museum relives past days when the community provided sanctuary for lepers.*

***Bathurst** is an upbeat coastal city that combines a French and English population and draws it's industry from nearby mining and forestry. As well, there are two farmers' markets, several beautiful churches and the stunning sands of Youghall Beach. Settled by Acadian Nicolas Denys and surrounded by picturesque falls, this is a popular area for water and land sports. And ask the locals about the legend of the Phantom Ship.*

GOWAN BRAE GOLF & COUNTRY CLUB

BATHURST, N.B. (On Youghall Dr., off Rte. 134)
Telephone: (506)546-2707

Manager: Keith Dougherty   Head Pro: Eric St. George
Course Supt.: Gilbert Vienneau   Architect: C.E. "Robbie" Robinson

18 Holes   Par 72   6553 yds.

This course has been referred to as the "Pebble Beach of New Brunswick" by SCORE magazine. There is a view of the Bay on 14 of the 18 holes.

$$		Golf Pkgs.	Public	Power Carts	Lessons	Lounge	Snack Bar	Meals	

A LANDMARK OF HOSPITALITY AND TRUE NEW BRUNSWICK FLAVOUR

When the explorer Jacques Cartier came to northern New Brunswick in 1604, he named the waters he sailed "Baie des Chaleurs" - Bay of Warmth. Bathurst is nestled in the heart of the bay and its hospitality is as warm as the waters it overlooks.

With distinct French flare, the city was the site of an earlier settlement established by Nicolas Denys, the governor of Acadia. Today the downtown features two farmers' markets where people congregate for conversation and fresh produce.

St. Peter Avenue "Bathursts Golden Mile" offers a thriving shopping district featuring many local and national commercial outlets.

Miles of sandy beaches, magnificent scenery and fresh seafood lure visitors back to Bathurst again and again. Some come to try and glimpse the illusive "Phantom Ship",

a ghostly apparition of a ship on fire, which many local people vow they have seen.

Some come to play Gowan Brae, one of the Maritimes' finest golf courses. SCORE, Canada's national golf magazine called Gowan Brae the "Pebble Beach of New Brunswick". Its 17th hole is probably one of the toughest par threes in the province- 241 yards usually played against the stiff breeze off the Bay. Then again, many players remember the 13th hole - par 4, 449 yards on the side of a hill. Gowan Brae's 14th green graces our colour title page.

A golfing vacation in Bathurst is enhanced by the executive accommodation of the Best Western Danny's Inn & Conference Centre. Danny's is a small, friendly and well-appointed resort with a heated pool, tennis and shuffle board courts and a nearby beach. The restaurant is one of the most popular in the region and features a variety of seafood, steaks and barbeque ribs.

At the Bathurst Marina, visitors can book deepsea fishing excursions, board-sailing, scuba diving and cruises into the Bay to try to site the Phantom Ship.

Best Western Danny's Inn & Conference Centre
P.O. Box #180, Bathurst, N.B. E2A 3Z2

Telephone: *(506)546-6621* • Facsimilie *(506)548-3266*
North America Toll Free: *1-800-528-1234*

The record salmon catch in the Restigouche River was a 72-pound giant in 1990, giving this area of New Brunswick, known as the "Restigouche Uplands", it's reputation as a sportsfisherman's utopia.

Explorer Jacques Cartier named the coastal water the Bais des Chaleurs, or "Bay of Warmth" when he discovered it's mild temperature in 1534. Settled originally by the Micmac Indians, and later by French and English immigrants, the area began and continues as a fishing, lumber and agriculture centre.

*The port of **Dalhousie** is located on the mouth of the Restigouche River on the shores of the Bais des Chaleurs, and the nearby Eel River Sandbar is believed to be the world's longest sandbar. One side of the sandbar is fresh water, the other is the salt water of the Bais des Chaleurs.*

Mountains over 2,600 feet high are part of the Appalachian Range, and offer spectacular views of the Bais des Chaleurs, the Atlantic Ocean and a good part of the rest of the province.

New Brunswick is the most French of the Maritime provinces, but it still maintains strong ties to its oceanside heritage. With fiddleheads growing fresh as far as the eye can see, and seafood the size and taste of which you can't find anywhere else, New Brunswick has become and remains an exceptional holiday destination.

QUEBEC

OWL'S HEAD • MANSONVILLE, QUEBEC ▲

Golf
Vacations

The Province of Quebec sits at a unqiue cross-roads between the Old and New Worlds; it is the only French-speaking territory in North America, and as such it feels like a part of Europe, but it is also a vibrant, progressive place that is perfectly at home in the West.

Thousands of years ago, the area was occupied by Amerindians in the south and Inuit in the north. In 1534, Jacques Cartier stepped onto the beaches of **Gaspe** and took possession of the territory in the name of Francis I, the King of France. He was followed by Samuel de Champlain who landed on the north shore of the St. Lawrence in 1608, in a place the natives called "Kebec". Known as New France, the region experienced massive expansion between 1660 and 1713, as France increased it's settlements along the shores of the St. Lawrence and in Acadia, (the Atlantic Provinces).

During the war between the British and the French, General Wolfe's armies besieged Quebec City and defeated Montcalm's troops on the Plains of Abraham in 1759. Four years later, with the Treaty of Paris, the French yielded Canada to the British Throne. This transfer prompted a host of English, Irish and Scots to settle in the New World.

The Constitutional Act of 1791 established a parliamentary system and granted French Canadians the right to their homeland. Canada was divided into two provinces, English-speaking Upper Canada (Ontario), and French-speaking Lower Canada (Quebec). The Lower Canada Patriotes rebelled against the British in 1837, but were defeated and conceded to the British North America Act in 1867. This established the Confederation of Canada, which included bilingual Quebec, Ontario, New Brunswick and Nova Scotia.

The 1960s marked the beginning of a period now refered to as the "quiet revolution", with confrontations over the use of the French language drawing often-violent protests in the 1970s. The Parti Quebecois won the 1976 elections, and under Rene Levesque, attempted to create a sovereign Quebec. The people decided otherwise, and in a 1980 referendum denied the government the mandate to became it's own country.

Today, Quebec remains committed to her future and the future of the entire country, and nowhere else in the province is that vibrancy more in view than in the city of **Montreal**. Although having recently celebrated it's 350th anniversary, the city shows no signs of stopping, or even slowing it's pace. Montreal is a cosmopolitan centre of commerce, finance and high fashion, with the best influences of both Europe and North America evident in all areas.

CARLING LAKE GOLF CLUB

PINE HILL, QUE (off Hwy #327, 55 minutes North of Montreal)
Telephone: (514) 476-1212   **Fax: (514) 533-5803**

Manager: Andre Gagnier   Head Pro: Jean Millaire
Course Supt: Patrick Chenier

18 Holes Par 72 6691 yds.   Rating: 72.5

One of Canada's finest 18-hole courses - a golf enthusiasts dream come true.

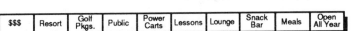

$$$	Resort	Golf Pkgs.	Public	Power Carts	Lessons	Lounge	Snack Bar	Meals	Open All Year

Founded in 1642, the island city once known as "Hochelaga", sports not only a huge and complex ground-level city, but is also home to a city under the ground. Connected to everything via a state-of-the-art Metro (subway system) and walkways, Montreal's Underground City is a waterproof, temperature-controlled prototype of the city of the future, and was based on a design by Leonardo Da Vinci. The Underground City features shopping, dining and other facilites far from the rain or snow.

Above-ground, there are three and a half centuries of history and architecture to absorb. On his second trip to North America in 1535, French navigator Jacques Cartier was looking for a shortcut to India on orders from King Francois I. The Lachine Rapids made it impossible to sail further west and Cartier became the first recorded European to view the Montreal archipegalgo from the top of Mont-Royal, to which he was led by friendly Indians from the village of Hochelaga.

Samuel de Champlain, the "Father" of New France, thought of setting up a town on Ile Sainte-Helene in 1611, but the colony of Ville-Marie de Montreal was not officially founded until May 18, 1642.

Conflict with the natives was common, and hampered the growth and development of the area until 1701, when the signing of a peace treaty produced a highly successful fur trade for a hundred years or more.

As a result of the Napoleonic Wars in Europe, the English began conquering New France in 1759, when it's population stood at 60,000. With the arrival of British merchants came a phenomenal growth. Lumber following fur as the main commodity. Little thought was given to defence and during the American Revolution, Montreal saw an 8-day occupation by the victorious rebels. They were unable to convince the French-Canadians to take up arms against the British rulers and left the city. The Americans tried to take Montreal again during the War of 1812, but were repelled.

Each street in Montreal is a new feast of history and culture. One of the favorite pastimes of both residents and visitors is to find a quiet streetside cafe, for which Montreal is famous, and sip a freshly-brewed espresso while absorbing the provincale feel of this most "European" of North American cities.

Following the St. Lawrence out towards the Atlantic Ocean, you'll find **Quebec City**, the only walled city in North America. The Algonquin Indians called this place "Kebec", meaning "where the river narrows", and it was here in 1608 that Samuel de Champlain chose to settle. Considered for many years the gateway to the continent, Quebec was repeatedly the object of conquest. In 1690, the Comte de Frontenac repelled the forces of English Admiral William Phipps and fortified the city. In 1759, the region was beseiged by General Wolfe's troops, and the shelled city fell into the hands of the English Army after the battle of the Plains of Abraham. It was through this battle that France eventually conceded its colony to the English.

Chalets
Montmorency

GOLF PACKAGE

30 MINUTES FROM HISTORIC QUÉBEC CITY

$**49**.^{95} Per Person, Double Occupancy
Minimum 4 persons

**1 Night Lodging
1 Round (18 holes) of Golf**

This package is available at all times during the golf season. In order to guarantee your starting time, reservations must be made 72 hours prior to your arrival. These rates are valid for the 2 to 5 bedroom condominiums and villas. Taxes are not included, no additional discounts apply. Based on availability.

1-800-463-2612

Direct: (418)826-2600 • Fax: (418)826-1123

1768, ROYALE AVENUE, SAINT-FERRÉOL-LES-NEIGES, QUÉBEC G0A 3R0

CHALETS MONTMORENCY GOLF COURSES
SAINT-FERRÉL-LES-NEIGES, QUE.
Telephone: (418)826-2600

Director: Denis Gagné

Beaupre Course: 18 Holes   Par 72   6700 yds.

St. Ferreol Course: 18 Holes   Par 72   6200 yds.

$$	Resort	Golf Pkgs.	Public	Power Carts	Lessons	Lounge	Snack Bar	Meals	

When calling or writing our advertisers, please mention *Golf Connections*.   53

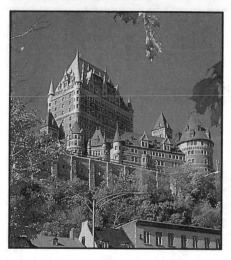

In 1774 the Quebec Act was signed, and allowed French-Canadians to retain their right to practice the Catholic religion, which was banned in England at the time. The act also allowed them to preserve their own language and customs. In 1775, the failure of the American Invasion led by General Richard Montgomery became the last military entanglement the city has seen. Nevertheless, the English army completed the fortifications of the city which are today an integral part of the landscape.

Quebec City's legacy as the political capital began in New France, then with the English colony, and it eventually became the Provincial Capital at the time of Confederation in 1867. Today, the area's main employer is the Provincial Government, with the major manufacturer being the pulp and paper industry. The city is home to five of the province's ten classified historical districts, illustrating just how culturally important Quebec City is.

Vieux-Quebec (Old Quebec), is the cradle of the French civilization in North America, and is the only fortified city north of Mexico. Perched high atop cap Diamant, the historic district overlooks the St. Lawrence River and offers numerous breathtaking views of the South Shore, Isle d'Orleans, the Lower City and the Laurentian Mountains.

The definitive Quebec City landmark is the Chateau Frontenac, visible from about every point in the city. It is a world-renowned hotel named after Count Frontenac, the governor of New France. Built in 1893, it was completed with the addition of a central tower in 1925. It was the site of several meetings during World War II, meetings between Winston Churchill, Franklin Roosevelt and Canadian Prime Minister MacKenzie King.

The Citadelle, located at the top of cap Diamant, constituted the eastern flank of Quebec City's defences. Inspired by it, many romantic writers have called Quebec the "Gibraltar of America". Construction on the Citadelle began in 1820 and lasted for more than 30 years. It is a star-shaped fortification composed of 25 buildings, and has been home to the Royal 22e Regiment, since 1920, making the Citadelle the largest fortified group of buildings still occupied by troops in North America.

Churches and sanctuaries are scattered throughout the region, testament to the French passion for religion and strong beliefs. Some noteworthy visits include the Chalmers-Wesley United Church, circa 1852, the Sanctuaire Notre-Dame-du-Sacre-Coeur, built in 1910 with tremendous stained-glass work, and the Holy Trinity Anglican Church, dating from around 1804. The Basilique-cathedrale Notre-Dame-de-Quebec is the oldest basilica on the continent north of Mexico, and marks the culmination of nearly 350 years of work. It is richly decorated with an impressive collection of rare art.

The Parliament Building, (Hotel du Parlement), is Quebec's most important national treasure. The building is an imposing structure with four wings which form a quadrangle approximately 100 metres square. The architecture is unique in North America, and was inspired by French classicism.

Twenty-eight stairways provide easy, if unusual, access to the Lower Town. Most of the stairs are narrow, and the hill into which they're carved is quite steep. The streets in Lower Quebec are also strangely narrow, but give way into exciting and upscale shopping districts like the Quartier du Petit-Champlain, an historic marketplace with roots back to the days when Quebec was a small port village.

Nearby, the Basilique Sainte-Anne-de-Beaupre is a shrine with a long history of rebirth. The original wood structure was built too close to the St. Lawrence, and was damaged by flooding and rebuilt at the foot of a hill in 1661. In 1676, it was replaced by a stone church that was then enlarged many times. In 1876, a new church was erected, and was soon declared a basilica. This was destroyed by fire in 1922, and the present basilica, neo-Roman in style, was built in 1923. It is admired for it's vast proportions and it's superb stained-glass windows. It also houses numerous incredible treasures.

Across the St. Lawrence is the Chaudiere-Appalches Region, an immense area stretching from the nearby Eastern Townships to the American border. The St. Lawrence River, the Riviere Etchemin and the capricious Rivier Chaudiere with its legendary ice-jams are an integral part of the region's history. The waterways provided the major means of communications in the early 18th century, enabling colonization to extend inward rapidly from their banks. The wood processing and export industry thrived on the acres of virgin woods, and agriculture was a central part of the economy due to the fertile soil.

CLUB DE GOLF TROIS SAUMONS
ST-JEAN-PORT-JOLI, QUE. (Highway 20, exit #414)
Telephone: (418)598-9719

Head Pro: Bruno Berube - CPGA   Course Supt.: Martin Gagnon - CGSA

18 Holes   Par 73   6293 yds.

Water hazards and sand traps make for challenging play.
Our #14 hole is a must see. Ask about our golf packages.

$$		Golf Pkgs.	Public	Power Carts	Lessons	Lounge	Snack Bar	Meals	

The geographical diversity of the region offers something for every type of outdoor enthusiast, including aquatic sports, cruises, hunting and fishing, snow goose watching, lush golfing and a day at the sugar shack to see how maple syrup is made.

East of the Chaudiere-Appalaches and across the river from Montreal lie the Eastern Townships, some of the most captivating and picturesque countryside in the province. The region sprawls across 13,000 square kilometres of mountains, forests and rolling farmland, and it shares a 300 kilometre frontier with the United States. It's southerly location makes it consistantly a few degrees warmer than other parts of the province.

Mountains herald the approach of the Townships; the northernmost chain of the ancient and mighty Appalachians cuts through the area. The mountains are a glorious backdrop to the inviting lakes and streams, and peaceful villages lying along sleepy rivers which meander around wooded hills.

*The original inhabitants, the Abenaki Indians, have left a lasting reminder of their time here in the form of place names, including **Memphremagog**, **Massawippi**, **Megantic** and **Coaticook**. When the Americans declared their independence from Britain in 1776, those loyal to the Crown decided that they did not want to live with the new republicanism, and many fled north to the Townships.*

The colonial government, only too happy to welcome the people, gave them generous land grants, and hundreds of Loyalists made their homes there. They were followed by tides of Irish Catholics in 1820, who left Northern Ireland after it became part of the United Kingdom, and again in 1840 during the Potato Famine.

During the 1850s, the population began to change from Anglophone (English-speaking) to Francophone (French-speaking) as many French moved down to the Eastern Townships to work on the railroads. By the beginning of the twentieth century, the area became predominantly French-speaking. The French named for the area, "Estrie", means "Kingdom of the East", and became its official name in 1981.

Long-known for it's asbestos mines, textiles and pulp and paper industries, the Townships is now increasingly switching to high-tech industries, including car manufacturing, medical equipment, computers, micro-electronics and precision machinery. The area has also earned a reputation as being an ideal year-round vacation spot, with outstanding golf and other summer sports.

OWL'S HEAD

3 - DAY GOLF GET-AWAY PACKAGE

$165 Per Person Quad Occupancy

- one round of golf per person per day
- one hour of tennis per unit per day
- free access to beach and hiking trails
- three nights / three days
- luxurious two-bedroom condo on Lake Memphremagog

At Owl's Head, you'll find a practice range with 4 target greens and a pitching green with 3 different bunkers featuring white silica sand. As well, you'll have access to our two-level putting green just beside the first tee.

Graham Cooke constructed this unique and breathtaking circuit to challenge your skills and amaze your senses. Every hole provides a panoramic view of the Appalachain countryside. Keep your eyes open and you may catch a glimpse of white tailed deer, ducks, and pileated woodpeckers. Local flora and fauna were conserved on a stretch of land overlooking 25 miles of spectacular views.

(514)292-3666

Autoroute 10, exit 106 (Eastman) follow the signs for Owl's Head.

OWL'S HEAD GOLF COURSE

MANSONVILLE, QUE (Autoroute #10 take exit #106 and follow the signs)
Telephone: (514)292-3666   Administration: (514)292-3342

Head Pro: Brian McDonald - CPGA

18 Holes Par 72 6705 / 6345 / 5905 / 5295

The clubhouse features B.C. timber, field stone, 45 foot ceilings, 5 fireplaces, a patio overlooking the course, terraced landscaping and full dining and refreshment services.

$$	Resort	Golf Pkgs.	Public	Power Carts	Lessons	Lounge	Snack Bar	Meals		

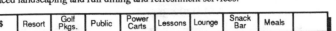

Club de Golf de Farnham Inc.
Chemin du Golf, C.P. #145, Farnham, Québec J2N 2R4
(514)293-3171

Club de Golf Les Cèdres
669, rue Coupland, Granby, Québec J2G 8C7
(514)372-0167

Club de Golf le Rocher de Roxton Pond
821, 4ᵉ Rang, Roxton Pond, Québec J0E 1Z0
(514)777-5888

Les Rochers Bleus
550, Route 139, Sutton, Québec J0E 2K0
(514)538-2324

Golf Bromont
95, rue Montmorency, Bromont, Québec J0E 1L0
(514)534-2200

Le Parcours du vieux village
475, rang des Patriotes, Napierville, Québec J0J 1L0
(514)245-3351

Waterloo
360, rue Leclerc, C.P. #1099, Waterloo, Québec J0E 2N0
(514)539-1055

Golf Inverness
511, chemin Bondville, C.P. #100, Knowlton, Québec J0E 1V0
(514)242-1595

Club de Golf Valcourt
Rue Champêtre, C.P. #280, Valcourt, Québec J0E 2L0
(514)532-3505

Inter Golf
1586, rue Principale, Granby, Québec J0E 1L0
(514)777-4653

Owl's Head
40 chemin Mont Owls Head, C.P. 35, Mansonville, Québec J0E 1X0
(514)292-3666

Eastern Townships
Take A Swing East!

IT'S VERY NEAR...VERY GREEN!

For more information about the golf courses and
packages, call or write:

MAISON REGIONALE DU TOURISME DE L'ESTRIE
Autoroute 10 - Sortie 68
St-Alphonse-de-Granby, Québe c
J0E 2A0
(514)375-8774

Québec, Ontario and Maritimes call 1-800-263-1068
and we'll send you our golf brochure.

The Outaouais Region, (French for "Ottawa"), is the westernmost part of the province and is a vast 33,000 kilometres offering visitors a dynamic, big-city vacation in harmonious partnership with extraordinary natural beauty.

Nestled in the heart of the lush Ottawa River Valley, it was first discovered by Samuel de Champlain during his journey through Algonquin Indian territory in 1613, in search of the Northwest Passage. In subsequent years, fur traders, explorers and merchants followed his path up through the Great Lakes. It was later, in 1800, with the arrival of the founder of Hull, American settler Philemon Writer, that the development of the Outaouais Region began. The lumber industry was key to it's future, and in the 19th century the area was known as Great Britain's woodyard because it supplied the timber for shipbuilding during the Napoleonic Wars.

TERRAIN DE GOLF
Champlain
GOLF COURSE

CHAMPLAIN GOLF CLUB

AYLMER, QUE. (On Aylmer Rd., Hwy #148)
Telephone: (819)777-0449

Owner: Golf Management Associates   Head Pro: Roseline Menard - CPGA
Course Supt.: Ken Schernosky - CGSA

18 Holes   Par 69   5755 yds.

Rating: Men's - 67, Ladies' - 69

A fully irrigated and well maintained course.

$		Golf Pkgs.	Public	Power Carts	Lessons	Lounge	Snack Bar	Meals	

Hôtels et Villégiatures 🚄 Canadien Pacifique

Le Château Montebello

- A WORLD CLASS RESORT FOR ALL SEASONS -

Chateau Montebello is the ideal resort, offering a wide range of activities for all seasons and styles. Located on a private 65,000 acre estate on the North Shore of the Ottawa River, between Montreal and Ottawa, this landmark of the Outaouais Region is of such charm and enduring quality it has gained world-wide recognition.

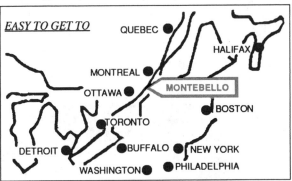

EASY TO GET TO

FROM NEW YORK
Interstate 87 north,
Hwy. 15 North,
Hwy. 40 West
Exit #9 (Hawkesbury),
Route 148 West.

FROM MONTREAL
Hwy. 40 West
Exit #9 (Hawkesbury),
Route 148 West.

**FROM TORONTO
(OTTAWA)**
Hwy. 40 East TransCanada,
Route 16 North (Ottawa)
Hwy. 50 East, Exit #221,
Route 148 East.

The GOLF CLUB at Chateau Montebello was designed in 1930 by Stanley Thompson, who also designed Jasper Park Lodge and Banff Springs (All Canadian Pacific properties). The course has undergone a multi-million dollar renovation in 1991 and this extremely interesting 18 hole, par 70 layout offers a special experience and a challenge that that is hard to forget.

- GOLF PACKAGES ARE AVAILABLE -

LE CHATEAU MONTEBELLO GOLF COURSE

MONTEBELLO, QUE. (On Route #148)
Telephone: (819)423-6341   Fax: (819)423-5283

Manager: Sarah Cruse   Head Pro: Francois Blambert
Course Supt.: Jacques Hebert

18 Holes   Par 70   5795

A mountain golf course situated at
the largest log castle in the world, with a host of activities.

$$	Resort	Golf Pkgs.	Public	Power Carts	Lessons	Lounge	Snack Bar	Meals	

The urban sector of the Outaouais shares in the liveliness of the whole capital region. There are five bridges linking Ottawa with Quebec. In **Hull**, a suggested visit is the Canadian Museum of Civilization, an architectural masterpiece as well as a treasure-house of artifacts, located downtown. Hull also features wonderful French cooking and a lively night life.

Gatineau Park is an historic site, conservation area and wildlife preserve with an excellent choice of outdoor activites including nature observations, bicycle touring, hiking trails and ice fishing. Hunters and fishermen will find the area interesting because of a special wildlife management program that allows them to practice their favorite sport without endangering an entire species.

The region has more than 20,000 lakes and dozens of rivers, with fishing, cruising, canoeing, sailing, pleasure boating and swimming. As well, some of the most scenic golf in the province is available in the Outaouais Region.

In a land of such tremendous contrast and historic wealth, it isn't hard to plan a vacation that leaves you feeling like you've travelled the world without ever leaving North America. Quebec remains truly the "crossroads of Europe and America".

ONTARIO

ROYAL WOODBINE GOLF COURSE • TORONTO, ONTARIO ▲

Golf Vacations

Ontario is an enormous province stretching from the southern tip of Canada to the extreme Arctic, along Hudson's Bay. It's topography is nearly as varied as its summertime activities, extending from the steamy shores of the southern Great Lakes, to the rugged Canadian Shield in the northeast, to the frozen tundra of the Far North.

Indians arrived about 10,000 years ago and found that Ontario was an ideal place for them to settle, because not only could they find an abundance of wildlife to hunt, in the southern part of the province they found they could grow their own food.

The Indians built longhouses surrounded by fields of corn, beans and squash, which became mainstays in their diet. In the summer, the men hunted, fished and made trading trips in birchbark canoes. In winter, they travelled with snowshoes and tobogans. Some travelling tribes fought, but by the 1600s most of the bloodshed was ended due to democratic confederacies formed by some of the warring tribes.

European settlers came in the mid-1600s, and with them brought goods to trade, gospel to preach and a whole new set of problems. Alliances were formed between the Hurons and the French, but the Hurons were virtually wiped out by disease and war with the Iroquois, who wanted to take over the illustrious fur trade. The site of the Hurons' last stand, Sainte-Marie-Among-The-Hurons, is located in **Midland**.

The Hudson's Bay Company opened fur trading outposts, the very first being at **Moosanee** on James Bay in 1673. Remnants of the site remain, along with a museum and artifacts. The fur trade would prove to be one of the major reasons for colonizing the area.

The British and French badly wanted to colonize North America. Caught directly in the middle, the Indians were important in the struggle between the two foreign powers. Most tribes lost badly in the wars, and eventually gave up their land and moved to reserves. Britain won control of the Canadian colony in 1759, only to lose the nearby American colonies twenty years later.

One of the heroes of the wars with the French was Joseph Brant, a Mohawk Indian who, after the war, was compensated by the British for his allegiance with land near **Brantford**, which is now an important native reserve and cultural centre.

The American Revolutionary War turned out to be beneficial to Ontario, helping to create Canada. 80,000 American colonists, still loyal to the British Crown, fled to Ontario and were given land grants. The land was cleared and farms and cities were built, and in 1791 the British Government declared the Constitutional Act, dividing Ontario and Quebec. Quebec was known as "Lower Canada", and Ontario was known as "Upper Canada". Ontario became it's own province, with it's own English legal system and provincial government.

*In 1812, the United States got fed up with the British searches of their ships, and took revenge on the British colonies of Upper and Lower Canada. The Americans thought the Upper Canadians would be thrilled to join forces and throw off the oppression of the British tyranny, but found the colonists to be resistant to the idea. British General Brock kept beating back the America insurgence, and, after the Americans burned the Legislature in **Toronto** and the town of Newark, (now **Niagara -On-The-Lake**), most people in Upper Canada took up arms against the Yanks. Laura Secord, a farmer's wife, started a legend that survives to this day by running nineteen miles through forests to warn of an American attack. Within two years, the war was over, ending in a draw.*

After the war, there was a revolt in Ontario led by William Lyon Mackenzie, a newspaper editor, against the conservative Family Compact government. This revolt managed to restore a system of democracy and a fair social system to the province.

*As the agriculture and lumber industries grew, immigrants from Britain flooded in. A few settled in **Toronto**, **Kingston**, **Peterborough** and other large settlements, but most lived in cabins trying to clear the vast wilderness into farmland. There are many pioneer villages either recreated or restored all through the province that offer a look at this rough existence.*

In 1867, Britain agreed to let the colonies become their own country. Led by Sir John A. Macdonald, Nova Scotia, New Brunswick, Quebec and Ontario became the first four provinces of Canada.

Western Ontario, beginning at the southern-most tip of Canada, is a golfers' and vacation-ers' paradise. Surrounded by Lake Erie to the South, and Lake Huron and Georgian Bay to the north and west, the region is lined with sandy-white beaches and quaint resort towns offering hospitality and an oasis from the stress of everyday life.

Jutting out into the calm of Lake Huron is the Bruce Peninsula, an outcropping of land re-nowned for it's scenic beauty and all-season fun. **Tobermory**, at the northern tip, is a harbour town with easy access to both Lake Huron and Georgian Bay. You can charter boats to fish or sightsee throughout these intricate waterways, and a large ferry boat, the M.S. Chi-Cheemaun, carries cars and passenger over to nearby **Manitoulin Island**. Down either side of the Peninsula are lakeside communities that cater to your every holiday need, like **Sauble Beach**, **Red Bay**, **Wiarton** and **Owen Sound**. For more hearty vacation-ers there is the "Bruce Trail", a hiking trail stretching through the Bruce Peninsula down the Niagara Escarpment into Southern On-tario, where you can find some of the most beautiful and well-preserved wilderness in southern Canada.

Heading south along Lake Huron, beachfront towns like **Goderich** and **Grand Bend** offer camping and lodging, and all the water sports you can handle. The port of **Sarnia**, a major border point with the United States, is one of Canada's largest centres of oil production and refinement. Further south lies **Windsor**, across the Detroit River from Detroit, and one of the most heavily travelled borders. Like its American counterpart, Windsor is an automotive giant, working closely with the "Motor City" and all the major auto companies. Through the weeks surrounding Canada Day and the Fourth of July, the "International Freedom Festival" is held along the border, with fairs, carnivals and fireworks celebrating the two countries' special relationship. Enjoy the quiet charm of rural Ontario without having to travel too far away from city life in communities like **Essex**, **Amherstburg**, **Leamington** and Canada's southernmost location, **Point Pelee** on Lake Erie. Further east along the shores of Lake Erie are more beachfront resort towns, like **Wheatley**, **Erie Beach** and **Port Stanley**, popular spots for sand-and-surf enthusiasts.

*The River Thames winds lazily through the southern tip of Western Ontario, and branches off into several tributaries around the city of **London**. Like its namesake across the "Big Pond", London is a richly historic and cosmopolitan city with elegance and sophistication, and is a rising star on the Ontario golfing scene.*

*Northeast lies the town of **Stratford**, most notably, the home of Canada's largest "Shakespearian" festival. One would be hard-pressed to find a more charming, artistic spot anywhere. **St. Marys**, 15 minutes from Stratford, is often called "The Stonetown", because of its mid-19th century stone architecture. It is also home of "The Quarry", Canada's largest outdoor swimming pool. The town of **Woodstock**, a short distance south, is a quiet, picturesque village that invites visitors to explore its beautiful history and excellent shopping.*

WESTMINSTER TRAILS

LONDON, ONT. (On Westminster Dr., east off Wellington Rd., south of 401)
Telephone: (519) 668-6121

Manager: Lenie Schrembri   Head Pro: Gary Harrison - CPGA
Course Supt: Fred Schmoelzl, CGSA

18 Holes Par 70 6150 yards Rating: Men's 67.5 Ladies' N/A

Water comes into play on 9 holes of this gently rolling course. Ramada® Inn - 401
Two Night/Three Day Golf Packages available from $136.80 Cdn./person

$$		Golf Pkgs.	Public	Power Carts	Lessons	Lounge	Snack Bar	Meals	
		Golf Pkgs.	Public	Power Carts	Lessons	Lounge	Snack Bar	Meals	

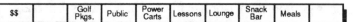

The Complete Golf Day...

Imagine a spectacular day of golf. A warm gentle breeze - bright sunshine - and the magnificent green fairways, glistening white sand traps, and the jewel blue waters of Acton's renowned Blue Springs Golf Club. You've mastered the exhilarating challenge of the famed "Turtle Lake" track... and now its time to relax.

Just a little more than a good golf swing away is one of Ontario's famous and most fascinating landmarks - the olde Hide House! The sheer size of this renovated 1899 tannery ware-house is awesome - and displayed under the cathedral-like wood beams are over 10,000 leather garments, plus woollens, accessories, leather furniture and gifts.

the olde Hide House

Built in 1899

(519) 853-1031

And to complete your day on the links, Jack Tanner's Table is a refreshing oasis. Located right inside the olde Hide House, Jack Tanners' proudly presents superbly prepared continental cuisine in a cozy atmosphere of rustic fire places, massive beams, warm brick and hanging plants... aah - the satisfaction!

For a complete golf day -

"Its worth the drive to Acton"

THE TORONTO NEWSPAPERS

On Acton's BLUE SPRINGS GOLF CLUB:

"The scenery is spectacular and the course is first class."

- TORONTO STAR -

"It may be the best new course in the country."

- GLOBE AND MAIL -

"A definite pleasure to play. . can't be passed up."

- TORONTO SUN -

JUST 45 MINUTES FROM TORONTO, HAMILTON OR KITCHENER, ACTON IS BEST KNOWN AS CANADA'S "LEATHERTOWN"

BLUE SPRINGS
GOLF CLUB

Acton is located 15km North of the 401 at highways 7 and 25.

BLUE SPRINGS
GOLF CLUB
- Home of the Canadian PGA -

In the golf world, where many new course descriptions strain credibility, few clubs can lay claim to being home of a national golf school and host of a CPGA Championship in 1994 - all before the first ball was driven off a tee! Such is the distinction of the **BLUE SPRINGS** Golf Club. Located in Acton, just 45 minutes Northwest of downtown Toronto.

The crowning jewel in the **BLUE SPRINGS** 540 acre complex is the magnificent "TurtleLake" course, a 6715 yard, 18 hole masterpiece which is truly a collection of signature holes.

This championship course is complemented by the 9 hole "Trillium" par three course, practice fairways and greens with quality equipment rentals, all just a few steps from a complete pro shop.

Mulligan's Grill (LLBO) offers express food service or casual dining in a relaxed air conditioned lounge. Groups up to 250 can be accommodated under the patio marquee.

A world class clubhouse, complete with racquet sports, fitness centre, conference rooms, banquet facilities and fine dining will complete the complex at maturity.

For public, group or tournament play . . . .
                    BLUE SPRINGS is a premier golf destination.

- Site of the SCORE Magazine Golf School -

BLUE SPRINGS GOLF CLUB

ACTON (On 1st Line, South of Hwy. 7, North of Mill St.)
Start Times: (519)853-0904   Administration: (519)853-4434

Director of Golf: Craig Guthrie   Head Pro: Shelley Woolner - CPGA
Course Supt.: Ted Ellis - CGSA

Turtle Lake: 18 Holes Par 72 6713 yds. Ratings: Men's - 74.5, Ladies' - 71
Trillium   : 9 Holes Par 3

2 practice fairways, 2 putting greens, 2 practice chipping greens
and green side bunkers. Start times up to 7 days in advance.

$$$			Public	Power Carts	Lessons	Lounge	Snack Bar	Meals	

Following the Niagara Peninsula, "Festival Country" offers an ideal climate for golf courses, which is why almost 20% of all Ontario courses are located in this region. It is also ideal for growing grapes used in world-renowned Niagara wine, as well as peaches, apples and many other delicious fruits and vegetables. The Niagara region is home to the "Niagara Falls", often called "the eighth wonder of the world". Tourists flock to this majestic spectacle year-round from all parts of the world. There are many ways to see The Falls, from a tunnel beneath the water, to a ferry that skirts the bubbling froth at it's base, to helicopter rides high overhead. The city of **Niagara Falls** caters to tourists, with several city blocks around The Falls devoted to wax museums, arcades and souvenir shops. Niagara Falls is the "Honeymoon Capital of the World", with no shortage of heart-shaped beds or bathtubs. Nearby, **Old Fort Erie** and **Queenston Heights** are reminders of the bloody War of 1812. Northeast is the quaint community of **Niagara-On-The-Lake**, a mecca for antique shoppers and browsers. Following northwest along the western edge of Lake Ontario, you'll find both **St. Catharines**, the "Garden City", and the wine region of Ontario, in communities like **Vineland**, **Thorold**, **Fruitland** and **Winona**. Here you can buy fresh fruit in season from vendors in booths along the side of the QEW Highway.

At the westernmost tip of Lake Ontario are the cities of **Hamilton** and **Burlington**. Hamilton is Canada's steel giant, boasting two of the largest steel companies as residents. Built up around this industry, Hamilton has grown into a truly world class city, drawing big names in entertainment to play at any of several large performance venues. It is a city with character, charm and an ethnic diversity you'd find only in much larger cities. Hamilton is also home to an international air show and the Warplane Heritage Museum, which draws thousands of visitors each year. Neighbouring towns like **Ancaster**, **Flamborough**, **Dundas** and **Waterdown** offer more rural diversions.

*Nearby Burlington, (Canadian home of "Golf Connections"), has outgrown it's role as a bedroom community to Toronto, into a city of 119,000 people. Nestled around the lip of Lake Ontario, Burlington boasts a revitalized lakefront and a downtown of shops and historic buildings that must be explored. As well, the Royal Botanical Gardens, Bronte Creek Provincial Park, the Crawford Lake Indian Village and Mountsburg Widlife Centre are all popular and fun outdoor amusements. West of Hamilton, the city of **Brantford** offers a look at history in the area, with the Alexander Graham Bell Homestead, (the birthplace of the telephone), and the roots of the Six Nations Indians, who have a reserve in the area.*

The most *private* public
golf facility in Canada

THE ULTIMATE IN SERVICE

36 - HOLE CHAMPIONSHIP COURSE

Extensive clubhouse facilities catering for full banquet service,
cocktail parties and wedding receptions.

- CORPORATE EVENTS
- BUSINESS ENTERTAINING
- INDIVIDUAL FOURSOME PLAY

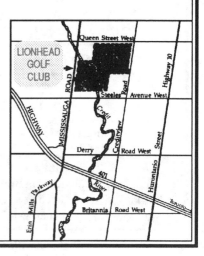

EASILY ACCESSIBLE FROM TORONTO
20 minutes away from
Pearson International Airport

5 km. N. of Hwy 401 on E. side of Mississauga Rd.

LIONHEAD GOLF & COUNTRY CLUB

BRAMPTON, ONT (3 Mi. N. of Hwy. 401 on E. side Mississauga Rd.)
Clubhouse: (416)455-8400   Pro Shop: (416)455-4900

General Manager: Alan Ogilvie - CPGA
Director of Golf: Chuck Lorimer - CPGA

36 Holes:
Legends Course - 18 Holes Par 72 5759 - 7184 Ratings: 70.1 / 77.0
Masters Course - 18 Holes Par 72 5553 - 7035 Ratings: 69.3 / 75.0

$$$		Golf Pkgs.	Public	Power Carts	Lessons	Lounge	Snack Bar	Meals	

Delta. Meadowvale

Resort & Conference Centre.

OFFICIAL HOTEL OF LIONHEAD GOLF & COUNTRY CLUB

Located just 5 minutes south of Lionhead Golf & Country Club on Mississauga Road, our facilities include:

- 374 guest rooms and suites
- 42 meeting and function rooms
- 4 restaurants and lounges
- indoor and outdoor pools
- whirlpools and saunas

- fitness and aerobics centres
- 4 covered tennis courts
- 8 squash and racquetball courts
- children's creative and activity centre
- complimentary airport and golf shuttle bus

$65.00 Cdn.* ($55.00 U.S.*)
* Per person per night based on double occupancy

Package Includes:
- Deluxe Accomodations • Breakfast Voucher • Welcome Gift
- Free Shuttle Service to Lionhead Golf & Country Club
- Free Parking • All Taxes Included

Note: Package does not include the price of golf. For golf rates and tee-off time availability contact Lionhead Golf & Country Club at (416)455-4900

For reservations contact:
1-800-887-1133 (U.S.A.) • **1-800-268-1133** (CANADA)
(416) 927-1133 (TORONTO) • **(416) 821-1981** (HOTEL DIRECT)

Delta Meadowvale
6750 Mississauga Rd, Mississauga, Ontario L5N 2L3

THE COURSE THAT JACK BUILT

"The idea was to build a championship golf course, a tough but fair golf course, but most of all, an easily viewable golf course."

Glen Abbey was the first public golf club in Canada to be specifically designed for major tournaments, with the spectator in mind. Spectator mounds have been built into this magnificent course so the public can view their favorite tour player in action.

Now home of the "Canadian Open", *Glen Abbey* has hosted this event fourteen times; 1993 will make fifteen.

The course is a favorite for many golfers who want to match scores where the pros compete. It is open for public play only and has four lakes, three of which are on the upper level of gently rolling fairways. The forth is in the spectacular valley area along with the Credit River, steep canyon walls and magnificent trees.

The history of *Glen Abbey* and its unique "Swinging Monk" symbol is quite interesting. Originally a large country estate, the property was bequeathed to Jesuit priests when the owner passed away. They used it as a retreat, but in time it became too difficult for them to maintain. Nonetheless, their stay left a mark on "The Abbey", an old stone building reputed to be haunted by "the ghost of the friendly monk".

A group of Oakville businessmen purchased the property, and turned it into *Upper Canada Golf & Country Club*. It then became the *Clearstream Golf & Country Club*, and finally *Glen Abbey*. Each in turn inherited "the ghost" and it was therefore decided to incorporate this legend into the club's logo.

"The Abbey" is now named, "Golf House" and is home to the Royal Canadian Golf Association, its museum, the Canadian Golf Foundation and the "Canadian Golf Hall of Fame". Once you have played your round and made full use of the clubhouse, you are welcome to visit Golf House (weekdays from 9:00am - 5:00pm). Who knows, you may even encounter ...

GLEN ABBEY GOLF CLUB

OAKVILLE, ONT. (On Dorval Dr., N. of Q.E.W.)
Clubhouse: (416)844-1800   Pro Shop: (416)844-1811   Fax: (416)844-2035

Dir. of Golf: Jack McClellan - CPGA
Course Supt.: Dean Baker - CGSA

Head Pro: Bob Lean - CPGA
Architect: Jack Nicklaus

18 Holes Par 73 7102/6618/6202/5577 yds.   Rating: Men's - 77, Ladies' - 73.5

Course Record: 62 - Greg Norman, L. Thompson, A. Bean

Home of the "Canadian Open".

$$$$$		Golf Pkgs.	Public	Power Carts	Lessons	Lounge	Snack Bar	Meals	

HOTEL OAKVILLE

Take your next GOLF VACATION with us.

Tee Off with us

While in Oakville plan to stay with us at HOTEL OAKVILLE, Howard Johnson and play these fine area courses:

- Glen Abbey Golf Club
- River Oaks Golf Centre
- White Oaks Golf Club
- Deerfield Golf & Recreation Centre
- Richview Golf & Country Club
- Oakville Executive Golf Course
- Saw-Whet Golf Club

(Courses are described in detail elsewhere in this section of the Directory)

Our GOLF PACKAGE includes overnight accommodation, breakfast, free parking, free in-room movies, special rates at area golf courses and much more . . .

Enjoy our Facilities:
- Indoor Pool • Whirlpool • Saunas • Exercise Room
- Fine Dining at "Chatt's" Dining Room
- "Schooner's" Atrium Lounge

HOTEL OAKVILLE, HOWARD JOHNSON

590 Argus Road, Oakville, Ontario L6J 3J3
Tel: (416) 842 -4780 Fax: (416) 842-5123
Toll Free: 1-800-654-2000

*Northwest is Mennonite Country, and the **Kitchener-Waterloo** Area. These twin cities offer some of the most dynamic and diverse activities anywhere, from exciting nightlife and shopping to quiet drives and scenic strolls through the gorgeous countryside. This is home to a large Mennonite community, so it's quite common to see a horse-and-buggy team pulling past the modern glass and concrete of Waterloo's two top-notch universities. With a heavy German population, the area has been called "Little Berlin", and, in mid-October, is host to Canada's largest, most enthusiastic "Oktoberfest" celebration.*

*Nearby, the city of **Guelph** is a smaller but no less exciting community, with many festivals including the popular "Guelph Spring Festival", held in May. Guelph is also home to Canada's premier agricultural university and veterinary hospital.*

The Canadian Academy
of
PURE GOLF

- 3 DAY & 4 DAY GOLF SCHOOLS -

LOCATIONS:

Chestnut Hill Country Club, Richmond Hill,
Leslie St. just south of Bloomington Sideroad

Glen Ayre Golf
Highway 8 between Mount Forest & Durham

Horseshoe Valley Resort
Barrie, Ontario

HORSESHOE

World-Renowned Professional Instructors
• Mark Evershed   • Bobby Wilson
• Moe Norman   • Jerry Anderson

• Fun
• Quality Accommodations
• Breakfasts & Lunches Included
• Video Analysis
• Course Management
• Beginners & Low Handicappers
• Playing Lesson & Unlimited Range Balls
• Small Classes of 4 to 6 Students/Instructor

FOR MORE INFORMATION CONTACT:

Sharon Kennedy-Menaul or Gary Menual

PURE GOLF

Box 1102, Durham, Ontario N0G 1R0
Tel: (416)449-6767 or (519)369-5457
Fax: (416)449-6821

*Canada's largest city is also perhaps its most enticing. When you visit **Toronto**, whether to work or to play golf, you are visiting the hub around which the rest of the country turns. You are also visiting the third largest golf market in the world, (after Chicago and San Diego).*

If you want to see Toronto, a good place to start is with a visit to the tallest free-standing structure in the world, the awesome CN Tower. Built less than 20 years ago, it has quickly become the Toronto landmark. Next door you'll find the brand-new SkyDome, home of the World Champion Toronto Blue Jays baseball team, with The Dome's state-of-the-art retractable roof. Lose yourself in each part of the city, from Chinatown to Kensington Market, an outdoor market nestled in the downtown core. From the mountainous highrises of Bay Street to the eclectic architecture of Spadina Avenue, including Casa Loma, Toronto's only castle, and from the street artists on Queen Street to the Royal Ontario Museum, Toronto is a "world-class city" with few rivals.

The Pheasant Run GOLF CLUB

PHEASANT RUN GOLF CLUB

SHARON, ONT. (On Warden Ave., 1/2 Mi. N. of Davis Dr.)
Telephone: (416)898-3917   or: (416)773-8475

Owner: Gordon Evans   Manager: Dave Evans

Highland Course - 9 Holes Par 37 3328 yds.
Midland Course - 9 Holes Par 36 3132 yds.
Southern Uplands - 9 Holes Par 35 2926 yds.

Breathtaking views, wandering water hazards, 89 sandy bunkers, naturally rolling terrain with narrow fairways framed by majestic forest. This course delights and reward golfers of all abilities.

$$$		Golf Pkgs.	Public	Power Carts	Lessons	Lounge	Snack Bar	Meals	

CROWNE PLAZA®

TORONTO AIRPORT
970 DIXON ROAD ❑ ETOBICOKE(TORONTO), ONTARIO, CANADA M9W 1J9
(416) 675-7611 FAX (416) 675-9162

BETTER THAN PAR!

The perfect combination ....
Holiday Inn Crowne Plaza & Royal Woodbine

- 5 minutes to Royal Woodbine
- Indoor and Outdoor Swimming Pools
- Sauna, Whirlpool, Fitness Centre
- Snookers Recreation Club Lounge
- Complimentary Airport Shuttle and Parking
- 30 minutes to Glen Abbey, Lionhead, Devil's Pulpit/
  Paintbrush and most Toronto-area courses

ROYAL WOODBINE GOLF CLUB

ETOBICOKE, ONT. (On Galaxy Rd. near Carlingview and Dixon Rd.)
Telephone: (416)674-4653(GOLF)

Director of Golf: Arnold Porter   Head Pro: Barry Wallis - CPGA
Course Supt.: Chris Dew - CGSA   Architect: M. J. Hurdzan

18 Holes   Par 71   6446/6109/5173 yds.   Rating: 71.4 /69.4/ 67.2

5 minutes from Highways 401 & 427. Three day advance
tee time reservations. Many hotels within walking distance.

$$		Golf Pkgs.	Public	Power Carts	Lessons	Lounge	Snack Bar	Meals	

Take a ferry out to Toronto Island for the day, where you can rent a bicycle and peddle along the meandering paths and view the city's impressive skyline in the distance. Toronto's lakeshore has great appeal, with Ontario Place, a huge waterfront complex of parks and entertainment, and, across the road, the Exhibition grounds, home of the Canadian National Exhibition, (The Ex), held at the end of each summer. Anybody who's anybody in show business has either sung, acted or made a film in town, with theatres of every shape and size to accommodate all performers. Each of Toronto's five boroughs are home to parts of this city's vibrant life, including the Metro Toronto Zoo in Scarborough, the Ontario Science Centre in East York, Black Creek Pioneer Village in North York, as well as Toronto's first post office, over 150 years old, in York, and Woodbine Racetrack in Etobicoke.

Mississauga, which rivals Toronto in size, is a relatively new city created by the amalgamation of five smaller towns. Mississauga is a planned community with each neighbourhood very nearly self-contained. Toronto's Lester B. Pearson International Airport sits on the boundary between Mississauga and Etobicoke.

Further west is Oakville, which is home to the Royal Canadian Golf Association, it's museum, the Canadian Golf Foundation, and the Canadian Golfers Hall of Fame. Downtown Oakville, and nearby Bronte Harbour, are picturesque shopping and marina districts. North of Toronto are the cities of Vaughan and Maple, through whose borders run Canada's Wonderland, an exciting amusement park.

East of Toronto lie the communities of Pickering, Ajax, Oshawa and Whitby,. Oshawa is the Canadian birthplace of General Motors, and its present Canadian headquarters.

Lodge & Golf Club

MAPLES OF BALLANTRAE LODGE & GOLF CLUB

STOUFFVILLE, ONT (West side of Hwy. 48, 1.5 km north of Bloomington Rd.)
Pro Shop: (416)640-6077   Lodge: (416)640-4882   Fax: (416)642-0469

Owner: Michael Wade   Mgr./Head Pro: Tom Aird - CPGA
Course Supt.: Don Kulba - CGSA   Architect: R.F. Bob Moote & Assoc.

18 Holes   Par 72   6300 yds.

Golf holiday packages. Stay, dine and relax in our
rustic lodge overlooking the golf course. Only 20 minutes from Toronto.

$$	Resort	Golf Pkgs.	Public	Power Carts	Lessons	Lounge	Snack Bar	Meals		

WOODLANDS
Golf & Country Club

— UNDER NEW OWNERSHIP & MANAGEMENT —

IMPROVED GREENS
&
CLUBHOUSE FACILITIES

NEW
GRASS DRIVING RANGE

- **TOURNAMENTS WELCOME**
- **WEDDINGS**
- **BANQUETS**
- **1992 MEMBERSHIPS AVAILABLE**

WOODLANDS GOLF & COUNTRY CLUB

BRAMPTON, ONT. (On McVean Dr., R.R. #8)
Clubhouse: (416)794-0850   Pro Shop: (416)794-0852   Fax: (416)794-0853

General Manager: Enzo Maggisano
Golf Course Manager: Ennio Ercoli

9 Holes Par 35 2773 yds.
9 Holes Par 35 2981 yds.
9 Holes Par 35 2986 yds.

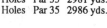

$$			Public	Power Carts	Lessons	Lounge	Snack Bar	Meals	

When calling or writing our advertisers, please mention *Golf Connections*.   81

The Lakelands region is home to numerous lakes and rivers, and also Algonquin Park, one of Canada's largest provincial parks. Running from Parry Sound on Georgian Bay to the Ottawa River Valley, and the resort and cottage country north of Toronto to North Bay on Lake Nipissing, this area is an oasis for anyone seeking some all-season escape.

Georgian Bay has the world's greatest concentration of islands along its eastern shore, with thousands upon thousands of beautiful islands sheltering quiet bays and channels like an endless series of interconnected lakes. **Parry Sound,** *is what a relaxing summer vacation should be; tranquil sunsets over still water, warm summer sun on the back nine, moonlit cruises past a dark shore. Calm summer days like this are found throughout the shores of Georgian Bay, south through the islands to Midland and* **Penatanguishene,** *and down the beaches to* **Wasaga** *and* **Collingwood.** *You've found the heart of the "Georgian Triangle", an area bounded by the scenic Blue Mountains, and the Niagara Escarpment's Bruce Trail. Some of Canada's best-known resorts are located in the Triangle, with great golf and all-year recreation available. Collingwood, originally know as "Hen and Chicken's Harbour", is a city that has carefully preserved its past as a shipyard, while being progressive and offering a first-rate vacation stay.* **Barrie,** *south of the Triangle and on the shore of Lake Simcoe, is the largest city in the Huronia region, offering top-name outdoor concerts and sporting events, as well as a revitalized harbour district and excellent places to stay.*

Stay 'n Play Golf

Now 27 Holes!
3 Days Unlimited Golf

2 nights weekend Friday & Saturday
2 golfers $325. ¹ golfer $274.
1 Non-golfer

2 nights weekday Sunday to Thurs.
2 golfers $281. ¹ golfer $246.
1 Non-golfer

Rates are double occupancy + GST + PST

Rates ★ 2 nights accommodation, 2 per room
include ★ 4 breakfasts ★ 3 days unlimited golf

★ 165 guest rooms - 4 star resort ★ Challenging 27 holes ★ Driving range ★ Practice green
★ Cart rentals ★ Pro shop ★ Instructional packages ★ Mini golf (18) ★ Twilight rates
★ Daily green fees - Frequency discounts ★ Tournaments ★ Indoor & outdoor pools
★ Exercise room ★ Whirlpool ★ Racquetball ★ Tennis ★ 2 Dining rooms ★ Cafe ★ Lounge
★ Live entertainment ★ Barbecue patio ★ Banquets ★ Conventions & more!

It's a short drive to our first tee!
45 min north of Toronto. 12 km west of Hwy 400 on Hwy 89 just east of Alliston

 NOTTAWASAGA INN
CONVENTION CENTRE & GOLF COURSE
1110 Hwy. 89, Alliston Ont. L9R 1A4

Toronto direct
(416) 364-5068
Barrie direct
(705) 458-9595
Alliston area
(705) 435-5501
Fax (705) 435-5840

NOTTAWASAGA INN GOLF CLUB

ALLISTON, ONT. (on Hwy. 89, 12 km west of Hwy 400)
Clubhouse: (705)435-5501   Toronto Line: (416)364-5068
Barrie Line: (705)458-9595   Fax: (705)435-5840

Director of Golf: Ron Harris - CPGA   Head Pro: George Clifton - CPGA
Course Supt.: John Vanderpost

Green Briar: 9 Holes Par 35 3188 yds. Valley: 9 Holes Par 35 3019 yds.
Briarhill: 9 Holes Par 35 3150 yds.

The 4-star resort is surrounded by 375 acres in the Nottawasaga Valley.
27 challenging holes with ponds and river in play on 14 holes.

$$	Resort	Golf Pkgs.	Public	Power Carts	Lessons	Lounge	Snack Bar	Meals	

COME SEE BLUE IN GREEN

Ranked 'Top 10' Canadian Resort Golf Course

Monterra Golf, opened in 1989, has quickly gained national attention. This spectacular layout plays away from the base of Blue Mountain towards Georgian Bay providing the course with many breathtaking vistas.

The strategic nature of Monterra is exemplified by the bent-grass fairways, changing elevations and ominous waste areas. The course features razorback mounding, multi-tiered greens and multiple tee positions challenging golfers of all levels.

Monterra boasts 6,601 yards, 76 sand traps, 6 water holes and mounding that could challenge the mountain itself.

Located at Blue Mountain Resorts, Monterra Golf is an ideal golf getaway.

MONTERRA GOLF

COLLINGWOOD (On Blue Mountain Rd., off Hwy. 26)
Telephone: (705)445-0231   Toronto Line: (416)869-3799
Fax: (705)444-2386

Owners: Blue Mountain Resorts Ltd.   President: Gord Canning
Dir. of Golf: Ron Heesen - CGCS   Architect: Thomas McBroom & Assoc.

18 Holes   Par 72   6601 yds.   Rating: Men's - 73.5, Ladies' - 66
Course Record: 66 - Brian French - 1989

Full course meals are available in the dining area.

$$$	Resort	Golf Pkgs.	Public	Power Carts	Lessons	Lounge	Snack Bar	Meals	

THE BRIARS
A Classic Country Resort

The Alluring Spirit of a Classic Country Resort, awaits !

Truly one of Canada's classic country resorts, The Briars is ideally situated just an hour north of Toronto. Nestled aside the fresh waters of Lake Simcoe, this authentic 200-acre heritage estate offers traditional hospitality in an unparalled natural setting.

John Sibbald, *"The Squire"* is justifiably proud of his family estate, now home to the fifth generation. The Briars' property has been gradually transformed by the Sibbalds into a unique year-round resort combining a distinctive Inn & Manor House, with a lakeside Country Club and the epitome of Golf Courses.

Choose from heritage accommodation in the restored Manor House, modern bedsitting rooms at The Inn - many with fireplaces, charming country club cottages or the special comforts of deluxe lodgings found throughout the resort.

The dining experience at The Briars is often described as *"country fresh with a gourmet touch."* Dining rooms at The Manor House seem to flow from one to the other and are cheerfully bright daytime, softly romantic in the evening. Panoramic views of Lake Simcoe can be enjoyed over drinks atop The Tower, or relax in Drinkwater Lounge with a view of the gardens.

The renowned Briars Golf Club is *"at your doorstep"* all season long. This challenging 18 hole, par 71 private course offers lush fairways and attentively kept greens in the classic Robbie Robinson design.

Other on-site facilities include five outdoor tennis courts, an indoor pool, sauna, whirlpool, exercise room, billiards & game rooms and wooded walking trails. Seasonal activities include cross-country skiing, skating, horse-drawn sleigh rides, bicycling, sailing and other resort activities.

The Briars is a Four Diamond property . . . . . its facilities, amenities and service impeccable.

For more information call toll- free from Canada & USA 1-800-465-2376. The local telephone number is (416)722-3271 - Fax number (416)722-9698.

THE BRIARS

Discover the charm of a country inn with the extras of a world class, five star resort, just one hour north of Toronto. Choose from gracious rooms in the manor or lakeside cottages on our beautiful 200 acre estate. Challenging golf, tennis, indoor & outdoor swimming, windsurfing and sailing are at your doorstep. There is a summer program for kids.

The Briars features a traditional 18 hole Scottish woodland course – a place where golf was meant to be played!

55 Hedge Road
Rural Route 1
Jackson's Point
Ontario. L0E 1L0

THE BRIARS
A Classic Country Resort

CALL TOLL-FREE
Can/U.S.A.
1-800-465-2376

THE BRIARS GOLF & COUNTRY CLUB
JACKSON'S POINT (On Hedge Rd.)
Telephone: (416)722-3772

Head Pro: Brad Johnston
Course Supt.: Grant Sedore - CGSA

18 Holes Par 71 6229 yds.
Rating: Mens' - 70, Ladies' - 71

Course Record: 63 - Robbie Phillips - 1987

	Resort	Golf Pkgs.	Private	Power Carts	Lessons	Lounge	Snack Bar	Meals	
	Resort	Golf Pkgs.	Private	Power Carts	Lessons	Lounge	Snack Bar	Meals	

The Muskokas are a popular vacation spot because of their close proximity to just about anywhere. Gravenhurst, the "Gateway to Muskoka", is nestled between Gull and Muskoka Lakes, and is a good jumping-off point from which to explore this incredible area. Ride the R.M.S. Segwun, a fully operational steamboat that offers one-of-a-kind tours through the lakes. Bracebridge is the jewel in the Muskoka crown, sporting a quaint downtown and the impressive "Bracebridge Falls", flowing with so much power they provide electricity to the whole area. Perhaps the city's biggest claim-to-fame is as the summer home to Santa Claus, who can be visited at the "Santa's Village Theme Park", which is located "halfway between the Equator and the North Pole". Huntsville is the district's largest city, with an extensive downtown shopping area. Huntsville is close to both Arrowhead and Algonquin Provincial Parks, the latter being one of the most impressive and stunning nature areas in the world. Turning 100 years old in 1993, Algonquin offers something exciting for every type of outdoor enthusiast, from bird-watching and nature tours to strenuous survival hikes and canoe portaging between the Park's hundreds of lakes and rivers. There's no better time than now to lose yourself in Algonquin's splendor.

North Bay, on the shores of Lake Nipissing, provides year-round adventure on some of the most exceptional land in the world. North Bay is noted for it's abundant fishing both during the summer and through the ice in winter, as well as brisk swimming in clean, clear water. The waterfront is an ideal place to view the inspiring northern sunsets, and, if you're lucky, perhaps the"Northern Lights". Following the Mattawa River to it's link with the Ottawa River, you skirt the edge of Algonquin and travel down the lush, scenic Ottawa Valley, with camping, cottages and fresh-picked vegetables at every turn. Heading west again, below the rim of Algonquin Park, is the northern portion of the Kawarthas, with family cottages, canals and quaint, lakeside towns like Bobcaygeon, Lindsay and Fenelon Falls.

You'll enjoy all that Haliburton's only 5-star resort has to offer.

A scenic two hour drive from Toronto delivers you to the heart of the Haliburton Highlands - the breathtaking backdrop for PineStone's challenging par 71, 18 hole championship golf course; one of Ontario's top rated resort courses streching out over 6,000 yards of magnificent wooded hills and countryside.

ENJOY OUR FACILITIES:

⇨ 103 spacious guest rooms, suites, chalets and villas - many with fireplaces and whirlpool baths
⇨ Indoor and outdoor pools, whirlpool, saunas and exercise room
⇨ Volleyball, shuffle board, tennis and pro shop
⇨ 13 conference and function rooms, fine dining and nightly entertainment
⇨ Children's Creative Centre, playground and fully supervised "Fun Zone"

PineStone

RESORT AND CONFERENCE CENTRE

1-800-461-0357

Phone: **(705)457-1800** • Fax: **(705)457-3432**

R.R. #2 (Highway 121) Haliburton, Ontario K0M 1S0

PINESTONE RESORT & CONFERENCE CENTRE

HALIBURTON (On Hwy. 121, via Hwy. 35 N. through Minden, then E.)
Telephone: (705)457-1800   Fax: (705)457-3432

General Manager: Alan Richards   Pro Shop Manager: Kathy Wallington
Head Pro: Doug Kirkham   Course Supt.: Brian Kuzmich

18 Holes Par 71 6023 yds.
Rating: Men's - 69.0, Ladies' - 73.5

Course Record: 67 by Hugh Nichol in 1988

$$$	Resort	Golf Pkgs.	Public	Power Carts	Lessons	Lounge	Snack Bar	Meals

Bracebridge Golf Club

Nestled in the Muskoka region of Ontario, this beautifully-groomed 9-hole course with rolling hills and seven water crossings offers golfers a challenge unlike anywhere else in the area. We offer a driving range, pitching green, putting green, fully stocked pro shop, club storage and fully licensed lounge and snack bar.

GREEN FEE PLAYERS &
TOURNAMENTS WELCOME
(705) 645-2362

CHALET INN

Being only 7 km from the Bracebridge Town Centre, we are close enough to enjoy choice Dining, Live Theatre, Boat Cruises, Santa's Village, Shopping and Tennis. We also offer GOLF PACKAGES with the Bracebridge Golf Course which is only 2 km away. Your Hosts: Neil & Sybil Brodie
Tim & Donna Brodie

"Discover a Gem", Where the Service is Excellent!
(705) 645-4152 or **1-800-363-4008** (Canada Wide)
R.R. #2, CEDAR LANE, BRACEBRIDGE, ONTARIO P1L 1W9

BRACEBRIDGE GOLF CLUB

BRACEBRIDGE, ONT. (On Hwy 117, E. off Hwy 11, N. of Bracebridge)
Telephone (705) 645-2362

Owners: Nancy & Allan Pratt
Manager: Nancy Pratt
Course Supt.: Allan Pratt - CGSA

9 Holes   Par 35   2730 yds.

$$		Golf Pkgs.	Public	Power Carts	Lessons	Lounge	Snack Bar	Meals	
			✓						

BROOKLEA INN GOLF & COUNTRY CLUB
MIDLAND (On Hwy. 93, 1-1/2 Mi. S. of Midland)
Clubhouse: (705)526-9872   Pro Shop: (705)526-7532

Manager: Michael Scherloski   Head Pro: Russ Howard
Course Supt.: Marlon Gieseler

18 Holes Par 72 6610 yds. Rating: Men's - 73, Ladies' - 71
 9 Holes Par 32 1735 yds.

Brooklea's 18 hole course is rated 73 by the
Ontario Golf Association. One of the highest rated in Huronia.

$$	Resort	Golf Pkgs.	Public	Power Carts	Lessons	Lounge	Snack Bar	Meals	

golf packages

Located on 1,000 acres of rolling wooded countryside on the shores of Peninsula Lake in the heart of Muskoka, Deerhurts Resort is an ideal golf destination, and welcomes golfers of all skill levels with a variety of affordable golf packages.

Deerhurst Resort offers two courses appealing to everyone from beginner to professional. The championship Deerhurst Highlands, designed by the renowned team of Robert Cupp and Thomas McBroom... 7,011 yards, 18-hole par 72. Deerhurst Lakeside... 4,500 yards, 18-holes par 65. Deerhurst Resort offers five golf Pros available for indiviual or group lessons, arranged in advance or upon arrival at the resort.

Other sports include: tennis, squash, racquetball, fitness room, indoor and outdoor pools, pedal boats, canoes, sail boats, windsurfing, and hiking trails. Horseback riding, waterskiing and fishing boats are available for hire.

1-800-461-4393 • (705)789-6411

Canadian Pacific ◀ Hotels & Resorts

Deerhurst Resort

DEERHURST RESORT GOLF COURSES

HUNTSVILLE, ONT. (On Canal Rd.)
Resort: (705)789-6411   Pro Shop: (705)789-7878

Manager/Head Pro: Paul Kennedy - CPGA
Course Supt.: Ed Farnsworth - CGSA

Highlands: 18 Holes   Par 72   7011 yds.
Lakeside: 18 Holess   Par 65   4500 yds.

\$\$	Resort	Golf Pkgs.	Public	Power Carts	Lessons	Lounge	Snack Bar	Meals	

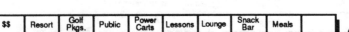

You don't have to travel very far outside of Toronto to feel the soothing nature of the Kawartha Lakes begining to overtake you. Sooner than you think, you arrive in Peterborough, where the scenic tranquility is broken only by the immense Peterborough Lift Lock, part of a series of canals that carry boats of all sizes between the thousands of lakes and river in the area. Peterborough is a town alive with culture, from modern art to the ancient and mysterious "Petroglyphs", a large bedrock slab emblazoned with the figures of Algonkian Indian spirits dating back thousands of years. Peterborough is also host to the "Molson Invitational Pro Am" golf tournament during the summer.

Southeast, on the beautiful Bay of Quinte, lie the sister cities of Belleville and Trenton. Trenton is a fisherman's delight, being the gateway to both the "Trent-Severn Waterway" and the Bay of Quinte. Some of the best fishing, including trout, pickerel and salmon, can be found in these waters. Belleville, known as the "Friendly City on the Bay", is the sport fishing capital of Ontario. The Moira River flows through Belleville, which has grown to become the largest metropolitan centre in the Quinte area, with the finest yacht harbours and the best walleye fishing you can find. Explore the rural beauty and historical tapestry of the Quinte area's many smaller towns, including Wellington, Picton, Stirling, Tweed, Madoc and Marmora.

Following the mouth of the mighty St. Lawrence River, you'll find the surprisingly youthful city of Kingston. Teeming with history, including Sir John A. Macdonald's home, the Royal Military College and Fort Henry, a major battlement in the War of 1812. The city has much that's new to offer, including a vibrant downtown core and Queen's University, one of the most popular in the country. Take a tour into some of the "Thousand Islands", each with histories more diverse than the last, then head back to Kingston for some outstanding shopping and accommodations.

Winding along the St. Lawrence, you'll come to **Brockville**, called the "City of 1000 Islands". In times past, Brockville was known for being the playground of the rich and famous, and was said to have more millionaires per capita than any other Canadian city. This heritage is reflected in the grandeur of its architecture, and in the outlying islands stretching through the area, many with only one family living on them. **Cornwall**, east of Brockville, was settled in 1784 by United Empire Loyalists, who found it the perfect site for farming and a port. Within quick driving distance from Ottawa, Quebec and New York State, Cornwall is an ideal place to enjoy small-town Ontario and all its charms.

Canada's capital, situated in a bend of the wide, winding Ottawa River, is truly one of the country's most affecting cities. One is touched by the understated grandeur of the Parliament Buildings, striking against the backdrop of this mighty river. Our forefathers could not have found a more deserving spot to place the heart of this nation; **Ottawa** is the crowning glory to the lush Ottawa River Valley. Each season has something to offer, with festivals and celebrations year-round. Sit in on a session of Parliament, or walk the bustling streets of this modern downtown. Ottawa is still only minutes away from country, and from the beauty of the rest of eastern Ontario.

Northern Ontario is the largest and most rugged area of Ontario. Its expanse runs from Sudbury and Sault Ste. Marie in the south and north to the southern shore of Hudson Bay, and from the Manitoba border on the west to Quebec's border on the east. The diversity in the land is overpowering, with mighty forests of fur trees along the shores of Lake Superior, and the frozen wastelands of the Far North. This is a land of majesty and silent, overwhelming beauty.

Take the ferry M.S. Chi-Cheemaun north from **Tobermory** and you will arrive on **Manitoulin Island**, a farming and recreation area that marks the boundary between Lake Huron and Georgian Bay. Accessible by boat, or by car along a unique suspension bridge from the mainland the activites are endless, with everything from nature walks and cycling, to swimming off sandy-white beaches and some of the finest fishing in the Great Lakes.

Along Lake Huron's northern shore are the cities of **Sudbury** and **Sault Ste. Marie**. Sudbury is home to a thriving nickel mine, the industry around which this city was built. The landmark giant nickel is a popular tourist attraction. Also recommended is "Science North", Ontario's newest science showplace where visitors will discover the dynamics of science up close. Sault Ste. Marie, affectionately known as "The Soo", is one of Northern Ontario's largest cities. A major steel producer, The Soo is also a great place from which to base your northern excursions. A principal port in the Great Lakes system, enormous ships from around the world use the city as a stopping point. It's also a sportsfisherman's paradise, with North America's "Big 10" sportfish well represented in the crystalline waters of Lake Superior. The drive along the eastern shore of Superior is an experience in itself, with the highway cutting through the rock of the Canadian Shield. And be sure to visit the town of **Wawa**, to see the giant Canada goose.

Your getaway to the Near North

Breathtaking scenery is what makes Mattawa Golf & Ski Resort the place to unwind. Come spend a day, a couple of days or even a week and find out for yourself what we're talking about.

GOLF PACKAGES

- Cross-Country Skiing
- Outdoor Skating
- Snowmobiling
- Downhill Skiing Nearby
- Trout Fishing
...and more

TOURNAMENT PACKAGES

WINTERIZED COTTAGES: Two Bedrooms, Four Piece Bath, Fireplace, TV, VCR, Fridge, Stove, Gas Barbeque
CLUBHOUSE: Restaurant, Licensed Bar, Patio

Contact us today for more information
MATTAWA GOLF & SKI RESORT - (705) 744-5818
P.O. Box 609 Mattawa, Ontario P0H 1V0

MATTAWA GOLF & SKI RESORT

MATTAWA, ONT (On Hwy. 17, 7 Mi. E. of Mattawa)
Telephone: (705)744-5818

Owner: Roland Martel   Manager: Mike Martel
Course Supt.: Mike Martel

9 Holes   Par 37   3229 yds.   Rating: 69.5

Course Record: 65 by Lou Latour in 1988

$	Resort	Golf Pkgs.	Public	Power Carts		Lounge	Snack Bar	Meals	

Thunder Bay is Ontario's northernmost big city. Located on the Trans-Canada Highway, Thunder Bay is the doorway to western Canada. When in Thunder Bay, look out over the water to an island offshore that natives call the "Sleeping Giant". This is the "Big Country", where massive granite outlooks rise high above vibrant forests, and skyscraping black cliffs dive into the "Big Sea Water". Lake Superior is a particular type of lake that, as the locals put it, "refuses to give up her dead". As such, there are countless shipwrecks to explore for those hearty enough to brave the frigid water; and for those who do, there will be an added thrill because everything below is perfectly preserved, as nothing decomposes in this water.

Following the Trans-Canada Highway northwest towards Manitoba, you will find a land of rugged beauty and vast, impenetrable vistas. Travel the lakes and rivers of this awesome, natural country, through *Lake of the Woods* to *Sioux Narrows*, to *Vermillion Bay* and the city of *Dryden*; north through places like *Mimmitaki Lake*, *Ojibway*, *Wabigoon*, *Mameigwess Lake*, to *Sioux Lookout* for a glimpse of how native peoples lived on this land centuries ago. Go where almost no one has ever gone by staying at one of many fly-in camps, where the only way in or out is by amphibious plane. For those who crave a vacation like no other, travel straight up the globe to the top of Ontario, to the shores of Hudson Bay, and see what the original fur traders and soldiers saw hundreds of years ago when they first settled this territory. Witness the supernatural wonder of the Aurora Borealis, the mystical "Northern Lights", and take a frozen dip in Hudson Bay, which is fed directly from the Arctic Ocean.

Visiting Ontario is like coming home to a favorite place; once you're here, you'll never want to leave. Come home to Ontario and explore a land unlike anything you've ever seen before.

MICHIGAN

HEATHER GOLF COURSE • BOYNE COUNTY, MICHIGAN ▲

Golf
Vacations

Michigan is a state with its feet in four of the five Great Lakes, inspiring an impressive sea-going heritage. The State of Michigan is known for many things and has any array of different faces. From the rugged, rocky Upper Peninsula to the Motown sounds of Detroit, this is truly a state of rich diversity.

The Upper Peninsula in Michigan encompasses an area larger than that of Massachussetts, Rhode Island, Connecticut and Delaware combined.

Called "Nature's Theme Park", you can find sand dunes, waterfalls and cliffs, pebbled beaches and squeaky-clean sand. And although this area is in the extreme north of the United States, Lakes Superior and Huron protect it from extreme temperature changes The average summer temperature reaches the high 70s, while winter nights only get down into the 20s.

Most of the land in the Upper Peninsula is public-owned, so you won't find "Keep Out" signs too often. So feel free to explore places like the sand dunes at **Grand Marias** on Lake Superior, where miles of the dunes roll down to the "Inland Sea". At Devil's Slide, tumble down towards the water far below on this smoothed sand slide. History says that lumbermen made the deep cut in the sand as they slid giant timbers down to the lake to be rafted to market.

There are nineteen State Parks, as well as the Isle Royale Park, which is a combination of dense forests and sparkling blue water, a splendid 45 mile long unspoiled island. The Pictured Rocks National Lakeshore, with 15 miles of rugged, 150-200 foot high sandstone cliffs, colored by minerals which seep from within the rock formations.The State Forests at **Hiawatha** and **Ottawa**, vary in their degree of ruggedness.The Seney National Wildlife Refuge, which is the largest contiguous national refuge in the U.S. east of the Mississippi occupies more than 95,000 acres with over 230 species of birds including the bald eagle and the sandhill crane.

With all this unspoiled nature, you are still never more than 30 miles from restaurants, hotels, motels and resorts. The Upper Peninsula is really a full-service vacation spot without seeming like its hovering around you constantly.

- A Golfer's Dream -

The Rock

The Rock ... a truly remarkable layout that is challenging and, at the same time one of the most relaxing rounds of golf you will ever enjoy. Each hole is totally separated from the next and wildlife seems to welcome golfers. Both team up to make The Rock a wonderous adventure.

This unique course was literally carved out of the forest and rock of Drummond Island and blends in beautifully with the rustic atmosphere. Trees, rock outcroppings, waterfalls, ponds and the wildlife combine to make it a breathtaking visual treat as well as a test of any golfer's skill.

Golf packages start at $62.50

- A Secluded Retreat -

Welcome to the world of carefree relaxation and challenging play. A place that reflects your preference for the very best.

Woodmoor

DRUMMOND ISLAND

A 40-room hotel with spacious 400-square-foot rooms, (many with lofts), full scribe log cabins and Frank Lloyd Wright-inspired Bayside cottages, plus elegant meals at Bayside Dining. Woodmoor also boasts a wide variety of casual recreation, including tennis, paddle tennis, outdoor pool and whirlpool, hiking and biking trail, an eight-lane bowling center and a full marina with boat rentals of all sizes.

For more Information Call:
1-800-999-6343
26 Maxton Road, Drummond Island, MI 49726

THE ROCK

DRUMMOND ISLAND, MI (Take ferry from DeTour, MI, or by Charter air service)
Pro Shop: (906) 493-1006   Toll Free: (800) 999-6343

Director of Golf: Larry Ledy   Course Supt: Mike Fairchild
Architect: Harry Bowers

18 Holes   Par 71   6830 Holes

Take the new car ferry from DeTour Village
or fly via charter service from your local airport.

$$$$$	Resort	Golf Pkgs.	Public	Power Carts	Lessons	Lounge	Snack Bar	Meals	

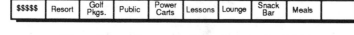

BOYNE MOUNTAIN.

THE MONUMENT:
A scenic mile long golf cart ride takes you to the summit of this 7086 yard jewel. Four sets of tees drop in giant steps to the pond-protected first hole. You end up at the 18th. island hole that Sam Snead calls one of the most intimidating anywhere. The Monument was a GOLF DIGEST runner-up for Best New Resort Course of 1987.

THE ALPINE:
The Alpine also starts at the Mountain's summit, dropping down in swoops to Deer Lake. Spectacular views are everywhere. Fairways are wide and inviting. Blind shots are non-existent. For all of its innocence, strategic bunkers and water hazards can take their toll. Like all Boyne courses, optional tees on holes make it enjoyable whatever one's playing ability. Woods and spaces separate players. During a round you will probably encounter more furry and feathered friends than golfers.

BOYNE HIGHLANDS.

THE MOOR:
Don't forget your sand wedge and ball retriever when you take on this Highland's test. You may need more than your driver. Besides the sand and water, there are marshes, woods, doglegs, and slick, tough-to-read greens. You should tackle The Moor with plenty of golf balls and good humor. The low handicappers who know all five Boyne courses consider it the most difficult. However it is much more forgiving when played from the forward tees.

THE HEATHER:
*In 1971 the Highland's Heather course by Robert Trent Jones, was recognized by GOLF DIGEST as one of America's 100 greatest courses, and in 1979 ranked **best** of all Michigan public and private courses. It's heavily wooded and features greens of up to 10,000 square feet, water hazards and deep bunkers. Heather course carts are equipped with computers, and feature the revolutionary YARDMARK™ distance measuring system, spelling out length of drive, distance to a hazard, the green and the pin.*

THE DONALD ROSS MEMORIAL:
Donald Ross is recognized as the father of golf course architecture in America, and he designed many of the country's classic courses. It's said, "You don't change a Donald Ross course, you copy it." Boyne went beyond mere copying, by duplicating 18 of his finest holes from such famous courses as Pinehurst No. 2, Oakland Hills, Seminole, Inverness and Royal Dornach. The course is strategic rather than penal. As Ross would say, playing it is "a pleasure, not a pennance."

FOR MORE INFORMATION CALL: 1-800-GO-BOYNE

AMERICA'S BEST GOLF VALUE. AND THE MOST FUN.

Boyne's Super 5 golf weeks are popular, one of a kind getaways. For singles, couples, groups and golfers of all abilities. Boyne also offers relaxing diversions like tennis, swimming, saunas, whirlpool, hiking and biking.

Play 36 or more holes a day on Boyne's fabulous five 18-hole championship courses.

Unlike golf instruction schools, the weeks are unregimented. You also get unlimited instruction with video analysis.

You'll play five top-ranked, 18-hole courses located at Boyne Mountain and Boyne Highlands resorts in scenic Northwest Michigan. The courses are lush, immaculate, world-class.

For just $845 per person, double occupancy, you'll get a full week of golf on Boyne's famed Heather, Donald Ross, Monument, Alpine and Moor courses, cart included. Plus unlimited instruction, five nights' lodging, breakfast and dinner daily, a dinner theater, cocktail parties, fun tournaments and special events. Taxes are included.

Book now for prime June, July or August sessions or call or write for free brochure. Video available for $5. Boyne Mountain, Boyne Falls, MI 49713.

Boyne's Super 5™ Golf Week.
1-800-GO-BOYNE. JUST $845

Canadian par value currency exchange to maximum of 15 percent.

Michigan wrapped its upper boundary around the Upper Peninsula as a condition of statehood in 1835 . Many considered it a poor bargain until the discovery of its rich copper and iron deposits, and the utilization of the forest and other natural resources further added to the value of the area.

The land was originally populated by the Chippewa and Menominee Indians. Explorer Father Jacques Marquette built missions in **Sault Ste. Marie** and **St. Ignace**, dating to the 1600s, and are among the oldest communities in the United States. Early European settlers began arriving in the mid-1800s, seeking a new life in the mines, the forests and later the farms that were carved from this fertile land.

The city of Sault Ste. Marie is the largest city in the Upper Peninsula, and is it's most easterly major community. The border with Canada and it's sister city, Sault Ste. Marie, Ontario, is linked by the International Bridge, one of the busiest border points between the two nations. Known as a port city, the enormous Soo Locks move the greatest tonnage of any locks in the world, (more than 10,000 vessels annually), and many visitors come to the city to see the gargantuan freighters sliding easily through on their way between lakes.

The Great Lakes Shipwreck Museum is in **Paradise**, not far from "The Soo", as well as the Point Iroquois Lighthouse, built in 1870 near the Hiawatha National Forest. As well, the rockiness of the terrain has created some spectacular waterfalls, including St. Mary's Falls, which often forced canoe portages in the old days before the Locks, and Tahquamenon Falls, known locally as "Little Niagara", which are the second-largest falls east of the Mississippi. The area is also the setting for Longfellow's epic poem, "Hiawatha".

South of the Upper Peninsula is a more mid-western landscape, with rolling hills, lush fields and some of the most beautiful golf you'll find anywhere in the northeast. Along the shores of Lake Michigan, and around Traverse Bay is **Boyne Country**. Hemingway spent twenty-two delightful summers here, declaring that "this is a priceless place". Located in the heart of America's "Summer Golf Capital", with over 20 spectacular public courses that play from glacier-carved hilltops and valleys, Boyne USA Resort's world-class championship links are ranked among the finest on today's golf circuit.

Summer activities are nearly endless in the Boyne area, with excellent fishing of trout, bass, panfish, walleye, and even salmon and steelhead, from the fresh-water lakes in the area. Boaters can take advantage of a 38-mile inland waterway that winds from Crooked Lake all the way to Lake Huron, at the other side of the state. Sandy beaches line Little Traverse Bay, and the dunes along the Lake Michigan shore offer colorful Petoskey stones which appear magically with each breaking wave.

*The towns of **Harbor Springs** and **Petoskey** invite evening strolls past turn of the century homes, churches, art centers, gingerbread houses and stately inns and hotels. On a quiet residential street in Petoskey, you'll even find Hemingway's former rooming house.*

HARBOR SPRINGS, MI

LITTLE TRAVERSE BAY GOLF CLUB

HARBOR SPRINGS, MI (On Hideaway Valley Drive)
Telephone: (616) 526-6200   Fax: (616) 526-9662

Head Pro: Paulo Rocha   Course Supt: Charles Menefee
Architect: Jeff Gomey

18 Holes   Par 72   6918 yds.

Designed in the traditions of Dr. Alister MacKenzie & Donald Ross, this course with its natural terrain of hills and valleys, is framed by mature stands of hardwood and pine. The panoramic views of Little Traverse Bay, Crooked Lake, Round Lake and Pickerel Lake provide golfers with dramatic vistas at every turn.

$$	Resort	Golf Pkgs.	Public	Power Carts	Lessons	Lounge	Snack Bar	Meals	Open All Year

*East of Boyne, in the heart of Michigan is **Gaylord**, which sits exactly on the 45th parallel, the imaginary line that runs around the globe directly between the North Pole and the Equator. Gaylord is the self-proclaimed "Golf Mecca of the Midwest", featuring 18 championship golf courses. It is also home to the largest elk herd east of the Mississippi, and is the sister city of Pontresina, Switzerland, with Gaylord garnering the name of "Alpine Village".*

MARSH RIDGE

Discover Gaylord's "Little" Resort where the concept of upscale is redefined, not by size but with friendly service, exquisite suites, meticulous greens and great food! A golfer's paradise in Gaylord's paradise of Golf. Take a week and play us all. For something a little special, stay and play at Marsh Ridge.

To make your reservations today call **1-800-743-PLAY** Gaylord, Michigan

* Per Person • Double Occupancy Sunday thru Thursday

THE GREAT ESCAPE
GOLF
LODGING
BREAKFAST
DINNER
$99.00 *

MARSH RIDGE RESORT
GAYLORD, MI (On Old U.S. 27 South)
Telephone: (517) 732-6794   In Michigan: (800) 624-7518

Manager: Dick Weber   Head Pro: Robb Medonis
Course Supt: Chris Whittman   Architect: Mike Husby

18 Holes   Par 71   6155 yds.

An intimate secluded resort that is easily accessible from I-75.

$$$	Resort	Golf Pkgs.	Public	Power Carts	Lessons	Lounge	Snack Bar	Meals	Open All Year

Pigeon State Forest nearby encompasses 80,000 acres of unspoiled nature and many beautiful resort facilities. At St. Ignace, one of the original settlements in northern Michigan, learn about early Ojibwa Indian culture and Michigan history, as well as a fascinating exhibit on shipwreck history.

Treetops
SYLVAN RESORT

TREETOPS SYLVAN RESORT

GAYLORD, MI (On Wilkinson Rd., Exit #282 at I-75 East to Wilkinson Rd.)
Telephone: (517) 732-6711   Toll Free: (800) 444-6711

Manager: Gerald Albert   Dir. of Golf: Rick Smith
Course Supt: Bruce Wolfram   Architect: Robert Trent Jones, Sr.

18 Holes Par 71 6399 yds.

This Robert Trent Jones masterpiece opened in 1987
and has received many State and National awards. A new
Tom Fazio course opened in July of 1992, and, with another course
scheduled to open in July 1993, the total holes at the resort complex will be 63.

$$	Resort	Golf Pkgs.	Public	Power Carts	Lessons	Lounge	Snack Bar	Meals	Open All Year
$$	Resort	Golf Pkgs.	Public	Power Carts	Lessons	Lounge	Snack Bar	Meals	Open All Year

Alpena, along the western shore of Lake Huron, is an ideal family holiday destination with every aspect of Michigan's outdoor recreation available. Alpena's successful "Discover Golf on the Sunrise Side" campaign continues to offer golf packages at affordable prices at any of several courses in the area.

Alpena boasts one of the few Underwater Preserves on the Great Lakes. The Thunder Bay Underwter Preserve, with around 80 wrecks, contains one of the heaviest concentrations of shipwrecks in the Great Lakes. A diving charter is available. As well, the 1870 Presque Isle Lighthouse is the tallest lighthouse on the Great Lakes.

Home to the annual Michigan Brown Trout Festival, Alpena fishing will appeal to anyone from a novice to a sportsfisherman. Fish native to the area include salmon, brown trout, rainbow trout, bass, pike, walleye, perch and panfish.

A-GA-MING GOLF CLUB

KEWADIN, MI. (10 miles N. of Elk Rapids, off U.S. 31)
Telephone: (616)264-5081

Owner: W.A. Siebenthaler	Mktg Director: Mike Terrell
Head Pro: Marv Roskamp	Course Supt: Jim Tollefson
Architect: Chick Harbert	

18 Holes Par 72 6572 yds.

One of the most scenic and challenging courses in Northern Michigan's golfing mecca. Situated on high bluffs, it has spectacular views of Torch Lake.

$$$	Resort	Golf Pkgs.	Public	Power Carts	Lessons	Lounge	Snack Bar	Meals

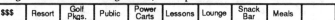

*South of Alpena is an area called "Michigan's Thumb", because of its position on the "hand"-shape of the state. This region is bounded by Huron County, with 93 miles of shoreline, 8 county and state parks, 12 boat launches and 3 state harbors. There are one-hundred and seventy-five centennial farms in the county, with 25 dating back to the 1850s, and 85% are still owned by the original families. **Bad Axe** is known as the "Shopping Mecca" of the Thumb, and is the county seat. **Pigeon** is a rural town nestled among picturesque farms and is called the "Land of Plenty", with one of the nation's richest growing areas. Nearby **Sebewaing** begins the shoreline drive along Saginaw Bay, and is host to the annual Michigan Sugar Festival, with parades and other activites. **Port Austin**, along the northern tip of the Thumb, declares itself the best spot in the state to view the sunrise and sunset.*

Port Huron is one of Michigan's oldest towns, and is located 56 miles from Detroit, across the famous Blue Water Bridge from Sarnia, Ontario. This marks one of the only four border crossings into Ontario. The Blue Water Bridge was begun in 1937, with a span over the river of 875 feet, and a total span of 8,020 feet. It cost $3.24 million to complete, and has a top height of 150 feet above the water. It's quite an impressive way to come in or out of the state.

*Neaby **Flint** is often called "The Vehicle City", as it was the birthplace of General Motors and is world headquarters for four divisions of the company. Prior to the automobile, Flint manufactured wooden carriages, so the motoring tradition is a long one. The Robert T. Longway Planetarium, Michigan's largest and best-equipped, is located in the Flint Cultural Center complex, a series of buildings including a library, the Flint Institute of the Arts, the Institute of Music and several theaters.*

TAWAS GOLF COURSE
On Michigan's Sunrise Side

TAWAS GOLF COURSE

TAWAS, MI (Just 5 min. NW of Tawas, call for specific directions)
Telephone: (517) 362-6262   Toll Free: (800) 235-8409 (US Only)

Manager: Steve Sonoga   Course Supt: Ted Smith

18 Holes   Par 72   6065 yds.

A stream flows through this scenic course which is accentuated
by mature hardwoods, cedars and pines. Excellent greens, water
hazards and traps make play interesting but not overly intimidating.

$		Golf Pkgs.	Public	Power Carts	Lessons	Lounge	Snack Bar	Meals	
$		Golf Pkgs.	Public	Power Carts	Lessons	Lounge	Snack Bar	Meals	

An excellent golf destination, the Buick Open is held here is August, with a $1 million purse. As well, the "Flushing Fabulous Fifties Festival" is held in June in **Flushing**, which has been designated the "Cruising Capital" of Michigan. In **Holly**, the Michigan Renaissance Festival offers a recreation of a 16th century English village during a harvest festival, with over 400 costumed participants and live jousting. The Genessee County Department of Parks and Recreation operates four public beaches during the summer, as well as public fishing, camping and picnic areas.

The town of **Mt. Pleasant**, near Lake Isabella, was originally known as "Ojibwa Besse", and was a hunting ground for Chippewa Indians. Isabella County is well-known as an oil capital and is the location of the Saginaw Indian Reservation.

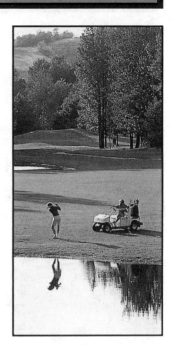

CRYSTAL MOUNTAIN RESORT

THOMPSONVILLE, MI (28 mi. SE of Traverse City, 4 hrs. NW of Windsor via I-75)
Pro Shop: (616) 378-2000   Reservations: (800) 968-7686

Owner: George Petritz   Golf Manager: Steve Kermode
Course Supt: Jim Meszaros   Architect: Robt. Meyer & Wm. Newcomb

27 Holes: 9 Holes Par 36 2897 yds.
           9 Holes Par 35 3036 yds.
           9 Holes Par 37 3296 yds.

Dramatic elevation changes, views & isolated rolling fairways amidst tall pines.

$$$	Resort	Golf Pkgs.	Public	Power Carts	Lessons	Lounge	Snack Bar	Meals	Open All Year

Cadillac, the name synonymous with the ultimate in luxury American automobiles, is a town surrounded by a million acres of state and national forests and numerous lakes and rivers. Named after the French founder of Detroit, Antoine de la Mothe Cadillac, it owes it existence to a thriving lumber industry there more than a hundred years ago. Called the "Snowmobile Capital of Michigan", the town has an outstanding trail system stretching hundreds of miles, and is host to the annual North American Snowmobile Festival. On a warmer note, there are four golf courses within ten miles of town. Morel mushrooms are a local delicacy, and can be found among the hardwood trees. White-tailed deer, grouse, woodcock, wild turkey and other game species abound in the woodlands around Cadillac.

STONEBRIDGE
G O L F   C L U B

STONEBRIDGE GOLF CLUB
ANN ARBOR, MI (On Stonebridge Blvd., between Lonk Rd. and Maple Rd., S. of Ellsworth)
Telephone: (313) 429-8383   Fax: (313) 994-5973

Head Pro: Jeff Graunke   Course Supt: Rick Bellers
Architect: Arthur Hills

18 Holes   Par 72   6458 yds.
The feature hole of Stonebridge is the par-4 #10 hole. Eight of the
back nine holes have water on them which, along with the wetlands, trees
and man-made obstacles make for one of the area's finer, more exciting courses.

$$$		Golf Pkgs.	Public	Power Carts	Lessons	Lounge	Snack Bar	Meals	Open All Year
$$$		Golf Pkgs.	Public	Power Carts	Lessons	Lounge	Snack Bar	Meals	Open All Year

Muskegon County has 26 miles of sandy beaches along the Lake Michigan shore, with water skiing, fishing, body surfing and jet skiing just some of the exciting watersport options. The County has three state parks, all of which are located on Lake Michigan. As well, it has the only two roller coasters in the state at Michigan's Adventure Amusement Park. Similar attractions include the Pleasure Island water fun park and horseracing at the Muskegon Race Course.

*In 1889, **Muskegon's** most prominent lumber baron, Charles Hackley, hired 200 skilled workers and artists to build a house for his family. Today, Hackley House and neighboring Hume Home amaze visitors with their craftsmanship and attention to detail. During the summer, old-fashioned trolley cars operate sight-seeing tours through Muskegon and area. The cost is only 25¢.*

America's most-decorated surviving WWII submarine, the U.S.S. Silversides, is docked on the Muskegon Channel, with guided tours available. She was commissioned into the Navy just 8 days after Pearl Harbor, and served in the Pacific Fleet along Japan's coast, sinking 23 ships, the third-highest among all WWII subs.

*Located just about midway between Chicago and Detroit is the city of **Kalamazoo**, home of Michigan's famous wine-producing region, and is called "Southwest Michigan's Golf Capital". Historic buildings are everywhere, from Gothic, Italianite, Greek Revival, Sullivanesque, Queen Anne, Art Deco and others, including eight different Frank Lloyd Wright designs. The Gilmore-Classic Car Club Museums feature displays of more than 150 antique cars on 90 acres of landscaped grounds.*

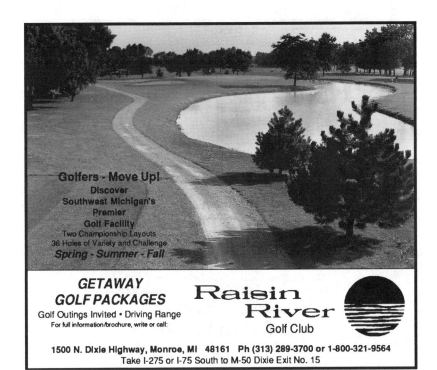

Nearby **Battle Creek** is home to Kellogg's, the largest producer of cereal in the world. As such, Battle Creek has earned the title of "Cereal Capital of the World". Founded in 1831, it began as a small pioneer town with early residents placing major emphasis on the importance of proper health and eating habits. The diet and health regimen at the former Battle Creek Sanitarium made the city famous as the "Healthy City".

Today, Battle Creek is home to the World's Largest Breakfast Table, as well as the Stan Musial Amateur Baseball World Series, the International Festival of Lights and the International Balloon Championship and air show.

The city boasts a foreign trade zone and Customs port of entry, as well as a variety of companies from Japan, Germany and England in its boundaries. Battle Creek industries continue to produce chewing gum, cookies, packaging machinery compressors, lighting, air conditioning and automotive interiors.

MICHIGAN GOLF GUIDE

FULL COLOR

8 ½" x 11", soft-cover guidebooks with color photos and feature articles on some of Michigans most interesting courses.

DETAILED MAPS & LISTINGS

Full-page maps of each county with all courses indicated, and listings that include green fees, course yardage, USGA rating, bar and restaurant services, availability of golf instruction, and more.

LODGING ACCOMODATIONS

listed on large center map for ease in planning extended trips.

FREE

GOLF PACKAGE INFORMATION INCLUDED WITH YOUR ORDER

	QTY.	PR. EA.	TOTAL
North Mich.		$6.95	
Southeast Mich.		$6.95	
Southwest Mich.		$6.95	
Set of all 3		$16.95	
4% Sales tax Michigan residents only			
Postage & handling		2.00	
Total Amount (U.S. FUNDS ONLY PLEASE)			

3 books available

Name _____

Address _____

City _____ State _____ Zip _____

Payment must accompany order. **Please make check or money order to:**

UNICORN GRAPHICS, INC.

P.O. BOX 232, FRASER, MI 48026   (313)792-6359

Lansing, Michigan's state capital, is located in the center of the lower part of the state. Its Capitol Building, a Victorian era design by Elijah E. Myers, was recently restored; the original construction took nearly seven years, and was completed in 1879. Lansing is the center for government for the state, and was the site of one of the 1992 Presidential Debates.

Lansing is marking the return of the LPGA during the spring of 1993 and 1994. As well, the city is home to the "Oldsmobile Classic", and is rimmed with exceptional golf courses. Michigan State University is a "Big 10" school, with a high echelon of college sports year-round.

The Michigan Museum of Surveying, the only one of its kind in the U.S., houses a collection of historical surveying artifacts. The Ingham County Courthouse is 88 years old and has had exterior renovations with interior renovations planned for 1993. The Michigan Library and Historical Center, nationally recognized for its architectural design, houses the Michigan Historical Museum, the State Archives and the Library of Michigan, which is the second largest library in the United States.

Festivals in Lansing include the Michigan Festival, held in August, which celebrates Michigan and its folklife traditions; Riverfest, over the Labor Day Weekend, with a carnival midway and family fun; and Silver Bells in the City, a celebration of lights held in November.

Detroit, "The Motor City", is the 6th largest city in America, with 4.3 million people living there. Downtown is dominated by the 7-tower Renaissance Center, from the 71st floor of which you can get a spectacular view of the surrounding skyline, and Detroit's Canadian neighbor, Windsor, Ontario.

Home of "Motown" records, the Motown Museum is a two-storey house north of downtown where Diana Ross and Smokey Robinson, among many others, began their careers. For a taste of the Blues, try a "blues burger" at the Soup Kitchen Saloon, Detroit's oldest pub, then visit the Rhinoceros for live blues and jazz.

A newly-renovated theater district, with the bejeweled 4,800-seat Fox Theatre, beckons visitors and residents alike downtown in the evening. The Fox, built in 1928, was once the queen of the nation's movie palaces, and sports a chandelier that weighs two tons and spreads thirteen feet across. The Fox now hosts travelling Broadway plays.

A visit to the "Motor City" would not be complete without seeing the Henry Ford Museum in *Dearborn*, which offers a look at Ford's inventions as well as American industry as a whole. One of Ford's hobbies was to collect buildings, and some are on display throughout his museum, including Thomas Edison's laboratory, the bicycle shop where the Wright Brothers built their first airplane, and the house where Noah Webster labored over his first dictionary. Ford's home itself, "Fair Lane", is open for viewing. Built in 1915 in Dearborn, it has 56 rooms, and pales only in comparison to his son, Edsel's, 60-room mansion.

Michigan's greatest strength is perhaps its incredible variety of everything it has to offer; from the solitude of a Lake Superior evening to the roar of the Detroit Grand Prix, from the "Cereal Capital of the World" to "The Thumb", the state of Michigan can boast something for just about everybody.

OHIO

QUAIL HOLLOW RESORT GOLF COURSE • CONCORD, OHIO ▲

Golf Vacations

Surrounded by water on three sides, (Lake Erie to the north, and the Ohio River to the west and east), the "Buckeye State" has a unique flavor. While technically the gateway state into the Midwestern United States, it is not entirely Midwestern; and although surrounded by water, it is not entirely Maritime. Ohio seems to be a perfect combination of both worlds, and the holiday traveller will reap the benefits.

Bordering five states and the balmy shores of Lake Erie, Ohio is tremendously accessable, and the range of vacation options are astounding. From the northwest, at the Michigan state line, and south along the Indiana border is the "Northwest Region". Often called "Big Sky Country", this is the land of farmland stretching as far as the eye can see, and barns as big as all outdoors. The Maumee River seems a mile wide as it rolls into **Toledo**, with grain elevators rising like skyscrapers against the far horizon. Small-town church steeples can be seen for miles along the flat horizon, which stretches along the Lake Erie shoreline and grows bountiful crops of tomatoes, cucumbers, celery, radishes and carrots. During the 1890s, gas and oil were discovered here, and made flamboyant overnight millionaires who had a taste for the extremely gaudy. On the northern shore is **Sandusky**, where you can get a ferry to or from Leamington in nearby Ontario. Sandusky is a garden-filled city of historic homes and museums, one where you can watch carousel restorers at work. Close by is Middle Bass Island, which is a small rocky island dominated by the Gothic castle of the Lonz winery, which pressed its first grapes in the 1860s and became the area's largest wine producer in 1875.

Also in Sandusky is the Cedar Point amusement park, the nation's largest amusement ride park including more roller coasters than any other park in the world, ten in total, and four vintage carousels, also the most in the world. The most popular non-ride is Berenstain Bear Country, which features a 35-foot treehouse. Off shore from Sandusky is Kelleys Island, which is the largest American island on Lake Erie, with archeological sites dating back to 12,000 BC. Also on the shores of Lake Erie is Toledo, home to the Toledo Zoo which has the world's only underwater hippoquarium, as well as the Toledo Museum of Art and the world-famous Toledo Mud Hens baseball team. Heading south into Ohio is **Wapakoneta**, home town of Neil Armstrong who was the first man to step on the moon. The Neil Armstrong Air & Space Museum relives his trip through models, authentic spacecraft, photos, film footage and the famous radio transmission heard across deep space on July 20, 1969 ... "That's one small step for man -- one giant leap for mankind". Thomas Edison's birthplace is in **Milan** in a small red-brick house which has been converted into a museum and offers insight into the genius who held 1,093 patents including the incandescent light, the phonograph, the movie camera and the mimeograph.

OHIO'S GOLF CAPITAL ™

NOT MYRTLE BEACH, BUT IT'S REAL CLOSE.

The Canton/Stark County area is fast becoming known as Ohio's Golf Capital.™ With 39 championship caliber courses and convenient accommodations,

•CANTON

SM

we offer a golf vacation that includes excellent dining, unique shopping, nighttime entertainment, all within minutes of the Pro Football Hall of Fame.

GOLF PACKAGES
per person, double occupancy, includes lodging, breakfast, green fees and shared cart.

starting at

$**49**

anton/stark county
CONVENTION & VISITORS' BUREAU

1-800-533-4302
Phone lines open 24 hrs., 7 days a week

The southwestern part of the state is the home of two of Ohio's major cities, **Cincinnati** and **Dayton**. Dayton is called "The Birthplace of Aviation". It was here that the Wright Brothers developed flight, and the city is a living museum to the importance of this discovery. The United States Air Force Museum is the world's largest aviation museum, complete with a 6-storey IMAX theater. The Dayton Art Institute is housed in a national historic building, and the Dayton Museum of Natural History is an interesting excursion. Historic southwest Ohio is alive at **Sharon Woods Village**, between Dayton and Cincinnati, with ten restored buildings including an 1804 log home, an 1880 railway station, an 1870 general store, an 1829 country inn, an 1860s-era doctor's office, an 1812 barn and two mid-1800s farmhouses.

Outside of Cincinnati is Kings Island Park, an amusement park which, this year, celebrating its 20th anniversary. The Park features Hanna-Barbara Land for the very young, and some terrifying roller coasters, including the "biggest, baddest wooden roller coaster", called "The Beast", as well as their steel coaster, "Vortex". Kings Island also houses a 100-acre Wild Animal Habitat with over 350 exotic animals, the "Phantom Theater", full of wierd visions and unexplained phenomena, as well as water rides, charming stores, live Broadway productions and fabulous food. Camping facilites and excellent indoor accommodations are available.

The center of Cincinnati is dominated by Fountain Square, where the "Genius of Water" statue sits high atop Tyler Davidson Fountain overlooking the broad open plaza. The Ohio River flows calmly through the city, and steam-powered riverboats right out of Mark Twain's time carry passengers up and down the River. The Cincinnati Reds were the first professional baseball team to play in the U.S., and you can catch a game at Riverfront Stadium. In the Fall, the Cincinnati Bengals wear their distinctive black-and-orange stripes on the field. Cincinnati's Museum Center is located in the art deco Union Terminal, which is often referred to as "the eighth wonder of the world". Inside, you can relive 19,000 years of history, and see films on the five-storey Omni-Max theater. The Cincinnati skyline at night is absolutely beautiful, and you can enjoy quiet strolls along the Ohio River, or dance the night away at one of countless nightclubs.

FORE!

Come **FORE**
the accommodations,
come **FORE**
the golf!

Kings Island Inn is a golfer's paradise,
with six golf courses just minutes
away, including two courses
designed by Jack Nicklaus.

- 288 guestrooms, 2 suites, 55 executive King rooms
- Indoor pool, sauna, whirlpool, exercise room, game room
- 20 minutes from downtown Cincinnati
- Located directly across from Paramount's Kings Island

GOLF PACKAGES INCLUDE:
Accommodations, green fee for
18 holes and golf cart

Kings Island Inn
& CONFERENCE CENTER

Individual Reservations
1-800-727-3050
Groups of 10 or more
(513)398-0115

5691 Kings Island Dr., Kings Island, Ohio 45034 (I-71 South to Exit 25A)

Midway through Ohio, on the I-71 highway from Cincinnati, is the state capital of **Columbus**. The largest city in the state, it is also Ohio's major city. Columbus is home to the Ohio State University, which has had many medical research breakthroughs in recent years, as well as the Battelle Memorial Institute, which is the world's largest private technology research and development organization. The neighborhoods of Columbus are vibrant with the heritage and culture of its early settlers, including German Village, a neighborhood that pays homage to Columbus' German heritage. At the waterfront of the Scioto River sits a replica of the Santa Maria, one of the ships used by Christopher Columbus when he discovered America, and a symbol of the city's namesake. Museums in the city include the Columbus Museum of Art, Ohio's Center of Science & Technology, which offers hands-on activites for kids and adults, as well as the Ohio Historical Society, which includes Ohio Village, a re-creation of a mid-19th century Ohio town.

Columbus is a large city with a modern skyline and all the amenities of big city life, and some terrific accommodation prices. This is also the land of the family farm, (and the designer golf course), where people raise corn, kids and Hondas.

Manufacturing and agriculture are strong forces in the Heartland of America, and the other side of Central Ohio are the farms and the small-town museums which celebrate local history, where the business districts have been preserved pretty much as they were in the 1800s. Some of the towns include **Dublin, Westerville and Granville**, as well as many vintage settlements dotting the countryside along US Route 40, reminding travellers of the days when the "National Road" carried the nation west. Knox County is 49 miles north-east of Columbus, and offers a good breakaway from the city, with unique shops, antiques, and Christmas walks through century-old neighborhoods. The county has 8 golf courses, as well as camping and outdoor activities.

QUAIL HOLLOW
A CLUB RESORT

Championship Golf
•
Conference Facliities
•
Fine Dining
•
Personalized Service

3 Day / 2 Night Golf Holiday
from $219.00 (ppdo)

- Elegant guest room
- 18 holes of golf each day with cart
- $25.00 of "Country Money" per person*
- Golf storage / cleaning
- Souvenir tees, divot repair tool and yardage book
- Taxes

* for purchase of pro shop or gift shop merchandise

"Home of the NIKE / Cleveland Open presented by REVCO"

(216)352-6201 • 1-800-792-0258

I-90 AT STATE ROUTE 44 (EXIT 200), CONCORD (CLEVELAND), OHIO 44077-9557

QUAIL HOLLOW RESORT GOLF CLUB

CONCORD, OH (I-90 at State Route 44, Exit 200, 30 miles E. of Cleveland)
Toll Free: 1-800-792-0258 ext. 3524 (Pro Shop ext. 3522)   Fax: (216) 639-1637

Owner: Club Resorts Inc.   Manager: Mike Srdjak, G.M.
Head Pro: Tony Milam, PGA   Course Supt.: Bob Blaylock, GSA
Architects: Bruce Devlin / Robert Von Hagge

18 Holes   Par 73   6400 yds.

Rolling terrain, wooded with narrow fairways. Home of the PGA NIKE Cleveland
Open (former Ben Hogan Tour), with the highest purse on tour.

$$$	Resort	Golf Pkgs.		Power Carts	Lessons	Lounge	Snack Bar	Meals	

SUGAR BUSH GOLF INC.

GARRETTSVILLE, OH (On Route 88 in Garrettsville)
Telephone: (216) 527-4202

Manager/Head Pro: Mike Koval

18 Holes   Par 72   Rating 72.4/121/6832

Sugar Bush is a scenic, rolling, challenging championship golf course. "Elevated tees, fast greens, lush fairways, rolling hills, mature maple trees, 2 lakes, a stream and some bunkers comprise our course."

$$		Golf Pkgs.	Public	Power Carts	Lessons	Lounge	Snack Bar	Meals	Open All Year
$$		Golf Pkgs.	Public	Power Carts	Lessons	Lounge	Snack Bar	Meals	Open All Year

OAK KNOLLS GOLF CLUB

KENT, OH (Located 1 mile north of Kent on State Route #43)
Telephone: (216) 673-6713

Manager: Scott Baker   Head Pro: Jon Wegenek
Course Supt: Greg Krak

East Course: 18 Holes   Par 71   Rating 68.7/108/6196 yds
West Course: 18 Holes   Par 72   Rating 68.0/110/6037 yds

Rolling, open terrain with excellent drainage. Driving range available.

$$		Golf Pkgs.	Public	Power Carts	Lessons		Snack Bar		Open All Year

GLENEAGLES GOLF CLUB

TWINSBURG, OH (On Glenwood Drive)
Telephone: (216) 425-3334   Fax: (216) 425-2042

Manager: Phil Giunta

18 Holes   Par 72   6214 yds   Rating: 71.1   Slope: 122

The newest public golf course in the area.
A beautiful setting with rolling hills, numerous waterways
and challenging greens. Lessons and driving range available.

$$		Golf Pkgs.	Public	Power Carts	Lessons	Lounge	Snack Bar	Meals	Open All Year

BOSTON HILLS COUNTRY CLUB

HUDSON, OH (Hines Hill Rd. E.)
Telephone: (216)656-2438   or (216)650-0934

General Manager: Jim Ballard   Head Pro: Ron Burke
Course Supt: Mike Vay

18 Holes   Par 71   5769 yds.   Rating: 65.9   Slope: 106

Featured in the Guiness Book of World Records for the most consecutive rounds played, Boston Hills is a beautiful 70 year old public course. Located on 156 acres in Hudson, it is a complete golf facility with ALL the amenities.

$$		Golf Pkgs.	Public	Power Carts	Lessons	Lounge	Snack Bar		Open All Year

AURORA WOODLANDS
Resort & Conference Center

NORTH EAST OHIO'S GOLF PARADISE

Enjoy four (4) beautiful golf courses with challenging fairways, undulating greens and a tremendous setting.

Sugar Bush GOLF *Inc.*

Oak Knolls Golf Club

GLENEAGLES GOLF CLUB

Boston Hills Country Club

Stay at the Aurora Woodlands Resort, one of North East Ohio's newly renovated hotels. For the golfers, we offer complimentary breakfast and drink coupons, spacious rooms or suites, exercise fitness room, indoor heated swimming pool, whirlpool, sauna, outdoor sports activities and Seasons Restaurant and Lounge with entertainment.

Also enjoy many different attractions including state parks, shopping, restaurants, Geauga Lake Amusement Park, and only a 30 minute ride from downtown Cleveland or Akron.

FEATURING **Sea World**. JUST STEPS AWAY!!!

GOLF PACKAGE INCLUDES:
* One nights lodging * one days green fees
* complimentary full breakfast * drink coupon
* golf cart an additional charge
* transportation * subject to availability

Golf Packages starting at
$57.00 (per person, based on availability, taxes not included)

- SENIOR GOLF PACKAGES ALSO AVAILABLE -

For more information or reservations call:
(216)562-9151 • 1-800-877-7849

800 NORTH AURORA ROAD • AURORA, OHIO 44202-9516

*Known as "Ohio's Outback", the southeast portion of the state, running along the Kentucky and West Virginia state lines, is a wild and beautiful place of few people and many natural wonders. This is the land of the wild turkey, the red-tailed hawk and the white-tailed deer, with fox and ruffed grouse as natural inhabitants. The area is part of the Appalachian foothills, with hidden lakes and majestic sandstone outcrops, and waterfalls that spill into deep-cut gorges. Quaint waterfront towns of **Marietta** and **Gallipolis** line the winding Ohio River, and the university town of **Athens** is where Ohio's first land-grant college was planted 188 years ago.*

*The land became the first permanent settlement in the Northwest Territory of the new Republic after the Revolutionary War, when a few of George Washington's men accepted land in payment for services rendered during the War. Bob Evans' home and farm allows visitors to take in the sights, including the Homestead, 19th century stagecoach stop, as well as a well-stocked general store, an authentic log cabin village, and an excellent farm museum. Hocking Hills State Park, with caves and hills for hiking, has campgrounds and bed-and-breakfasts nearby to help experience the friendliness of the area. The Wilds is a co-op venture between government, private industry and eight zoological parks to create a 9,154-acre endangered species haven from the remains of an old strip mine, which is soon to be constructed 15 miles from **Zanesville**. Southeast Ohio is a haven for artists looking for a place to find seclusion.*

The Canton/Stark region, in the northeastern section of Ohio, has been called "Ohio's Golf Capital", with over 39 courses and nearly 600 holes to play. Museums and attractions in the area include the Pro Football Hall of Fame, which is a 4-building complex complete with a movie theater and exciting display, as well, the Glamorgan Castle, built in 1904, was a private dwelling to a wealthy entrepreneur, and is now open for viewing. The Canton Classic Car Museum features antique and classic cars restored to their original condition. The Hoover Historical Center, birthplace of William Hoover, founder of the Hoover Vacuum Company, reflects on the growth of his company. The Palace Theatre, built in 1926 and on the National Register of Historic Places, contains the "atmospheric theater" concept, the illusion of being outdoors, under the stars. The nearby McKinley National Memorial, the national historic landmark dedicated to William McKinley, the 25th President of the United States, is located in the 23-acre Monument Park.

TAM O'SHANTER PUBLIC GOLF COURSE

CANTON, OH (On Hills & Dales Rd. NW, 5 minutes from Pro Football Hall of Fame)
Telephone: (216)477-5111   Toll Free: 1-800-462-9964   Fax: (216)478-6505

President: Chuck Bennell

"Hills" Course: 18 Holes   Par 70   6385 / 6054 / 5076 yds.   Slope: 104 / 103 / 92
"Dales" Course: 18 Holes   Par 70   6569 / 6249 / 5384 yds.   Slope: 110 / 107 / 100

These two courses are maintained to private club standards. Golf Packages are
available in cooperation with the Parke Hotel, located off I-77 just 5 minutes from
the course. For package information call 1-800-344-2345 (U.S.A.) or (216) 499-9410.

$$		Golf Pkgs.	Public	Power Carts	Lessons	Lounge	Snack Bar	Meals	Open All Year

WILKSHIRE GOLF CLUB

BOLIVAR, OH (Next to I-77 exit #93)
Telephone: (216)874-2525

Pro/Manager: Jeff Willis   Course Supt.: John Easterday

18 Holes   Par 72   6539 yds
Rating: 70.8   Slope: 114

Our plush, well manicured fairways will reward the accurate
tee shot with a picturesque approach to a putter's "dreamland".

$$		Golf Pkgs.	Public	Power Carts	Lessons	Lounge	Snack Bar	Meals	Open All Year

*Akron is the corporate headquarters for major rubber companies and is an internation-
ally-recognized polymer research center. Called "The Rubber Capital of the World",
Akron is the original home of the Goodyear Blimp, and the Goodyear World of Rubber
museum is located in town. Akron is also the birthplace of Quaker Oats, and there is
a shopping complex called Quaker Square built from the original factory. The Akron
Art Museum is considered the finest contemporary art museum between New York and
Chicago, featuring American works from the 1850s and up. Kent State University is just
outside Akron, with sports and theatrical events, as is the National Inventors Hall of
Fame.*

*Cuyahoga Valley National Recreation Area was set aside by Congress in 1974 as an
unspoiled National Park. There is a 22-mile long river valley bordered by steep,
forested hills undercut with surprising sandstone gorges and secret waterfalls. The
National Park Service has removed all the modern "intrusions", making it possible to
hike these trails without seeing a telephone pole or a house. Ashtabula County, in the
extreme northeast corner of the state, is known for its twelve covered bridges. Wayne
County, south of Cleveland and southwest of Akron, is America's largest Amish
settlement. Towns like **Kidron** and **Dalton** are host to Amish auctions and markets,
where you can buy quilts and other traditional Amish and Mennonite goods.*

*Ohio's borders stretch from the fertile farmland to the foothills of the Appalachian
Mountains, and from the southern shores of Lake Erie to the forests of the Kentucky
border. Even with this diverse landscape you can still find the trademark Buckeye
hospitality at every turn, making any vacation in Ohio a terrific vacation.*

WINDMILL LAKES

WINDMILL LAKES GOLF CLUB

RAVENNA, OH (On State Route 14)
Telephone: (216) 297-0440

Head Pro: Herb Page - PGA   Course Supt: Bob Doty - GSA

18 Holes   Par 72   6936 yds.

"Northern Ohio's Award Winning Golf Shoppe".
Home of CIPRIANO'S Restaurant.
"Northern Ohio's Most Challenging Public Golf Course".

$$		Golf Pkgs.	Public	Power Carts	Lessons	Lounge	Snack Bar	Meals	Open All Year	

PENNSYLVANIA

CULBERTSON HILLS GOLF COURSE • EDINBORO PENNSYLVANIA ▲

Golf
Vacations

America began here, in **Philadelphia** with the signing of the Declaration of Independence, and it is here that the greatest parts of what America has become continue to flourish. But Pennsylvania is so much more than the bitrhplace of the United States; it is Amish and Mennonite communities untouched by time, living "Plain" in Lancaster County; it is the historic battlefields of Gettysburg and Valley Forge, where you can witness re-creations of these bloodiest of Civil War confrontations; it is the staggering white-peaked Pocono Mountains and the lush Susquenhanna Valley's majestic forests and mighty rivers, immense cities and tiny towns, and everything in-between. It is not hard to see why Pennsylvania says, "America Starts Here".

And the best place to start a tour of Pennsylvania is at the beginning. **Philadelphia** was founded in the early 1700s by William Penn, and was the capital of the British colonies for a time. Perhaps the most important and well-known attractions in Philadelphia is Liberty Bell Pavilion, a glass-encased building preserving the nation's most hallowed symbol of liberty, and Independence Hall, the spot where the U.S. Constitution and Declaration of Independence were adopted into law. Independence Hall was built as the Pennsylvania State House, and now hosts millions of visitors each year. At each turn is another page from the American history books; the Betsy Ross House is a restored 2-storey Colonial home where Betsy Ross lived when she was credited with making the first American Flag; the Tomb of the Unkown Soldier is erected in memory of the unknown Revolutionary War soldier, with an eternal flame installed in 1976. The Tomb is located in Washington Square, one of Philadelphia's five original squares.

Germantown, founded in 1683 when German settlers were given an area 6 miles north-west of Center City Philly. Germantown Road was the main route to **Reading**, **Bethlehem** and points north. The Germantown Mennonite Church was built in 1770, and is the home of America's first Mennonite congregation. Fairmont Park, in Philadelphia itself, is the largest landscaped city park in the world, with more than 8900 acres of scenic beauty a mere few steps from the downtown core.

Philadelphia is also home to the world-famous Philly Pretzel, a soft-pretzel served on street corners throughout the city. Philadelphia also has a host of fine restaurants and friendly, tucked-away eateries. "Lily Langtry's" is an elegant Victorian-style restaurant featuring glittering chandeliers, antiques, sweeping staircases, lavishly-costumed musical revues and an award-winning menu.

Valley Forge is the nearest Civil War battlesite to Philadelphia. It was here that George Washington and his army of 12,000 men made their encampment during the winter of 1777. Now, on 3600 acres hardly touched by time are reconstructed soldiers' huts, fortifications, rows of cannons, Washington's headquarters and the Washington Memorial Chapel.

THE POCONOS
Get Away To It All.

More than 30 golf courses are located in the Pocono Mountains of Northeastern Pennsylvania, and every major Pocono resort prides itself on its outstanding golf course. Each one boasts of its unique features and signature holes.

Furthering its reputation as the "Myrtle Beach of the North", the Poconos are expanding the scenic and challenging courses which dot the region's 2,400 square miles of woodlands, mountains, streams and rivers.

Lodging facilitites here offer a variety of inclusive golf and stay packages to suit every taste and budget. Those who would like to have some fun off the greens will find family attractions, shopping, fine dining, entertainment and a host of other outdoor sports and activities.

For your **FREE** Pocono Mountains Vacation Planning Kit, containing all the information you need to plan a golf vacation in the Poconos, call **1-800-762-6667** today.

1-800-POCONOS

Pocono Mountains Vacation Bureau, Inc.
1004 Main Street, Box GV,
Stroudsburg, PA 18360

PENNSYLVANIA
★AMERICA STARTS HERE★

Other fun stops in the Philadelphia area include Sesame Place, a "Sesame Street" theme park with over 40 play and water activities, shows, educational exhibits, characters, Sesame Island and brand new Twiddlebug Land. Championship golf courses surround Philly, offering challenges steeped in history.

John James Audubon, the world-famous naturalist and artist, came to nearby **Mill Grove** in the early 1800s to settle and study. His home is now a museum with his work on display and also a wildlife sanctuary on site. South through the Brandywine valley is a wine-growing region, as well the home of many mushroom farms. On September 11, 1777, Washington was defeated by the British at Brandywine Battlefield, where today both Washington's and British General Lafayette's headquarters are restored and open to the public.

Allentown, in the Lehigh Valley, is home to the Liberty Bell Shrine, which marks the post where the Bell was hidden from the British during the Revolutionary War. Easton's Center Square, in the middle of Allentown, is the site of the third public reading of the Declaration of Independence. Nearby Bethlehem was founded in 1741 by the Moravians, a group of deeply-religious, middle-European missionaries whose influence lives on 250 years later, most notably in the yuletide traditions that have helped earn Bethlehem the designation of "The Christmas City". A recommended side trip is the Lehigh Valley Covered Bridge Tour, a self-guided tour beginning in Allentown and passing seven covered bridges.

As far back as 1815, vacationers journeyed to the Pocono Mountain counties of Carbon, Wayne and Monroe as a summer getaway. Carbon County, nestled in a quiet corner of the Poconos, is famous for the Switchback gravity railroad, which was the first railroad built on any large scale in America, and for the beautiful Glen Onoko Falls. The area is known as the "Switzerland of America", and its main town, **Jim Thorpe**, was renamed from the original "Old Mauch Chunk" in honor of the famous athlete, who is buried there. Mauch Chunk State Park is a secluded outdoor recreational facility near Jim Thorpe, on a picturesque 350-acre lake with boating, fishing, swimming and camping facilities. Lehigh Gorge Park is Pennsylvania's newest state park, it follows the course of the Lehigh River for 26 miles through the rugged terrain of the Lehigh River Gorge. An abandoned railroad bed follows the river through the park. The Lehigh is one of the finest, most popular rivers in the East for whitewater rafting, kayaking and canoeing. It is a sportsman's paradise, with excellent hunting and fishing in season. The Francis E. Walter National Recreation Area was originally built as a flood control project by the Army Corps of Engineers to tame the turbulent Lehigh River. The Army Corps stores water for periodic dam releases, providing higher water levels to the Lehigh River for even better white-water rafting.

SHADOWBROOK INN & RESORT

TUNKHANNOCK, PA (On Route 6, 2 miles east of Tunkhannock)
Telephone: (717)836-2151   Toll Free: 1-800-955-0295
                            Fax: (717)836-5655

General Manager: William Renfer
Pro Shop Manager: Alan Wiser

18 Holes   Par 72   5828 / 5629 / 4811 yds.

For golf package infromation see our ad on facing page.

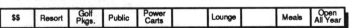

$$	Resort	Golf Pkgs.	Public	Power Carts		Lounge		Meals	Open All Year	

SHADOWBROOK
INN & RESORT

The traveler in search of friendly accommodations, fine food, a wide range of recreational activities and a warm atmosphere will find all this, and more at Shadowbrook.

Backdropped by one of Pennsylvania's beautiful mountain settings is our ever popular 18 hole golf course. If lodging, meals and recreation are on your agenda, we specialize in designing packages to suit your needs.

GOLFERS GETAWAY WEEKEND

- ✦ Golf Saturday & Sunday Unlimited
- ✦ Golf Cart each day for 18 Holes
- ✦ Lodging Friday and Saturday Nights
- ✦ Entertainment Friday & Saturday Nights
- ✦ Breakfast Saturday & Sunday Mornings

$113⁰⁰
TWIN DOUBLE RATE

$128⁰⁰
QUEEN STUDIO RATE

WEEKDAY PAR THREE

(AVAILABLE MONDAY THRU FRIDAY)

- ✦ Golf four days Unlimited
- ✦ Golf Cart each day for 18 Holes
- ✦ Lodging for three nights
- ✦ Breakfast three mornings

$177⁰⁰
TWIN DOUBLE RATE

$200⁰⁰
QUEEN STUDIO RATE

SUNDAY GOLF FLING

- ✦ Golf Sunday & Monday Unlimited
- ✦ Golf Cart each day for 18 Holes
- ✦ Lodging Sunday Nights
- ✦ Breakfast Monday Morning

$69⁰⁰
TWIN DOUBLE RATE

$76⁰⁰
QUEEN STUDIO RATE

Above Golf Package Rates are Per Person, Based on Double Occupancy

1-800-955-0295
(717) 836-2151

ROUTE 6, TUNKHANNOCK, PENNSYLVANIA 18657

Major cities like **Scranton** and **Wilkes-Barre** preserve America's industrial heritage. Anthracite coal was first mined here, and tours of the Lackawanna Coal Mine and Ashland's Pioneer Tunnel Coal Mine give visitors a first-hand look at the coal-mining industry. In **Tunkhannock**, the Wyoming County Historical Society preserves the timeless history of the area outside Scranton. In 1762 setlers from New England came to the Wyoming Valley, but were driven out by Indians. It was not until after the Sullivan expedition in 1779 that families were able to establish a permanent settlement in the Tunkhannock area. The name Wyoming is an Indian word meaning "extensive meadows", which describes the area perfectly.

Towanda is part of the newly-developed "Pennsylvania Trail of History" which winds to the French Azilum, located on a horseshoe bend of the meandering Susquehanna River. **Azilum**, (or "Asylum"), was appropriately named because it provided a natural setting of undisturbed calm to a group of French exiles fleeing their native France and the mulatto and slave uprising of Haiti, who settled in Pennsylvania in 1793. The French fled after the French Revolution, and, according to an unverified story, even Marie Antoinette, the Queen of France, and her two children were said to have settled in Azilum. Today, of the fifty structures erected by the settlers, not one remains.

In Scranton, visit one of several Anthracite coal museums, dedicated to exploring the lives and labors of the people of Pennsylvania's hard coal region, with exhibits and living museums extending 70 miles. Visit Eckley Miner's Village, surround by black-silt ponds and strip-mining pits, which was settled in 1854 and remained a privately-owned company "patch" town until 1971. It is now home to more than 50 residents, including retired miners, their widows and children.

The Susquehanna River has been called the "Currier & Ives" of rivers by many artists. Here you'll find traditional river towns like **Lock Haven**, **Selingsgrove** and **Lewisburg**. Covered bridges dot the river's feed-streams, and paddlewheel riverboats, like the Hiawatha in **Williamsport** still transport visitors in high style. Williamsport is also the birthplace of Little League Baseball, and is now the home of the Little League Baseball World Series, held at the end of August.

The Susquehanna River's rich bottom lands are farmed by Old Order Amish and Mennonites, who also live their enviable simple life throughout the region. The Boal Mansion in Boalsburg began construction in 1789, and includes the Columbus Chapel, which belonged to Christopher Columbus' family in Spain and contains his family heirlooms dating back to the 1400s. You'll also find the Northumberland County home of Joseph Priestly, the 18th century theologian who discovered oxygen.

Festivals in the area include the Strawberry Festival held in **Turbotville** in June, Central PA Festival of the Arts, held at the State College in early July, and the Clinton County Fair, which is held the first week of August in **Mackeyville**. Clinton County, in the northern part of the Susquehanna Valley, is a great place to hike, canoe, hunt and fish. In Center Hall is **Penn's Cave**, America's only all-water cavern toured by guided motorboats.

The Allegheny National Forest spans more than a half million acres, and is the only National Forest in Pennsylvania. It is a dense forest with tall, pristine pine trees. In spring, wild rhododendron, dogwood and Mountain Laurel, (the state flower), bloom brightly. The Allegheny National Forest is popular for forest hiking or backpacking trips, camping, lakeside picnics, a refreshing swim on a hot day, fishing, hunting, boating, canoeing, waterskiing, and much more. Six isolated boat-access campgrounds on the shores of the Allegheny Reservoir offer anywhere from 8 to 32 sites.

The Reservoir itself extends 27 miles, with more than 91 miles of shoreline. There are more than 600 miles of trails in the Allegheny National Forest for hiking or cross-country skiing. Heart's Content and Tionesta Scenic Areas offer virgin stands of white pine 300-400 years old, and have been virtually unchanged for a hundred years.

The "Allegheny National Forest Region" of Pennsylvania spans four counties and offers over one million recreation areas.

Warren, the anchor city of Warren County, is an historic city of 12,000 people, called the "western gateway" to the Allegheny Forest. Early wealth from timber and oil is reflected in the stately homes of the late 19th century. The largest mail-order house in America makes its home in Warren because of its easy access to all other parts of the country.

Several golf courses in the area offer 18 holes of beautiful play and Warren is a good spot to begin a canoe trip down the Allegheny River.

WARREN, PA

GOLF PACKAGE FOR TWO*

$**225**.00   (Based on double occupancy tax and gratuity included)

• Two nights lodging - 2:00 PM Check Out • A complimentary cocktail • One breakfast - Morning of your choice • One dinner - night of your choice • One round of golf for two with shared cart • Golf widow package available • Non-meal package also available

Hotel Amenities: Indoor pool and sauna, Tootsie's Nightclub with entertainment, DJ, and dancing, Fine Dining restaurant, Plenty of free parking, Exercise and game room, Banquet facilities for large groups, Beautiful garden atrium, Box lunches available

FOR RESERVATIONS CONTACT:

210 LUDLOW STREET, WARREN, PENNSYLVANIA 16365

(814) 726-3000 • 800-H-INN-814

136   When calling or writing our advertisers, please mention *Golf Connections*.

COREY CREEK GOLF CLUB

MANSFIELD, PA
Telephone: (717)662-3520

Head Pro/Course Supt.: Art Connelly
Architects: Herb Peterson/Jack Marsh

18 Holes Par 72 6571 / 6164 / 5573 / 4920 yds.
Rating: 71.1 / 69.1 / 66.1 / 66.0

This scenic course is set in the Appalacian Mountains of northern Pennsylvania.
It features quick, undulating greens with creeks and lakes on 12 holes.

$		Golf Pkgs.	Public	Power Carts	Lessons	Lounge	Snack Bar	Meals		

Sugar Grove is located in northern Warren County between Warren and Chautauqua, New York. Lovely Victorian homes line the streets, and many Amish buggies pulled by fast-trotting horses pass through the town. Tidioute-on-the-River is home to the annual Pennsylvania Championship Fishing Tournament each September. At thirty-years old, this is the oldest tournament of its kind in the U.S.A. Near **Kellettville** is the largest dude ranch in Pennsylvania.

The Warren County Fairgrounds are located in **Pittsfield**, the Fair is held early in August. **Youngsville** is home to the July Jubilee of square dancing, as well as the annual Fireman's Festival. Brokenstraw Airport is also located in Youngsville, which is where many fly-in fishing and camping excursions are based.

Pennsylvania Route 6 is part of what is known as the Grand Army of the Republic Highway, the longest highway in the United States. Stretching from Cape Cod, Massachussetts to Long Beach, California, parts of the Pennsylvania portion of this highway have been rated among the top 10 most scenic highways.

The Kinzua Bridge State Park is highlighted by the Kinzua Viaduct. Originally completed in 1882, the Viaduct was advertised as the Eighth Wonder of the World when it was unveiled, with a span of 2053 feet and 301 feet high at its center. Today it is still the second-highest railroad bridge in the U.S.A., and the third-highest in the world. The Viaduct is studded with legend, one of the most appealing being that, within sight of the Viaduct lies $40,000 in buried gold currency in glass containers. They were buried by a bank robber at the turn of the century and to date no one has claimed discovery.

Bradford is close to the New York border, and a mere two hours from Canada, thus earning the title, "Northern Gateway" to the Allegheny National Forest. There is a major ski resort in the area, as well as a one-of-a-kind Seneca/Iroquois National Museum, where you explore the culture and heritage of these Natives tribes. Bradford is also home to world-famous Zippo Manufacturing, manufacturer of the Zippo lighter. Visit the 1840s Crook Farm and the Penn-Brad Museum, which features the only working and accurate wooden oil rig in existence.

Rt. 68 & I-80
CLARION, PA
16214

GETAWAY GOLF PACKAGES:

from
$59.00 (per person)
(Based on double occ.)

PACKAGE INCLUDES:

- Complimentary Welcome Cocktail
- One Nights Lodging
- One Full American Breakfast
- 10% Discount on Lunch or Dinner
  in our Dining Room
- 18 Holes Championship Golf
- Shared Cart Rental

PLAY THESE FINE COURSES:

Mayfield Golf Club
One of Western Pennsylvania's premier championship courses, Mayfield's 18 holes and 6990 yards of challenge are nestled in the heart of the Magic Forest. Long, tree-lined fairways, water hazards and bunkers will test every club in your bag.

Hi-Level Golf Club
This executive course is easy to walk and perfect for tuning up your game. Take advantage of the 5 hole practice course before enjoying 18 holes of fun filled golf.

Foxburg Country Club
Enjoy two rounds of golf on this scenic 9 hole course, the oldest in continuous play in the U.S. View the wild waters of the upper Allegheny River and be ready to spend time in the quaint Log Clubhouse which is the present home of the American Golf Hall of Fame.

Pinecrest Country Club
Minutes from either Days Inn is the Pinecrest Country Club. Slick greens and winding tree-lined fairways are but two of the challenges that await you on this 18 hole course.

FOR MORE INFORMATION & RESERVATIONS CALL:

(814) 226-8689

Perhaps the greatest claim-to-fame of the Allegheny National Forest Region comes from the tiny town of **Punxsutawney**, home of "Punxsutawney Pete", the world-renowned forecaster of the remaining duration of the winter. Pete is the groundhog who, if he sees his shadow on Groundhog Day, means an additional six weeks of winter are on their way.

Erie is called the "Gem City" because of its sparkling bay, and derives its name from a fierce band of Indians known as the Eriez who numbered about 12,000 at the beginning of the 17th century. The combination of the Indian Wars in 1653 and pestilence brought about the demise of the Eriez tribe. The French arrived on the Lake Erie shore in 1753, but French rule ended in 1759. In 1760, small British garrisons occupied the area until an Indian uprising, known as "Pontiac's Conspiracy", attacked and destroyed the frontier outposts. Even though a treaty of peace of instituted in 1764, there was no attempt to rebuild the forts. Erie County remained a wilderness until after the American Revolution.

American General "Mad" Anthony Wayne was victorious over the Western Indians at the Battle of Fallen Timbers in 1794. That victory, in conjunction with various treaties signed with the Indians, paved the way for an American settlement in 1795. The first settlers, primarily farmers, came from Eastern Pennsylvania, New York, New Jersey and New England. In a short time, Erie became one of the most important ports on the Great Lakes.

Erie's greatest historical moment occured during the War of 1812, when Commodore Oliver Hazard Perry, commanding the Flagship Niagara, forced the British squadrom to surrender.

By 1851, Erie had shown tremendous growth, and it hasn't stopped since. Erie, called the "Flagship City", is the third-largest city in Pennsylvania, and the only port on the Great Lakes. Erie is visited by about 4 million people each year, due in large part to their nice, warm summers because of the proximity to the southern shore of Lake Erie.

Presque Island, *which shelters Erie from storms and cold winters from Lake Erie, is a peninsula that is both geologically and biologically significant, offering ecologists that rare opportunity to study plant life successions. A sand and water lakeshore changes to a climax forest within two miles. Presque Island State Park was aquired by the State of Pennsylvania in 1921.*

Historical sites include the Flagship Niagara, which defeated the British Lake Erie fleet in 1813. A reconstruction of the ship was commissioned in 1989, and the ship now sails as the flagship of the Commonwealth of Pennsylvania. The Land Lighthouse, the first lighthouse built on the Great Lakes, was built in 1813 and reconstructed in 1867, and overlooks the tip of the Presque Isle Peninsula.

There are covered bridges scattered throughout the Erie area, including the Harring-ton and Carmen Bridges over Conneaut Creek, Gudgeonville Bridge over Elk Creek, and the Brothern Crossing Bridge over LeBeouf Creek. As well, the first monument dedicated to those who died in the Civil War, and the only statue of George Washing-ton in British uniform are in the area.

There are a number of annual festivals in the Erie region, including the popular "We Love Erie Days" Festival, held in August. Planned as a family experience, the festival attracts top-name entertainment and offers tours of the reconstructed Flagship Niagara.

The area's rich soil makes it prime farmland, and one of the most popular commodities is the largest stretch of Concord grapes East of the Mississippi, which are harvested at prize-winning wineries.

CULBERTSON HILLS GOLF CLUB

EDINBORO, PA (2 Mi. E. of I-19, from exit #38)
Telephone: (814)734-5650   Fax: (814)734-1332
                              Canadian Toll Free: 1-800-227-8448

Manager: Bob Orr, Sr.   Head Pro: Bob Orr, Jr.
Course Supt.: Janet Gibas

18 Holes   Par 72   6444 yds.

Accommodations available on site at the EDINBORO INN, see facing page.

$		Golf Pkgs.	Public	Power Carts	Lessons	Lounge	Snack Bar	Meals	

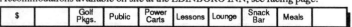

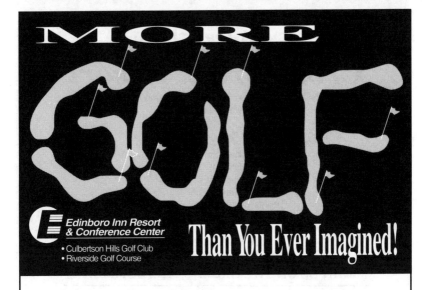

PAR 5. SUNDAY SRETCH GOLF

Sunday (After 1 p.m.), Monday & Tuesday
Two Nights Lodging
1 Dinner for 1 • 1 Breakfast for 1
$139.00

Edinboro Inn Resort
& Conference Center

• Culbertson Hills Golf Club
• Riverside Golf Course
814-734-5650

For Reservations Only Call:
Continental USA.....................................1-800-352-3182
Canada...1-800-227-8448

Located just 20 minutes
South of Erie, Pennsylvania
on I-79, Exit 38

Per person, double occupancy. Based on U.S. Funds.
Other Golf Packages available, Call for more Information.

There's Always A Tee Party At...

Cross Creek Resort

Just a 2-1/2 hour drive south of the Canadian / USA border
Titusville, Pennsylvania

Cross Creek Resort Features:
- 27 hole Championship Golf Course
- Gourmet Dining
- 94 Luxurious Guest Rooms
- Outdoor Heated Pool
- Tennis Courts
- Crystal Ring Lounge with Revolving Bar
- 19th Hole Lounge
- Amiable Staff and Attentive Service

JOIN US ON THE GREENS THIS SUMMER

Golf Packages starting at just

$209. PER PERSON
(US FUNDS, PLUS 6% TAX)

All of our Golf Packages Include:
- Unlimited Golf
- Riding Cart (18 holes per day)
- Buffet Breakfasts
- Buffet Dinners
- Lodging
- AND NO HIDDEN COSTS

Experience all the pleasures of resort golfing
without extensive travel and prices.

CALL US TODAY! (814)827-9611

4 miles south of
Titusville, Pennsylvania
on Route 8. One hour
south of Interstate 90.

BUTLER, PA
139 Pittsburg Road
Butler, PA 16001
(412) 287-6761

MEADVILLE, PA
240 Conneaut Lake Road
Meadville, PA 16335
(814) 337-4264

DAYS INN

GOLF PACKAGE FROM $49*

(* Per person , per night, based on double occupancy. Subject to availablity.
Not valid with any other discounts. All rates are plus 6% tax.)

Includes:
* Pre-arranged tee times for 18 holes of golf
* Shared golf cart • One nights lodging
* Complimentary full-American breakfast • complimentary beverage • Late Sunday check-out of 6 p.m.
* Group packages available

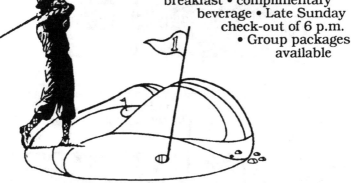

BUTLER COURSES:
* The Aubrey's Dubbs Dred • Highland Golf Course
* Lake Arthur Country Club • Lake Vue North

MEADVILLE COURSES:
* Oakland Beach Golf Course • Whispering Pines Golf Course
* Riverside Golf Course

HOTEL FEATURES BUTLER / MEADVILLE:
* Spacious, Comfortable Rooms • Heated Indoor Pool • Jacuzzi • Full Service Restaurant • "Frisco's" Lounge with Nightly Entertainment in Butler. "Referee's" Sports Bar & Grill in Meadville • Room Service
* Remote Control cable TV with Free HBO and ESPN • In-Room Movies
* Hospitality Rooms and MeetingFacilities Available

Conley Resort Inn

CONLEY RESORT INN GOLF COURSE

BUTLER, PA (18 mi. N. of Pittsburgh on Rte. 8, PA Turnpike esit 4)
Telephone: (412)586-7711   or: (412)562-0693
Toll Free: 1-800-344-7303

Director of Sales & Marketing: Betty Hengelsburg

18 Holes   Par 72   6200 yds.

Special weekday and twilight rates.
Special corporate packages for groups of 15 or more.

$$	Resort	Golf Pkgs.	Public	Power Carts		Lounge	Snack Bar	Meals	

*Over two million people live in **Pittsburgh**, which is the center of a nine-county area filled with every imaginable opportunity for business and pleasure. Pittsburgh first entered history in the mid-1700s, as it is the point of land where the Mononogahela and Allegheny Rivers meet to form the great Ohio River, and was first surveyed by George Washington, who was then a 21 year old major in the Virginia milita. It was captured by the French and then won back by the British in 1758. Within two years, mining and manufacturing established Pittsburgh as a major settlement.*

For nearly two hundred years, the city was known for its industrial might. However, within the past twenty years, the area is gaining a reputation as a recreation area. Now a lively, sophisticated place to visit, Pittsburgh is one of the safest cities of its size in the country. The streets are safe enough to draw people back downtown at night to hear the internationally-acclaimed symphony at Heinz Hall, superstars at the Civic Arena, or the hottest Broadway musicals at the Benedum Center.

The city is surrounded by three sparkling rivers, which are excellent spots to fish, boat or swim. As well, there are acres of lush parkland, and nearby is a real working farm for guests to tour.

Kennywood Park is a traditional amusement-type park, while Sandcastle is one of the country's largest water slide parks. The Pittsburgh Zoo has an enteraining Tropical Rain Forest Complex which delights visitors of all ages. Also, families enjoy touring the Carnegie Science Center's interactive exhibits.

*Pittsburgh is a sporting town, with a professional hockey team, (the 1991 Stanley Cup Champion Pittsburgh Penquins), a pro Football team, (the Pittsburgh Steelers), and a pro Baseball team, (the Pittsburgh Pirates). **Pittsburgh** was named one of the top 10 healthiest cities to live in a recent survey, and boasts more golf courses per capita than any other city in America.*

The "Laurel Highlands" Region marks the boundary where the Allegheny Mountains begin. Lake Raystown, in the foothills, is a favorite amongs boaters, hikers, bikers and nature lovers. Dozens of year-round resorts feature golf and other amenities.

The Laurel Highlands was the site of the Whiskey Rebellion in 1794, which marked the first revolt against a Federal tax. Battlefields and forts like Busy Run, Fort Neccessity, Fort Ligonier and Fort Roberdeau serve as reminders of the French and Indian War and territorial conquests that pushed America's frontier westward. **Old Bedford** is an authentically reconstructed pioneer town depicting the 1790s, with frontier towns-people, shops and craftsmen. Architectural history is also part of this beautiful corner of Pennsylvania, and it is here you'll find Frank Lloyd Wright's "Fallingwater", a remarkable house built over a rushing mountain waterfall.

The city of **Altoona's** landscape is dotted with family farms, which carry on throughout the beautiful countryside, in places like **Sinking Valley** and **Morrison's Cove**. Special effort has been made to preserve the very best in historic architecture, and magnificent designs from all periods can be seen in **Altoona, Hollidaysburg, Tyrone** and **Duncansville**.

Visit **Roaring Spring's** restored vintage railroad station, the Allegheny Portage Railroad, and Lemon House in Cresson, as well as Altoona's Baker Mansion, Allegheny Furnace, World Famous Horseshoe Curve, the Railroaders Memorial Museum and two exciting amusement parks, the Lakemont Park, which has been operating since 1894, and Bland's Park. Shop at a large regional enclosed mall, or in small country boutiques. As well, the area is an antique and flea market-lover's paradise.

The Southwestern Pennsylvania Heritage Preservation Commission has begun a 47-mile Heritage Tour Highway through the area, looking at points of particular importance to the legacy of America's industrial heritage. The tour takes you from Altoona to **Johnstown**, with fifteen sites including an exhibit dedicated to the devastating Johnstown Flood.

*Along Pennsylvania's southern boundary with Maryland, and between the Laurel Highlands to Philadelphia is the heart of the Pennsylvania Dutch and Amish communities, located mostly around **Lancaster**. Thousands of residents still wear distinctive Plain clothing and speak the German of their ancesters as a unique dialect called "Pennsylvania Dutch". Lancaster County is home to the nation's largest settlement of "Plain", (Amish, Mennonite and Brethren), peoples, and is not an historical re-creation but a fascinating, living community where change comes very slowly. Places like the Amish Village in **Strasburg**, and the Amish Farm and House in **Lancaster** offer visitors a look at a real working Amish settlement.*

Settled in 1719, Lancaster County's fertile land and talented craftspeople made it an important source of supplies during the American Revolution. The first hard-surfaced, long-distance road in America, the Philadelphia to Lancaster Turnpike, was authorized in 1792. Following the Revolution, traffic became too heavy for dirt roads, so the 62-mile long road, which cost roughly $450,000 to build, became the primary artery.

The Battle of Gettysburg in July of 1863 was the turning point of the Civil War. It was a quiet first of July when 75,000 men of General Robert E. Lee's Confederate Army met 97,000 men of the Northern Army of General George C. Meade, by chance, when a Confederate brigade sent to Gettysburg for supplies observed a forward column of the Northern cavalry. For the next three days, more men fought and died than in any other single battle before or since on American soil. When the dust settled, 51,000 men had lost their lives.

There are more than 1000 Civil War monuments along a 40 mile stretch of scenic avenues in Gettysburg. Gettysburg itself, is preparing the 130th anniversary re-enactment of the Battle of Gettysburg for the July 3-4 weekend of 1993.

VALLEY GREEN GOLF COURSE

ETTERS, PA (On Valley Green Rd, off I-83 at exit 14 and follow the signs)
Telephone: (717)938-4200

Manager: Roger Van Etten   Head Pro: Roger Van Etten - PGA
Course Supt.: Duane Van Etten

18 Holes Par 71 6000 yds.

A course with scenic views and natural beauty.

$			Public	Power Carts	Lessons	Lounge	Snack Bar	Meals		

Camping in Gettysburg is popular, and there are also many fine indoor places to stay. When you're in Gettysburg, be sure to stop in at the Eisenhower National Historic Site, and tour the house and farm of the 34th President.

*The Cumberland Valley stretches from **Carlisle**, Pennsylvania to Winchester, Virginia, which is the late Patsy Cline's hometown. **Chambersburg** was the only town north of the Mason-Dixon Line to be burned by the Confederates during the Civil War. A festival is held each July to commemorate the spirit of rebirth and rebuilding.*

*The Mason-Dixon Line, the legendary Civil War dividing line between the North and the South, runs along the southern Pennsylvania boundary with Maryland and West Virginia. **Mercersburg**, close to the Line, is the birthplace of former President James Buchanan, the only U.S. President to be born in Pennsylvania.*

a golf course recreational community

PENN NATIONAL

FAYETTEVILLE, PA (On Clubhouse Dr., off Route 997 S.)
Pro Shop: (717)352-2193   Toll Free (US & Canada): 1-800-231-0080

Manager: Dennis Zimmerman   Head Pro: David Beegle
Course Supt.: Terry Morgan   Architect: Edmund Ault

18 Holes   Par 72   6451 yds.

Challenging but "fair" 18 hole course located at the foothills of the
Appalachain Mountains. Site of the 1977 ECAC and 1992 Atlantic 10
College Championships. Golf packages available at the Penn National Inn.

$$	Resort	Golf Pkgs.	Public	Power Carts	Lessons		Snack Bar	Meals	Open All Year
$$	Resort	Golf Pkgs.	Public	Power Carts	Lessons		Snack Bar	Meals	Open All Year

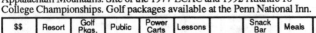

Outside Philadelphia are a trio of cities described as, "a capital city, a chocolate kingdom and a colonial town". **Harrisonburg** was founded in 1710, and became the state capital in 1812, replacing nearby Lancaster. The State Capitol Buildings are striking and enormous, and the entire city is bounded by the Susquehanna River. **Carlisle** has an important place in military history; settled in 1720, the city is home to a memorial to Revolutionary War heroine Molly Pitcher, and also has Confederate cannonballs still embedded in the courthouse walls. The Carlisle Barracks houses the town's Indian School, which was the first non-reservation school for Indians. Visit the Octubafest, which combines the traditional Oktoberfest celebrations with a tuba finale that won't soon be forgotten. Carlisle is also called the "Car Collecting Capital of the World", with antique car shows and auctions.

The town of **Hershey** can only be described by one word: chocolate. Called "The Sweetest Place on Earth", Hershey was from the start a model company town, with a touch of the amusement park atmosphere thrown in. Hershey's past can be seen at the Hershey Museum and Founders Hall, with rides and history lessons and comfortable gardens. The Hershey Park Christmas Candyland shines with over 300,000 lights each year. And the streets of Hershey are lined with street lights shaped like Hershey's Kisses™.

GOLF'S GATEWAY
TO THE SOUTH ...
YORK COUNTY, PA

is sometimes called the "Myrtle Beach of the North". The over abundance of well-conditioned, mature courses and highly trained professional staff has given York this reputation. A diverse golf destination, York County offers exceptional attractions, gracious hospitality services and outstanding outlet shopping. So much to experience, yet only a days drive for many Canadians.

It only seems fitting that America's first capital should become the "FIRST CAPITAL OF GOLF".

YORK COUNTY GOLF PROMOTIONS, INC.
I-83 and Rt. 30, 222 Arsenal Road
York, Pennsylvania   17407-1925

TO PLAY THE BEST YORK COUNTY GOLF, CALL:

Briarwood Golf Club	(800) 432-1555
Briarwood West	(717) 792-9776
Cool Creek Country Club	(717) 252-3691
Grandview Golf Course	(717) 764-2674
Heritage Hills Golf Resort	(717) 755-4653
Honey Run Golf & Country Club	(717) 792-9771

FOR RESERVATIONS CALL (800) 942-2444

York County has been called "America's Golf Capital", and justifiably so. The area has dozens of courses, with all levels of play to put the vacatioing golfer to the test. York also served as the nation's first capital, when the Articles of Confederation were signed in 1777. The town of York itself dates back to 1741, and was one of the many settlements in the area around that time. The York County Colonial Courthouse is the place where the Continental Congress adopted the Articles of Confederation, and a nearly exact replica details the historic courtroom and holds many Revolutionary-era relics.

When planning a trip to play the best golf courses in York County, why not plan on staying at the areas finest hotel... The Yorktowne Hotel.

This National Historic Landmark is a completely restored world-class hotel conveniently located in the heart of charming center-city York... within walking distance of the city's business, financial and legal districts, and only minutes away from York County golf courses.

We offer special amenities to please every guest. Free Valet parking is always available. Oversized modern guest rooms with sitting areas make socializing convenient and comfortable. There's a complimentary snack and beverage tray, a next-day weather forcast, and complete room service with an all-night sandwich menu.

We also offer a choice of dining: an elegant, formal dining room full of sophistication and romance serving fine Classical cuisine... and a casual restaurant and lounge, offering a congenial setting for an early breakfast, an informal dinner, or a relaxing escape after a tough 18 holes.

GOLF PACKAGES

$89.⁰⁰

1 Day/1 Night (Per Person Double Occupancy)
18 Holes of Golf and Cart ✦ 1 Bucket of balls
Free Guest Pass to a nearby Health Club
1 Dinner and Breakfast in *Autographs Lounge*
1 Oversized Yorktowne Room

$159.⁰⁰

2 Days/2 Nights (Per Person Double Occupancy)
36 Holes of Golf and Cart ✦ 2 Buckets of balls
Free Guest Pass to a nearby Health Club
1 Dinner and 2 Breakfasts in *Autographs Lounge*
1 Oversized Yorktowne Room

1-800-233-9323
(717)848-1111

The Yorktowne Hotel
48 East Market Street York, PA 17401

WHO WOULD
KNOW BETTER HOW
TO PUT THE

SWING

IN YOUR WEEKEND?

Get ready to tee-up and drive your way into
a great golf getaway. Come enjoy our friendly service
and inviting accommodations. We offer a pool,
restaurant and room service at a price that is
hard to resist. We know how to put your
vacation safely on the green.

✳ Holiday Inn®

$**49**
Per Room / Per Night

2 GREAT YORK LOCATIONS:

334 ARSENAL ROAD
(717) 845-5671

2600 EAST MARKET STREET
(717) 755-1966

The Central Market is an 1888 Romanesque Revival market hall which replaced an earlier one on the town square. Fresh farm produce from the outlying areas are available at Market on Tuesdays, Thursdays and Saturdays. Agriculture is York's #1 industry, following country traditions rather than national statistics.

Farms there are still family-owned; with over 2000 farms in York County, less than a dozen are "corporate" owned. York has the second-highest number of farms of Pennsylvania's 67 counties, with each farm averaging about 135 acres in size.

A country roads driving tour is recommended, along which you can follow the Susquehanna River past spectacular bluffs and river views, then through deep valleys that reveal the streams that flow eventually to the river. Neatly painted farm buildings dot the countryside, and picturesque little towns lie on roads not on the beaten track.

HONEY RUN GOLF & COUNTRY CLUB

YORK, PA (On Salem Church Rd. just 5 mi. W. of York)
Telephone: (717)792-9771

Head Pro: Nevin Parr - PGA   Course Supt.: Rod Chronister
Architect: Edmond B. Ault

18 Holes   Par 72   6797 / 6477 / 5976 yds.
Rating: 72.4 / 71.0 / 74.0   Slope: 123 / 121 / 125

A mature, rolling course with plenty of length from the championship tees.
Honey Run hosted the Christa McAullife Futures Classic for four straight years.

$$		Golf Pkgs.	Public	Power Carts	Lessons	Lounge	Snack Bar	Meals	Open All Year

Herald Hills

**18 Holes Public
Lighted Driving Range
Miniature Golf
Discount Golf Store**

 Featuring

Windows
ON THE GREEN
FINE CONTINENTAL CUISINE

Champagne Sunday Brunch
Serving Sunday 11:00 a.m. - 3:00 p.m.

Critic's Acclaim: "This one has it all"
Enjoy veal, poultry, seafood, rack of lamb and certified
Angus beef in an elegant but casual atmosphere.

OPEN 7 DAYS A WEEK

 2700 Mount Rose Avenue, York, Pennsylvania 17402

HERITAGE HILLS GOLF RESORT
YORK, PA (1 mi. E. of I-83, Exit 7 - Prospect St.)
Telephone: (717)755-4653

Head Pro: Fred Schultz   Course Supt.: Tony Goodley

18 Holes Par 71   6330 / 6015 / 5075 yds.
Rating: 70.6 / 69.1 / 69.5 Slope: 120 / 118 / 116

Challenging scenic course with 18 holes of championship golf.
Lighted driving range and miniature golf course on site. Enjoy *Windows
on the Green* for fine dining and banquets, or the *Fairway Pub* for casual dining.

$$	Resort	Golf Pkgs.	Public	Power Carts	Lessons	Lounge	Snack Bar	Meals	Open All Year

BRIARWOOD GOLF CLUB

YORK, PA (7 mi. W. of I-83, on Route 30.)
Telephone: (717)792-9776   Toll Free: 1-800-432-1555

Head Pro: Rick Saxton

36 Holes: 9 Holes   Par 37   3306 / 3181 / 2615 yds.   Rating: 35.3 / 34.8 / 34.4
              9 Holes   Par 35   3240 / 3069 / 2503 yds.   Rating: 34.8 / 33.9 / 33.3
              9 Holes   Par 35   3196 / 2926 / 2457 yds.   Rating: 35.0 / 33.8 / 33.7
              9 Holes   Par 35   3105 / 2757 / 2362 yds.

The first 3-9's are fairly open so you can hit away with the driver, but then you must hit to relatively small greens. The last 9 has larger, more heavily bunkered greens.

$$		Golf Pkgs.	Public	Power Carts	Lessons	Lounge	Snack Bar	Meals	Open All Year

GRANDVIEW GOLF CLUB

YORK, PA (Rt. 74, 3 mi. N. of West Manchester Mall)
Telephone: (717)764-2674

Manager: Robert Little

18 Holes   Par 72   6639 yds.

At 6639 yards from the blue, Grandview can be a tough par 72. A creek meanders through most of the front side, and there's a large pond on No. 13.

$$		Golf Pkgs.	Public	Power Carts	Lessons	Lounge	Snack Bar	Meals	Open All Year

The Bridgeton Hotel
AND CONFERENCE CENTER

Home of the
"TEE TIME" Reservation Center

The Best Kept Secret in York

*The most centrally located lodging facility for York County golf courses.
Located on a grassy knoll, tastefully decorated, very confortable
and Triple-A rated. Outdoor pool, Satellite-cable TV featuring
Showtime, and in-room coffee.*

THE HEARTHSIDE COCKTAIL LOUNGE
A cozy, quiet and relaxing hideaway.

ROUND THE CLOCK DINER
Open 24 hours - On premise
Bright and airy, featuring good family-style cooking at affordable prices.

THE BRIDGETON CONVENTION CENTER
*Impeccably designed for business and social needs. It is the
most modern conference/banquet facility in York.*

A GOLFER'S PACKAGE DELIGHT
☆ Double Occupancy Room
☆ Dinner and Breakfast ☆ Cocktails
☆ Green Fees ☆ Golf Cart

The Comforts of Home
Near the Greens of York County

(717)843-9971

222 Arsenal Road, I-83 and U.S. 30 York, Pennsylvania 17402

York County's history is diverse and spans many hundreds of years. The Fire Museum of York County, built in 1911, houses two centuries of firefighting equipment, and highlights major firefighting developments. The Strand-Capital Performing Arts Center is a former vaudeville hall and 1920s movie palace which has been restored and now caters to every taste in live performing and classic film. The 1,214-seat Strand showcases national touring theater and dance companies, symphony and chamber music events, and the York Symphony Orchestra.

Area celebrations and festivals include the "Sign of the Plough" Oyster Festival in October, with historical tours and entertainment served with fresh oysters, which have been popular in the area since the 18th century. "First Night York" is a New Year's Eve celebration of the performing arts, with family entertainment all evening throughout downtown.

A wide panorama of history and industry awaits you in Pennsylvania. Reach out and touch American history in the form of the Liberty Bell, or visit company mining towns that are still in use. Lose yourself in vibrant downtown Pittsburgh, or lakeside Erie. From the relaxing, powerful Pocono Mountains, to the dense, secluded Allegheny National Forest and the sandy shores of Lake Erie, Pennsylvania is the best of all worlds, and all types of terrain. The state offers so much, you'll need several trips just to touch on all of it. Make Pennsylvania part of your golf holiday some time soon.

COOL CREEK COUNTRY CLUB

WRIGHTSVILLE, PA (1 mi. S. of Rt. 30 off the Wrightsville exit, just E. of York)
Telephone: (717)252-3691

Head Pro: Sherm Keeney

18 Holes Par 71   6671 / 6356 / 6002 yds.
Rating: Men, 70.0, Ladies' 73.4

The front nine is quite open, while the back runs up
and down a valley, with a creek and/or pond coming into
play on four holes. Small greens demand accurate iron play.

$$		Golf Pkgs.	Public	Power Carts	Lessons	Lounge	Snack Bar	Meals	Open All Year

NEW YORK

SCOTT'S OQUAGA LAKE HOUSE GOLF COURSE • DEPOSIT, NEW YORK ▲

Golf
Vacations

New York is a state that has always known how to host a perfect family getaway and New Yorkers have built a reputation on it. It's a land of skyscrapers and towers, and of mountains of rock and mighty rivers that flow through its grand regions. It is this ruggedness and beauty that brought New English pioneers from the crowded east to establish a new settlement and a new way of life.

Nowhere is this diversity of history, scenic beauty and urban efficiency more evident that in **Albany**, the state capital. Albany is the oldest continuous settlement of the nation's original thirteen colonies, and was discovered by Henry Hudson as he sailed up the Hudson River in 1609. Over the next decades, Fort Orange, as it was called, was established as a trading post for the Dutch West Indies Company; however, it was taken from the Dutch by the British in 1664, and renamed Albany in honor of King James II, who had been the Duke of York and Albany. In 1686, the British granted Albany's founding charter as a city, although Dutch customs, language and traditions still continued under British dominion.

Albany was named the state capital in 1797, and in 1809 the first capitol building was completed. The capital buildings housed today in the Empire State Plaza were completed in 1899 under the governorship of Thedore Roosevelt.

Today, modern Albany and the surrounding region offer many different cultural and theatrical attractions, as well as world-renowned art galleries and museums. You can tour the city by boat, trolley car, motorcoach, a public transit system counted among the best in the country, or by hot air balloon. Any number of sports and recreation activities are available, including 7 public golf courses with a total of 162 holes, horse racing at nearby Saratoga Springs, boating down the Hudson River, the New York Yankees baseball farm team, basketball, football and many beautiful campsites.

No-WAIT GOLF, MONEY-SAVING PACKAGES & SPECTACULAR MOUNTAIN AND LAKE SCENERY

A multi-day vacation to Lake Placid and Essex County can provide you with an enjoyable "full-course" sample of the range of golf courses available amidst the scenic vistas of the beautiful Adirondack Mountains and lakes.

Essex County's distinctive courses attract golf enthusiasts of all abilities. The 9 hole executives, found at the Port Kent, Saranac Lake, Willsboro, Schroon Lake, Cobble Hill and Ausable Valley Golf Clubs, are complemented by their 18 hole championship counterparts in Westport, Lake Placid and Ticonderoga, all with virtually no waiting to tee off. There are 12 public courses available, surrounded by the spectacular beauty and diversity found in Essex County.

The area attractions, cultural events and historical sites will keep the whole family entertained during your visit here. From the historic forts at Ticonderoga & Crown Point and the scenic wonder of Ausable Chasm & High Falls Gorge, to the excitement of Frontier Town and Santa's Workshop, people of all ages are entertained and educated by the natural wonders and pure family fun.

Whether you're interested in a luxury hotel, a cabin, or the relaxing atmosphere of a bed and breakfast, the tremendous range in accomodations are sure to suit all of your vacation needs. Many offer money-saving golf packages. Just call the central reservations office for complete details.

You can choose from accomodations conveniently located near trailheads to hiking trails in the High Peaks, or the internationally-known Olympic sites in Lake Placid, but wherever you choose to stay, you're sure to be close to yet another wonderful golfing experience on Essex County's plush fairways and challenging greens.

CALL TOLL-FREE FOR MORE INFORMATION

1-800-44-PLACID

*North of the Capital region lie the Adirondack Mountains, which are known as "New York's Mountain & Lake Country". Perhaps the first thing one thinks of when mentioning this area is **Lake Placid**, and the 1980 Winter Olympics. While this was an important event, and served to highlight Lake Placid and Essex County's superb winter sports conditions, there are many other sides and many other seasons to this area. The Adirondacks are home to over 2,300 lakes and ponds, crystal clear water nestled between lush green mountains which provide excellent swimming, boating and fishing in the summer. The Adirondacks are also home to more than 36 golf courses, with literally hundreds of challenging holes and natural beauty just waiting for you to give them a swing. And when you're not on the course, there's so much to do you could fill an entire vacation simply exploring.*

Wandering through Franklin County is like putting your feet up, this is a great place to relax. A pathway of warm, fresh-water lakes settle through the area, and you can rent a canoe to explore much as the early settlers in the 1700's did. Franklin is an antique collector's dream, with many unexpected finds available around every corner. The county offers year-round entertainment, from white beaches lining their warm lakes in summer to exceptional snow and ski centers all winter long.

*Franklin's eastern neighbor is Clinton County, which hugs the western shores of Lake Champlain. The largest city is **Plattsburgh**, which has the State University, and all other urban amenities. There are gorgeous sandy white beaches all along the lake, the 6th largest in the U.S., with year-round yachting and chartered sailboats at your disposal. As well, there is exceptional fly fishing, windsurfing, camping, and, of course, great golf. And who know, you may even catch a glimpse of "Champ", the sea monster who is rumored to live in the calm, still waters of Lake Champlain.*

CRAIG WOOD GOLF COURSE
LAKE PLACID, NY
Telephone: (518)523-9811

Manager: Butch Martin
Course Supt.: Lynn Wilson - GSA

Head Pro: Brian Halpenny
Architect: Seymour Dunn

18 Holes   Par 72   6554 yds.

A championship course laid out with
breathtaking views of the Adirondack Mountains.

$		Golf Pkgs.	Public	Power Carts	Lessons	Lounge	Snack Bar	Meals		

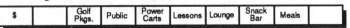

WHITEFACE INN RESORT & CLUB

LAKE PLACID, NY (On Whiteface Inn Road, off Route 86)
Telephone: (518)523-2551

Manager: Robert Vojnick   Head Pro: J. Peter Martin - PGA
Course Supt.: Kevin Geesler   Architect: John Van Kleek

18 Holes   Par 72   6490 yds.

This superbly conditioned course has been challenging golfers of all levels since
the turn of the century. The fairways, inlaid in 360 acres of valleys and forests,
offer breathtaking views of the surrounding mountains and beautiful Lake Placid.

$$	Resort	Golf Pkgs.	Public	Power Carts	Lessons	Lounge	Snack Bar	Meals	
$$	Resort	Golf Pkgs.	Public	Power Carts	Lessons	Lounge	Snack Bar	Meals	

Essex County, long-known for its breathtaking skiing and winter sports, has also become synonymous with summer fun. The Lake Placid Olympic Training Center is there, and you could perhaps watch the next great Olympic athletes training. The quaint shops of Main Street in Lake Placid will delight any lover of antiques and hand-crafted goods. The mountains which seem to be everywhere have some of the best and most challenging hiking trails around, and the views for those hearty enough to reach the peaks are simply without compare. In the same area is **Wilmington**, home of Whiteface Mountain which was used in the '80 Olympics. In addition to "The Mountain", this alpine town has the West Branch of the AuSable River, one of the best trout-fishing

streams in the East. Wilmington is also home to the "Santa's Workshop" theme park, featuring rides, a peting zoo where you can touch Santa's reindeer, and a visit to Santa's house.

In the southern corner of Essex County, the town of **Ticonderoga** is nestled on the shore of Lake Champlain. There you'll find the historic Fort Ticonderoga, a battlement dating back to the first settlers in the area, which is truly a unique find and a fascinating piece of local history. The area is also well-known for its fishing derbies and tournaments that lure fishermen throughout the spring and summer. Up the shoreline lies the town of **Essex**, one of New York's most remarkably well-preserved historic villages. Over 160 structures built between the 1790s and 1860, (essentially the entire town), appears on the National Register of Historic Places. Inland slightly is **Elizabethtown**, the county seat and government center with an eye for historic beauty and preservation.

At the southernmost tip of the Adirondacks is Warren County, encompassing most of Lake George it is the starting point of the Hudson River. Warren County is one of the most popular areas in New York for camping and fishing; with over 160 lakes and ponds, it has long been known as the "Grand Slam Fishing Capital of the Northeast". The Lake George region boasts 9 major gamefish, as well, there is excellent hunting with some of the best and wildest game country in the area. The town of **Lake George** was settled by a treaty between a French-Canadian Jesuit missionary named Father Isaac Jogues and the Iroquois Indians in 1646. Father Jogues was so taken with the lake that he called it the "Lac due Saint Sacrement", meaning "Lake of the Blessed Sacrament".

Spectacular Scenery of the
ADIRONDACK MOUNTAINS
in Upstate New York

the LAKE GEORGE area

LAKE GEORGE AREA
18-HOLE USGA GOLF COURSES

BOLTON LANDING: **Sagamore Resort & Golf Club,** 518-644-9400
Weekdays $50, Weekends $50

LAKE GEORGE: **Queensbury Country Club,** 518-793-3711
Weekdays $15, Weekends $15

QUEENSBURY: **Hiland Park,** 518-761-GOLF
Weekdays $25, Weekends $30

WARRENSBURG: **Cronin's Golf Resort,** 518-623-9336
Weekdays $12, Weekends $14

NOTE: Four USGA 9-hole golf courses are also located in Warren County.
All area golf courses are listed in the Warren County Travel Guide.

For free Travel Guide and further information:
WARREN COUNTY TOURISM
729 Municipal Center, Lake George, NY 12845-9795
1-518-761-6366, ext. 729 (business office M-F 9-5)
518-761-6368 FAX

1-800-365-1050 Ext. 729

THE SAGAMORE

BOLTON LANDING, NY (On Lake George)
Telephone: (518)644-9400   Toll Free: 1-800-358-3585

Manager: Robert McIntosh   Head Pro: Tom Smack
Course Supt.: Rick DeMeo   Architect: Donald Ross

18 Holes   Par 70   6950 yds.

Back in 1928, the legendary Donald Ross carved a golf course out of birches
and evergreens, routed the holes to take full advantage of Adirondack vistas,
even planted heather from his native Scotland. Come and play this scenic test of golf.

$$	Resort	Golf Pkgs.	Public	Power Carts	Lessons	Lounge	Snack Bar	Meals	Open All Year
$$	Resort	Golf Pkgs.	Public	Power Carts	Lessons	Lounge	Snack Bar	Meals	Open All Year

LOON LAKE GOLF COURSE

LOON LAKE, NY (On Route 99)
Telephone: (518)891-3249

Owner: Carol Long   Manager: Nancy Price
Course Supt.: Leo Collins

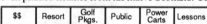

18 Holes   Par 70   5400 yds.

The oldest in the Adirondacks... in continuous operation since 1895,
the Loon Lake Golf Course has been praised for almost four generations
as the most scenic 18 holes in the Adirondacks. This, coupled with a
"Scottish Links" design, make a round at Loon Lake a memorable experience.

$$$		Golf Pkgs.	Public	Power Carts			Snack Bar	Meals	
$$$		Golf Pkgs.	Public	Power Carts			Snack Bar	Meals	

South of the Adirondacks, and skirting the state line with Pennsylvania are the Catskills. Long-known as one of the vacation resort capitals of the United States, the Catskills with its mountain-top chalets and family-run resorts, is everything its reputation claims. Greene County is the center of things, with festivals year-round that attract big-name music stars from all poles of the music industry. There is always something new and exciting to do, from the Carson City & Indian Village, an authentic wild-west recreation in the town of Catskill, to the Catskill Game Farm with rare and exotic animals from around the world. The best views available are from the highest chairlift in the Catskills on the Hunter Mountain Sky Ride, where you can also find go-kart rides and scenic aerial tours. Outdoor enthusiasts will find the Catskills a mecca of all-season activity, from championship fishing to over 350 holes of golf at 22 courses throughout the area. Sail through the many rivers and lakes which run through the Catskill mountains, or hike over the pine-covered peaks for some breathtaking scenic views. Mountain-biking is encouraged, but be ready to work hard at it.

The Catskills are also known for their summer theater festivals, where some of the best and brightest performers from Broadway come to hone their craft. The "Woodstock Music Festival" was held at Woodstock in 1969, and a plaque commemorating the event was laid on the site. This is family fun country, and there really is something for everyone. There are many childrens' camps, which specialize in vacations and summer adventures for the younger set. In winter, the lush mountains turn to white, and some of the best skiing can be found, as well as ice fishing, snowmobiling and an abundance of winter carnivals. The excitement never seems to stop in the Catskills, no matter what the season.

RAINBOW GOLF CLUB

GREENVILLE, NY (On Rte. 26)
Telephone: (518)966-5343

Head Pro: Walter J. Birmann - PGA Class "A"

9 Holes   Par 36   3030 yds.

Free golf for registered guests. An interesting and challenging course. The signature 7th hole is among the finest. Other amenities include fishing, hunting, tennis and an airport with a 1800 foot grass runway.

$	Resort	Golf Pkgs.	Public	Power Carts	Lessons	Lounge	Snack Bar	Meals	

The CONCORD
R E S O R T   H O T E L

GOLF | PACKAGES

MIDWEEK & WEEKEND

Unlimited free golf on all courses (including the world famous "Monster") ✦ Free club storage ✦ Free bucket of balls ✦ Two clubhouses ✦ Pro golf shops

HOTEL FEATURES:

Full American Plan
• 3 gourmet meals daily
• Special diets
• Cocktail party
  Saturday night
• Children's dining room

Entertainment and Dancing Nightly
• All Star Show nightly
• No cover of minimum
• Discotheque music
• Little Club for late dancing

Children's Program
All facilities for pre-school to teens. A full program daily keeps the youngsters happy from sun-up to sun-down.

• Babysitters available
• day camps year round for youngsters over 3 years
• Choice of eating in Main or Children's dining room at no extra charge

Sports Activities
• 45 holes of golf
• Indoor swimming pool
• 16 indoor tennis courts
• 24 outdoor tennis courts
• Indoor & outdoor basketball
• 18-hole miniature golf course
• Fitness center
• Men's & Ladies' steam rooms, saunas, health club and plunge
• Volleyball, Ping Pong
• Class lessons and exhibitions in golf & tennis

1-800-431-3850
Hotel: **(914) 794-4000**   Fax: **(914) 794-7471**

CONCORD RESORT HOTEL, THE

KIAMESHA LAKE, NY
Telephone: (914) 794-4000   Toll Free Reservations: 1-800-431-3850
Fax: (914)794-7471

Director of Golf: Billy Burke, PGA

18 Holes Par 72 7672 / 7205 / 6793 yds.
18 Holes Par 71 6660 / 6025 yds.
 9 Holes Par 31 2200 yds.

The Concord golf school.

$$	Resort	Golf Pkgs.	Public	Power Carts	Lessons	Lounge	Snack Bar	Meals	

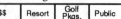

TENNANAH LAKE GOLF & TENNIS CLUB

A GOLFER'S DREAM!

Tennanah Lake Golf & Tennis Club is located on 1000 spacious acres in the beautiful Catskill Mountains of Roscoe, New York. Our facilities include an 18 hole Championship Golf Course, Har-Tru Tennis Courts, Olympic Size Pool and Overnight Accommodations.

• Professional Lessons • Pro Shop
• Twilight Golf 5:00 PM • Lodgings • Coffee Shop
• Outing Dates Available • Tennis Courts
• **Golf Packages Available**

For more
information or
reservations call:

(607) 498-5502

or Fax:
(607) 498-4177

ROSCOE- HANKINS ROAD, ROSCOE, NEW YORK 12276

TENNANAH LAKE GOLF & TENNIS CLUB INC.

ROSCOE, NY (Exit 94 Quickway North)
Telephone: (607)498-5502   or: (914)794-2900

President & CEO: Robert James Frankel   Head Pro: Gregory Scott Smith
Course Supt.: Bruce Petrelli   Property Manager: James Amback

18 Holes   Par 72   6737 / 6297 / 5822
Rating: 71.2 / 69.3 / 72.5   Slope: 119 / 115 / 115

Enjoy our 18 hole championship golf course designed by
PGA Professional Sam Snead, complete with a 60-mile panoramic view!

$$	Resort	Golf Pkgs.	Public	Power Carts	Lessons	Lounge	Snack Bar	Meals	

We the **Scott** FAMILY invite you to join us

For a Super
VACATION
with Plenty of
GOLF

UNLIMITED PLAY
on our own two
Scenic Mt. Top
9 HOLE COURSES

at our 1100 acre N.Y. State MOUNTAIN RESORT on Beautiful OQUAGA LAKE

LIVE BALLROOM MUSIC 7 nights a week
3200 Square ft. Hardwood Dance Floor

Live Cabaret Type Shows EACH NIGHT

Each Morning **FUN DANCE SESSIONS**
SQUARE - FOLK - LINE

GOLF - TENNIS - SHUFFLEBOARD

Bocce, Swedish exercise course, Putting, Pitch and Putt, Hiking, Fishing, Showboat, Sing-alongs, Speedboat rides, Waterskiing, Sailing, Canoeing, Mini-bus tours, Programs throughout the day, Fashion Shows, Talent Shows, Video Fun, Cookouts, Bowling, Pocket Billiards, Ping Pong

*3 FABULOUS MEALS EACH DAY
**COMFORTABLE ACCOMMODATIONS
One rate includes all of this, and there is NO TIPPING

We **Scott's** love fun, and we love people.

Give us a call
607-467-3094
for brochures and rates

Scott's OQUAGA LAKE HOUSE

P.O. BOX 47 • OQUAGA LAKE • DEPOSIT, NY 13754

For 123 years the Scott family has been entertaining summer vacationists at this 1,100 acre resort on beautiful Oquaga Lake on the edge of the Catskills near Deposit, N. Y.

Although open to the public, Scott's guests enjoy unlimited free golf on their golf courses, which include a main nine hole course built in the early twenties with two alternate holes added later on, an executive nine hole course about one-half mile away with connecting trail through the woods for cars. Both courses are on top of the mountain and provide some beautiful panoramic views. Also available is a pitch and putt nine hole course and practice putting green.

The charm of the unique resort may be the members of the Scott family, who personally provide a large number of programs, activities, tours, music, shows, and entertainment. People agree that the Scott's byline "The Excitement of a Cruise - Friendliness of a Bed & Breakfast" fits them very well.

SCOTT'S OQUAGA LAKE HOUSE GOLF COURSE

DEPOSIT, NY (From Rte 17 take exit 84, follow the signs to Oquaga Lake.)
Clubhouse: (607)467-2447   Main Office: (607)467-3094

Manager: Ron Drumn   Course Supt.: Ron Bowerman

9 Holes   Par 36   3080 yds.
9 Holes   Par 32   1555 yds.

Two very scenic mountain top courses, about 1/2 mile apart.
One green fee covers both courses. Unlimited free golf to guests
of Scott's Hotel. Power carts extra. Also a nine hole pitch and putt.

$	Resort	Golf Pkgs.	Public	Power Carts	Lessons		Snack Bar	Meals	

*Slightly upstate but still on the Pennsylvania state line is the "Central/Leatherstocking" region, most famous for the National Baseball Hall of Fame and the National Soccer Hall of Fame, both in **Cooperstown**. Cooperstown is also the home of the New York State Historical Association, as well as the nationally-known Glimmerglass Opera Company, who perform in the Alice Busch Opera Theater overlooking the beautiful Lake Otsego. This is small-town New York, with all its charms and relaxing atmosphere. It is an exciting place to explore, no matter what time of year.*

There are several championship golf courses, as well as some for the more novice player. The lakes and rivers which dot the countryside are perfect for boating, swimming or white-water rafting. You can also enjoy some great fishing or just lie on one of the many white, sandy beaches. Perhaps your taste runs more into hang-gliding, flying in a glider or hot air ballooning. Hundreds of campgrounds are nestled within the dense forests, and you can hike, bike or even ride through them on horseback, along the trails and over the rolling mountains and hills.

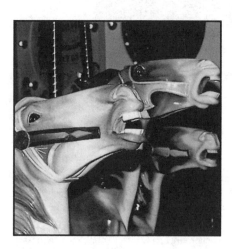

One of the most unusual attractions in the area is the world's largest collection of wood-carved carousels. In fact, Broome County, on the southern border with Pennsylvania, is the self-proclaimed "Carousel Capital of the World". The county has six painstakingly restored vintage carousels, which have been nominated to the National Register of Historic Places. Admission to this fascinating exhibit is one piece of litter.

LEATHERSTOCKING GOLF COURSE

COOPERSTOWN, NY (In Cooperstown, off Route 28)
Telephone: (607)547-9931

Manager:Frank J. Maloney
Head Pro: Will Pijnenburg

Head Pro: Ed Kroll
Architect: Devereux Emmett

18 Holes   Par 72   6500 yds.

An outstanding test of golf with magnificent vistas of Otsego Lake.
The course has played host to a number of New York State Tournaments.
Accommodations available on site at THE OTESAGA HOTEL.

$$$$	Resort	Golf Pkgs.	Public	Power Carts	Lessons	Lounge				

GENEVA ON THE LAKE
America's Premier Small Resort

Golf Getaway Package

Treat yourself to a wonderful Golf Getaway at this elegant small resort. Located on Seneca Lake in the scenic Finger Lakes Wine Country — just 2 minutes from the 18 hole Seneca Lake Country Club. **Golf Getaway Package** includes: a beautiful suite, each with a ready kitchen and some with fireplace, whirlpool or canopied bed; a complimentary bottle of wine, fresh fruit, and flowers on arrival; continental breakfast each morning; *The New York Times* at your door; 18 holes of golf with a cart; and friendly hospitality. Additional — candlelight gourmet dining Friday to Sunday with live music and Sunday Brunch year-round and Lunch on the Terrace July 1 to September 6. "The food is extraordinarily good," reports *Bon Appetit*. **Recipient of AAA's ◆ ◆ ◆ ◆ Award for 11 consecutive years.** Write P.O. Box 929 Geneva, N.Y. 14456.

Call 1-800-3-GENEVA

West along the Pennsylvania state line lies the Finger Lakes region, so named for the half-dozen long, thin lakes that cut north-to-south through the area. Indian legend has it that the Creator looked down upon the Finger Lakes and was so taken with its beauty that He left behind His hand print, which is what the Finger Lakes are said to resemble. Regardless of how they were formed, the diversity of the topography, with long narrow lakes lying side by side, and deep gorges with rushing falls and fertile, wide valleys, is unique to this area.

*The Finger Lakes are steeped in history, with many communities and landmarks named after their Native American heritage. Cities like **Ithaca**, **Syracuse**, **Oswego** and **Canandaigua** are just a sampling of the distinctive names. The area is a wealth of antique finds, as well as museums and historical properties, and is one of the major wine regions of the world, having flourished for a hundred years. One of the more popular attractions is wine tasting in the fall.*

This area isn't mired in the past, however; far from it. The Finger Lakes was named by the National Geographic Society as one of "America's Great Hideaways", and was rated one of the "Top 30 Vacation Destinations in the United States", according to Rand McNally & Co.'s "Vacation Places Rated". The Finger Lakes region boasts 3,200 rooms to accomodate groups from 10 to 600, all with some of the nation's best scenery and recreation in its backyard. You can find just about anything you'd like to do there, from fishing and flower festivals in the spring, golfing at over 50 courses, boasting several hundred holes, swimming and water skiing in the summer, hunting and wine tasting in the fall, and skiing, snowboarding, ice sailing and skating in the winter.

BRISTOL HARBOUR
On Canandaigua Lake

At the BRISTOL HARBOUR GOLF CLUB in Canadaigua, NY you will experience one of Western New York's most talked about golf courses.

This 6700-yard championship course, designed by Robert Trent Jones in 1972, is nestled in the breathtaking Bristol Hills overlooking Canadaigua Lake . . . the gem of the Finger Lakes.

A superb test of golf, the course combines natural settings with an outstanding sequence of holes.

Perhaps the most underated hole on the course is #11, a par 3 that plays 148 yards from the reds, 173 yards from the whites and 216 yards from the blues . . .

The green is diagonal with bunkers protecting the right front and left rear. Club selection is the key and a par here usually picks up one to two strokes on the field.

Keeping your mind on your game can be difficult as this hole offers a most spectacular view of Canadaigua Lake, one of many you will experience as you play your round.

BRISTOL HARBOUR offers many different golf packages with accommodations in their Lakeside Condominiums or Lakeside Townhomes.

To find out more or to book your reservations, just call 1-800-288-8248 and . . . experience the difference !!!

1-800-288-8248

The major cities of **Rochester** and **Syracuse** are both true world-class cities, urban centers with an abundance of upstate hospitality. Syracuse boasts 26 golf courses in and around the city, with an art and culture center playing host to a symphony orchestra, art galleries, an opera company, live theater and a museum of art. You can take boat cruises over Onondaga Lake or visit the Burnet Park Zoo.

The city of Rochester is the 3rd largest metropolitan area in the state, with well over a million people, but don't let its size daunt you; Rochester is truly a "welcome surprise". It was the home of George Eastman, founder of the Eastman Kodak Company, and there is the International Museum of Photography at his former home, with exhibits spanning 150 years. A major attraction in the area is the Darien Lake amusement park, with over 100 midway rides, exciting shows and attractions, including America's tallest ferris wheel, "The Viper" super-coaster, and a campground with more than 2,000 campsires. There are over 30 public, private and semi-private golf courses in Rochester and area to challenge every skill level.

Southwest of the city is Watkins Glen, a professional auto racing track featuring NASCAR racing and many high-profile competitions. The skyline of Rochester is one of the most unique anywhere, with historic buildings and distinctive new skyscrapers sharing the space and making for an aesthetically fascinating view.

B R I S T O L   H A R B O U R
On Canandaigua Lake

The Bristol Harbour Golf Club, designed in 1972 by ROBERT TRENT JONES offers championship golf, an on site restaurant in a resort setting with tennis, private beach and marina. Located just 30 miles south of Rochester, on Canandaigua Lake, the Gem of the Finger Lakes.

Golf Packages Starting at $148.00 per Person

Package Includes:
- 2 nights accomodation in lakeside Condominium or Golfside Townhomes
- 3 Rounds of Golf with Riding Carts

- Free Driving Range
- Bag Storage
- Preferred Tee Times
- Breakfast

"Bristol Harbour Golf Club is one of the Premier Golf Courses the Finger Lakes has to offer. The tees are in immaculate condition, the fairways are expertly manicured and the greens are simply perfect"
. . . . FINGER LAKE TIMES, July 5, 1991

Listed in GOLF DIGEST *as one of The Places to Play in New York State*

Call 1-800-288-8248 Today!!

BRISTOL HARBOUR GOLF CLUB

CANANDAIGUA, NY (Rte. 332 S. to Rte 21 S. follow signs to Bristol Harbour)
Office: 1-800-288-8248   Pro Shop: (716)396-2460

Manager: Mark Knickerbocker	Head Pro: Suellen Northrup
Course Supt.: Ken Leach	Architect: Robert Trent Jones

18 - R - 6100 - 72

Course Record of 67 held by Jack Nicklaus.
Host of the 1992 New York State Men's Mid-Amateur.

$$	Resort	Golf Pkgs.		Power Carts	Lessons	Lounge	Snack Bar	Meals	

Foxfire Golf & Tennis

FOXFIRE GOLF & TENNIS

BALDWINVILLE, NY (I-90 Thruway exit 39, 690 N. 1 mile, Van Buren Rd. exit)
Clubhouse: (315)638-2930   Pro Shop: (315)638-1362

Manager: Joel Fitzgerald   Head Pro: Grag Natale
Course Supt.: Dick Perry   Architect: Hal Purdy

18 Holes Par 72 6451 yds.

Foxfire is a well maintained course that meanders through various
residences. It is fully irrigated and well trapped with lurking water hazards which
test the average as well as the expert golfer. Accommodations only 2 miles away!

$$		Golf Pkgs.	Public	Power Carts	Lessons	Lounge	Snack Bar	Meals	

LIVINGSTON COUNTRY CLUB

GENESEO, NY (On Lakeville Rd., exit 8 off Rte. 390 S., at Rte. 20A W.)
Clubhouse: (716)243-9939   Pro Shop: (716)243-4430

Manager: Thomas C. Burke   Head Pro: Jeff Kaye - PGA
Course Supt.: Leonard Geary - GSA

18 Holes Par 72 6200 yds.

18 hole championship course located in the scenic
Genesee Valley. Special weekday rates including carts.

$		Golf Pkgs.	Public	Power Carts	Lessons	Lounge	Snack Bar	Meals	

THE • LODGE

Aommodations ✧ Dining ✧ Entertainment ✧ Fitness
Golf ✧ Conferencing

Golf Package:

CHECK IN ON ANY THURSDAY OR SUNDAY
TWO NIGHTS DELUXE ACCOMMODATIONS
TWO BREAKFASTS FOR TWO
TWO LUNCHES FOR TWO
ONE DINNER FOR TWO
GREEN FEES AND CART
45 HOLES OF GOLF

$450.00 per couple

includes all taxes and gratuities.

Possible Itineraries:

Check in Thursday, 9 holes of golf and dinner at Woodcliff
Friday - 18 holes of golf and lunch at Shadow Lake
Saturday - 18 holes of golf and lunch at Shadow Pines
- or-
Check in Sunday, 9 holes of golf and dinner at Woodcliff
Monday - 18 holes of golf and lunch at Shadow Lake
Tuesday - 18 holes of golf and lunch at Shadow Pines

THE LODGE AT WOODCLIFF IS A FOUR DIAMOND RESORT
FEATURING LIVE JAZZ EVERY NIGHT

1-800-365-3065

Rochester: **(716) 381-4000**   Fax: **(716) 381-2673**

The Lodge at Woodcliff, 199 Woodcliff Drive, Fairport, New York 14450
(Just off New York State Thruway, at Exit #45)

Following the Pennsylvania state line, you come to the "Chautaqua/Allegheny" region, one of New York's premier wine regions. This area is very relaxed and a great place to unwind, and is a relatively short drive from the Canadian borders at Buffalo and Niagara Falls. The area is home to the Chautaque Institution, a unique facility which, since 1874, has been a center for the performing arts, symphony orchestras, opera, theater, ballet, top-name celebrity entertainment, as well as classes, workshops and world-renowned lecture series'.

*One of the major attractions of the area is the "Lucille Ball Festival of New Comedy", which is held in Lucy's hometown of **Chautaqua** in May. It is a festival focused on developing new comic talent, and is always very popular. South of Chautaqua is the town of **Gerry**, which has been home to the "oldest consecutive rodeo East of the Mississippi", and is held in August. You can go on a scenic rail excursion for dinner or take a ride on a paddle wheel steamboat; visit a recreated pioneer village or stop in at a buffalo ranch. For a complete change of pace, visit "Panama Rocks" or "Rock City", the world's largest outcroppings of glacier-cut, ocean-quartz rock, with thousands of crevices and gargantuan dens to explore. The area proudly boasts 17 golf courses and resorts offering golf, and some fabulous skiing.*

Peek'n Peak

RESORT & CONFERENCE CENTER
CLYMER, NEW YORK

ALL THE RIGHT INGREDIENTS

Spectacular Recreation Amid Gracious Amenities . . . a great 18-hole golf course with its superior mix of challenges, indoor and outdoor pool, new fitness center with its ten station Universal gym, tennis courts, cycling and much more . . . all blending perfectly with the timeless beauty of a country resort setting.

GOLF GETAWAY PACKAGES

FOR MORE INFORMATION AND RESERVATIONS

TEL: (716)355-4141   FAX: (716)355-4542

PEEK'N PEAK is the home of the ROLAND STAFFORD GOLF SCHOOL, unquestionably the very best instruction you can get, because it gets results.

Small classes, video analysis, PGA trained instructors and a specially designed practice area all work together to provide excellent instruction. There's even a covered tee to assure that the weather won't interfere.

FOR MORE INFORMATION CONTACT:

THE ROLAND STAFFORD GOLF SCHOOL RESERVATIONS OFFICE

Toll Free: 1-800-447-8894 or call (914)586-3187

PEEK'N PEAK RESORT & CONFERENCE CENTER
CLYMER, NY (On Ye Olde Rd., I-90 to Rte. 17, exit at Findlay Lake)
Telephone: (716)355-4141

General Manger: John Gallagher   Head Pro: Steve Card - PGA

18 Holes Par 72 6260 yds. Rating: Men's - 69, Ladies' - 72

A natural playground amidst one of
Western New York's most beautiful settings.

$$	Resort	Golf Pkgs.	Public	Power Carts	Lessons	Lounge	Snack Bar	Meals	Open All Year

*Due north of the "Chautauqua/Allegh-eny" is the "Niagara Frontier", with the city of **Buffalo** its major hub. One of the area's most important assets is its proximity to the Canadian border; Canadian shoppers and visitors account for much of the area's retail economy, and as such are welcome guests. The Peace Bridge is, in fact, the major port of entry for Canadians into the United States.*

Buffalo has been called "The Crown Jewel of the Great Lakes", and is New York's 2nd largest city. Its Lake Erie waterfront continues to be revitalized, and its shores are home to the only inland naval park in the country. Buffalo has a clean, new theater district and has introduced a Light Rail Transit (LRT) system ranking among the most efficient in the country. The city is considered one of the best values for overnight guests anywhere, with abundant shopping catering to Canadians, but with an eye for American customers, too. There are literally dozens of public golf courses in and around Buffalo, but if you have a taste for something different, Buffalo is home to two professional sports teams, the Buffalo Bills football team and the Buffalo Sabres hockey team, as well as amateur baseball and basketball teams, and is proud to be the host of the 1993 World University Games.

TERRY HILLS GOLF COURSE

BATAVIA, NY. (On Rte. 33, 10 Min. from N.Y. State Thruway exit #48)
Telephone: (716)343-0860   Toll Free (US and Canada): 1-800-825-8633

President: Joseph Rotondo   Dir. of Golf: Nicholas J. Rotondo
Architect: Ed Ault

18 Holes Par 72 6038 yds.

18 exciting holes with watered fairways.Tee times taken seven days
a week - call in advance. "The best kept secret in Western New York"

$			Public	Power Carts	Lessons	Lounge	Snack Bar	Meals	

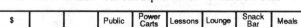

Holiday Valley

GOLF • SCHOOL

- ONLY 3 HOURS FROM TORONTO -

A THREE DAY GOLF SCHOOL

- 5 hours of golf instruction daily incl. on course play
- Daily videotape, review and critique
- Green fees and golf carts during and after class
- Only 4 students per professional - grouped by ability
- Use of all resort facilities
- Arrival gift and cocktail party
- Lunch each day

TOTAL COST $517.00

. . . Imagine what three days of living and breathing golf could do for your game . . .

Large Pro Shop - Discount Prices
Yonex ADX 200 . . . $249.00
Hogan Edge $425.00

FOR RESERVATIONS AND ADDITIONAL INFORMATION:

Call Dick Eaton, Golf Director, Holiday Valley Resort

(716) 699-2346

P.O. Box 370 Ellicottville, NY 14713-0370

HOLIDAY VALLEY RESORT

ELLICOTTVILLE, NY. (On Rte. 219, 45 Mi. S. of I-90, in Buffalo)
Resort: (716)699-2345   Pro Shop: (716)699-2346

Head Pro: Dick Eaton   Course Supt.: Don Wagner

18 Holes   Par 72   6555 yds.   Rating: Men's - 71, Ladies' - 74

Spectacular scenery and variety makes this
one of the most exciting courses in Western New York.
Plenty of water, traps and natural hazards add to the challenge.

$$	Resort	Golf Pkgs.	Public	Power Carts	Lessons	Lounge	Snack Bar	Meals	

*Buffalo was the home to Millard Fillmore, the 13th President of the United States, and there is a museum in his honor in nearby **East Aurora**. As well, on "Millionaires Row" in downtown Buffalo is Wilcox Mansion, site of the inauguration of President Theodore Roosevelt. Within a few miles of the city, many historic battlesites from the War of 1812 can be seen, including historic **Lewiston**, the Erie Canal and locks, and **Old Fort Niagara**. Buffalo's city hall is a shining example of the grand architecture of its period, with a 28th-floor observation deck open to the public. On Allen Street is the heart of the Allentown Historic District, host to Buffalo's largest concentration of antique shops. On Delaware Avenue is the Allen Herschell Carousel Factory, once the world's largest manufacturer of carousels and band organs.*

*Following the Niagara River northward, you come to one of the true wonders of the modern world, **Niagara Falls**. The Falls are the major attraction of the area, with many different ways to view them, including the "Maid of the Mist", a boat that takes drenched passengers directly beneath the deafening, roaring water; or there's always a helicopter, which is probably the best overall view of The Falls you could get. Niagara is known as the "Honeymoon Capital of the World", and lives up to its reputation. A larger array of heart-shaped beds and bathtubs would be difficult to find. There are several bridges to and from Canada, and both Niagaras, the Canadian and American, are excellent neighbors.*

BYRNCLIFF RESORT & CONFERENCE CENTER

VARYSBURG, NY (On Route 20A, 12 mi. E. of East Aurora)
Telephone: (716)535-7300

Manager: Scott Meidenbauer
Course Supt.: Sandy Zeeb

Head Pro: Keith Buttles
Architect: Russ Tryon

18 Holes   Par 72   6783 yds.

Challenging and Scenic 18 hole layout for summer
golfing pleasure along with 12 miles of Cross Country Ski
trails for year round recreation. Lodging available on premis.

$	Resort	Golf Pkgs.	Public	Power Carts	Lessons	Lounge	Snack Bar	Meals	
$	Resort	Golf Pkgs.	Public	Power Carts	Lessons	Lounge	Snack Bar	Meals	

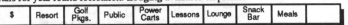

Some other interesting attractions in the area include "Artpark", a 200-acre state park with artists, craftsmen and performers working daily in an artists-colony atmosphere, with a large indoor/outdoor theater which features jazz, opera and pop concerts, as well as ballet, live theater and dance performances all summer long. "The Turtle" is a Native American living arts center, a turtle-shaped complex renowned for its extensive collection of American Indian history and culture. Fishing on both Lake Ontario and Lake Erie is abundant, and the area is well-known for fresh-water salmon. Area state parks offer breathtaking views and excellent hiking and camping.

BATAVIA COUNTRY CLUB

**BATAVIA, NY (On Batavia-Bryon Rd., from thruway exit 48 to Main St. to Rte. 33)
Telephone: (716)343-7600**

Manager: Karen L. Pompa   Course Supt.: William McDonald

18 - R - 7134 - 72

Golf Packages - Monday, Wednesday and Friday
during the season. Includes green fees, cart and dinner for two.

$		Golf Pkgs.	Public	Power Carts	Lessons	Lounge	Snack Bar	Meals	

Northeast along the shore of Lake Ontario, on the far side of the Finger Lakes region, is the "Thousand Island/Seaway" district. This area marks the beginning of the St. Lawrence River and the end of Lake Ontario, and is full of, quite literally, one thousand islands. Here you'll find great game to hunt and some of the best fishing you can get.

Try your hand at golf courses overlooking the mighty St. Lawrence River, with water hazards that really mean business, You can also go canoeing, white water rafting, boating, and watch the enormous ships travelling through the St. Lawrence. This is a great place to unwind, and you'll discover cosy cottages and campsites with outdoor activites including hiking and exploring all the islands in the area.

Of particular note is Heart Island, on which sits the unfinished "Boldt Castle".

Originally commissioned in 1900 by George C. Boldt, proprietor of the Waldorf-Astoria Hotel, it was to be a gift to his beloved wife, Louise. It was a replica of the German Rhineland Castle, but, with work underway on eleven buildings and $2.5 million invested, Mrs. Boldt suddenly died, and George abandoned the project and never returned to the island.

In 1977, the Thousand Island Bridge Authority assumed ownership of the island and castle, and will preserve it for future generations. Hundreds of hearts adorn the castle as a testament to Boldt's undying love for his wife.

Other historical areas include Jefferson County, which boasts a museum of fresh water boats, a turn-of-the-century museum and store in **Alexandria Bay**, and stretegic battlesites and harbors that were important during the War of 1812.

In nearby **Redwood**, visit the Thousand Islands Zoo, which features a large collection of exotic wild animals and a petting zoo.

Watertown, the county seat and largest city in the region, is expanding and growing while managing to hold on to its rich history.

Play the Jewel   **CLUB**   *of the 1000 Islands*

THOUSAND ISLANDS GOLF CLUB

WELLESLEY ISLAND EAST, NY (Exit 51 off Route 81 to Wellesley Island E.)
Telephone: (315)482-9454   Fax: (315)482-9321

Owner/Manager: Doug Horton   Head Pro: Frank Picone
Course Supt.: Richard Shaver   Architect: Seth Reiner

18 Holes   Par 72   5997 yds.

Scottish Links Style. Rolling hills, scenic holes bordering the St. Lawrence River.

$		Golf Pkgs.	Public	Power Carts	Lessons	Lounge	Snack Bar	Meals	

Jumping downstate, we find the most densely populated area in the Western world, New York City and area. No other place on Earth has greater instant name recognition. It has been said that most people in America have either themselves, or have ancestors who have lived in Brooklyn. Ellis Island, and the Statue of Liberty, was the major port of entry for Europeans for many years, and the museum at Ellis Island pays tribute to the vastly different cultures who have helped make America a land of such diversity.

New York has been called "The Big Apple", "The City That Never Sleeps", "Metropolis"; no matter how it's known, New York City is the center of just about everything that happens, anywhere. Every part of this city is well-known, from Central Park to the Guggenheim Museum; from the Empire State Building to Grand Central Station; and from Soho to Wall Street. There are boat cruises around Manhattan Island, bus trips throughout the city, and, of course, you are always invited to walk.

Long Island, the tip of New York State that extends into the Atlantic Ocean, prides itself on being both a terrific getaway from the bustle of the city, and close to all the amenities of New York City. You'll find sandy white beaches and rocky outcroppings from which you can take a dip in the Atlantic or one of several isolated Sounds. Historic Long Island begins in Old Bethpage with a village restoration, including replicas of tools and machinery, a working farm, costumed interpreters and antique-furnished houses re-creating the feel of life in the 19th century. Fire Island, which separates the Atlantic from the Great South Bay, has recreation parks and 17 resort communities with exceptionally clean, white sand beaches. Some of the wealthiest people in New York have or continue to live on the Island, with some of the largest mansions anywhere, especially Hempstead House, which was the Guggenheim Mansion at Sands Point Preserve. You can take whale-watching tours and visit working fishing villages to buy fresh lobster and seafood right off the boat.

To the immediate north of New York City is the "Hudson Valley" region, where most New Yorkers from the city go when they want to get away to the country. This area is steeped in history and tradition; visit Franklin Roosevelt's home and museum, and the Vanderbilt museum, both in Dutchess County. As well, the region is home to many fine colleges and education centers, including Vassar College, the best-known. This is wine country, and you are invited to tour one of many wineries in the region. There are festivals throughout the year, as well as antique and specialty stores. There are many championship golf courses, as well as well-kept campgrounds and some fine fishing and hunting along the shores of the Hudson River.

NEW ENGLAND

VILLAGES AT KILLINGTON GOLF RESORT • KILLINGTON, VERMONT ▲

Golf Vacations

Connecticut, known as the "Commuter State", prides itself on putting the visitor in touch with America's beginnings, and celebrating the beauty of outdoor New England and the creative Yankee spirit which has left, and continues to leave, a lasting impression on how America views the world.

The history goes back as far as the dinosaurs, and you can still find bones and prints of Jurassic dinosaurs, as well as visible reminders of the Native American culture, vestiges of the China trade and the heyday of the wooden whale ships. George Washington rode this land, and supplies for his rag-tag army were funneled through Governor Jonathan Trumbull's tiny store at Lebanon.

The scenery is still open and green, laced with quiet lakes and meandering streams. To preserve this serenity, there are more than one hundred state parks and forest, dozens of wildlife preserves, arboretums, public gardens and nature centers.

Connecticut's southern border lies along Long Island Sound, with over 250 miles of shoreline for stretching, lazing and strolling on a warm New England summer day. There are scores of small coves and harbors, once home to commercial fishing and now the host to fleets of pleasure craft.

In 1776, Connecticut was the birthplace of the submarine, and the world's first nuclear-powered sub, the USS Nautilus, was built there and is open to the public in Groton. Other accomplishments of Connecticut's people include the creation of lollipops, cylinder locks, payphones and shelf clocks, as well as the launching of today's insurance industry, developing modern techniques of mass-production, and the founding of America's first school of law.

Along its border with New York, "Commuter Country" is home to many of New York City's elite, who don't mind the short drive from the Big Apple to the truly New England towns, with white clapboard houses, winding streets, overbranching shade trees, small streams and ponds, and a quiet change of pace.

Hartford gives more than 350 years of history, with gravestones in the Center Church Cemetary displaying markers from as far back as 1640. The city is also home to interesting historical buildings, namely Charles Bullfinch's 1796 statehouse, and Mark Twain's stately 1874 mansion. Hartford is the capital of Connecticut, whose Capitol Building is a gold-domed Gothic structure which has served as the seat of government since 1879.

*Facing Long Island Sound and the Atlantic, the towns of **New London** and **Mystic** drew restless, venturesome Yanks of centuries past, and set them around the world in search of whale oil, porcelain, rum and spices. For a time, New London was the busiest whaling port on the east coast, and mansions built by her sea captains testify to the success of their voyages. Mystic Seaport recreates the seagoing, shipbuilding era, from shops and homes to skills and folklore, and even to the preservation of the last of the great wooden whaling ships, the Charles W. Morgan.*

In spite of the rocky soil and hilly landscape that provided materials for miles of stone walls, Eastern Connecticut yields many crops, including herbs. The area is home to schoolteacher Nathan Hale's family home, a reminder of the state's role in American history. Surrounded by farmland is the University of Connecticut, which began as a land grant school of agriculture, and has working barns you can still visit. In nearby **Woodstock** *is Henry Bowen's spectaculr carpenter-Gothic pink home, "Roseland".*

ELMRIDGE GOLF COURSE, INC

PAWCATUCK, CT (On Elm Ridge Rd., just East of I-95)
Telephone: (203)599-2248   Fax: (203)599-4145

Owners: Joseph & Charles Rustici   Head Pro: Tom Jones - PGA

18 Holes Par 71 6501 / 6082 / 5279 yds.
Rating: 71.2 / 70.8 / 70.4 Slope: 121 / 117 / 113

Enjoy the scenic Connecticut countryside as you play on the most challenging course in the area. The hilltop site offers cool breezes and remarkable views. Accommodations nearby. *"Any friend of golf is a friend of ours."*

$$		Golf Pkgs.	Public	Power Carts	Lessons	Lounge	Snack Bar	Meals	Open All Year
		✓	✓	✓	✓	✓	✓	✓	✓

The ivy-coated walls of Yale University continue to provide a rich backdrop for the emerging cityscape of *New Haven*. The Peabody Museum of Natural History is one of the oldest and most prestigious university museums of its kind. New Haven itself has no trouble mixing old and new; jazz concerts enliven the Green that was laid out in 1638, and each spring city leaders re-enact the drama of Benedict Arnold demanding the keys to the ammunition so that he and his troops could join the Revolution in 1776. The Shoreline Trolley offers nostalgic rides over historic rail tracks along the shore.

Along the Connecticut River, called the "Long Tidal River" by the Native population, is Gillette Castle, a latter-day Rhenish fortress of stone and wood designed by actor-author William Gillette, who introduced Sherlock Holmes to the American stage. In Essex, the Valley Railroad offers steamtrain rides along the riverbank, then a mid-stream view aboard a connecting riverboat. In *East Haddam*, you'll find the Goodspeed Opera House, built in 1876, as well as the Nathan Hale Schoolhouse, circa 1750, and what is perhaps the oldest surviving church bell in Christendom, dated to about 815AD.

Vermont is called the "Green State", and it lives up to that name very well. Home to the beautiful Green Mountains, the Vermont countryside is like a tapestry of grassy velvet dotted by farmland and red frame barns. The state was founded by Ethan Allen and the Green Mountain men, heroes of the American Revolution, and Ethan Allen's 1787 homestead has been preserved outside Burlington.

Burlington*, Vermont's largest city, is called the "Queen City", and offers a contrast to the rural countryside. It's home to the University of Vermont, contemporary shops and restaurants, and one of the most successful pedestrian malls in the nation. Lake Champlain, upon whose shores Burlington is built, is the 6th largest lake in the country, and is rumoured to be home to "Champ", a mythical, rarely-sighted creature similar to Scotland's "Loch Ness Monster". Vermont seems a welcome home to beasts of this kind; Lake Memphremagog, at* **Newport** *near the Quebec border, is rumoured to have an inhabitant of it's own, dubbed "Memphre".*

Perhaps Vermont's most popular destinations are the innumerable resorts throughout the mountains. Communities like **Killington, Barre, Sugarbush** *and* **Stowe** *are all familiar names to both golfers and skiers, as these exceptional resort towns offer year-round fun.*

The state's claim-to-fame is, of course, it's maple syrup, which can be bought just about anywhere. For other sweet treats, a visit to the world-famous "Ben & Jerry's Ice Cream" factory, outside Burlington, is recommended.

SUGARBUSH RESORT

WARREN, VT (S. of Burlington off Route 100 on the Sugarbush Access Road)
Telephone: (802) 583-2722   Toll Free: 1-800-53-SUGAR

Head Pro: Michael Aldridge - PGA

18 Holes   Par 72   6524 /5886 / 5187 yds.
            Rating: 71.7 / 69.0 / 70.4   Slope: 128 / 122 / 119

Designed in 1962 by Robert Trent Jones, Sr., our classic mountain
course is built right into the natural Vermont landscape. Featuring tree-lined
fairways, rolling greens, hidden traps, plenty of doglegs and spectacular views.

$$	Resort	Golf Pkgs.	Public	Power Carts	Lessons	Lounge	Snack Bar	Meals	

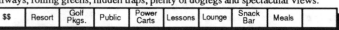

Architecturally, Vermont is a visual feast, with historical preservation a mainstay in the state. **Montpelier**, *chosen as the state capital in 1808, includes the marble-domed State House, Blanchard Block, City Hall and the Washington County Courthouse.* **St. Johnsbury**, *near the New Hampshire border, is lined with historic buildings, including the Fairbanks Museum and Planetarium, founded during the Victorian era. The Planetarium's exterior is a towered design of carved red sandstone, and a large stuffed polar bear greets you in the natural science exhibit, where their 19th century display has been preserved perfectly.* **West Arlington**, *in southern Vermont, is home to former homes of Norman Rockwell.*

The Shelburne Farm is the state's largest historical institution, with thirty-seven historical buildings and homes set on 45 acres. Collections of Americana and art occupy visitors for at least a full day. Bennington Museum in the southwest features Vermont native Grandma Moses art, as well as local pottery and the oldest U.S. flag in the nation.

The "Northeast Kingdom", along Vermont's three-county border with Canada, is miles of unspoiled scenery, thick woods and rural vistas. Lake Willoughby, a 600-foot deep glacial lake, is tucked between two mountains and sports a little-known, uncrowded beach with spectacular views at its north end.

Near the resort town of **Stowe**, *you'll find Smuggler's Notch, a natural phenomena of sheer cliffs rising skyward and large roadside boulders along a winding highway, which made it a natural route for smugglers in older times. The road is closed during part of the winter, but makes an exceptional trip during the warmer months.*

Quechee Gorge near **Woodstock** *features spectacular rock formations leading down 163 feet to the cascading Ottauquechee River. North of Woodstock, the "Rock of Ages" quarry in* **Barre** *is the world's largest granite quarries, yet has only scratched the surface of the tremendous veins of stone which descend ten miles into the earth. Much of the unfinished marble that adorns the buildings and monuments of the nation's capital came from this area of Vermont.*

Lake Morey Inn Resort COUNTRY CLUB

With a championship golf course out the front door and beautiful Lake Morey out back, we offer a complete resort vacation you'll never forget. Tennis courts, a full health club, a practice green, a variety of water sports on the lake, bicycling, pools, jacuzzi, sauna and racquetball offer you the entire world of sports. Children's supervised activities, most days and evenings. Horseback riding and hot air balloons are available nearby.

Mid-week Special Pricing
Ask About Our Million Dollar Hole-in-One Tourney

Introducing Our New Three Day Golf School

- welcome and farewell reception
- professional staff • extensive video taping and review
- three on-course playing lessons • greens fees and carts for 3 days
- minimum of 5 hours instruction daily
- maximum of 5 students to each pro
- club fitting suggestions
- take home video of your swing
- diploma

1-800-423-1211
1-802-333-4311

Lake Morey Road
Fairlee, Vermont 05045

LAKE MOREY INN RESORT COUNTRY CLUB

FAIRLEE, VT (On Lake Morey Rd., just off I-91)
Telephone: (802)333-4311

Owner: Michael V. Buzzeo
Head Pro: Bill Ross - PGA

Manager: Jeffrey A. Boughrum

18 Holes Par 70 6024 yds.

A million dollar renovation of the golf course has been completed. With a flat front nine and rolling back nine it features stunning views of the Green Mountains. Home of the Vermont Open Golf Championship for the last 39 years.

$$	Resort	Golf Pkgs.	Public	Power Carts	Lessons	Lounge	Snack Bar	Meals	Open All Year

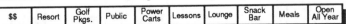

BASIN HARBOR CLUB

VERGENNES, VT (On Lake Champlain)
Resort: (802)475-2311   Pro Shop/Tee Times: (802)475-2309

Manager: Head Pro: John Uzdilla

18 Holes   Par 72   6513 / 6232 / 5745 yds.

Ratings: 71.5 / 70.4 / 68.1 Slope: 122 / 120 / 116

This course winds past the Lake, through woods and along natural meadows.

$$	Resort	Golf Pkgs.	Public	Power Carts	Lessons	Lounge	Snack Bar	Meals	Open All Year

Voted in 1991 the "most livable state" by an independent research company, New Hampshire was the first state to declare it's independence from England, the first state to adopt it's own constitution, and the ninth and deciding state to ratify the Constitution. New Hampshire shares borders with Maine, Vermont, Massachussetts and Quebec, which makes it a terrific, central place to be based when touring and playing the New England States.

Called the "Granite State", New Hampshire takes pride in the preservation of it's unique identity, character and appeal. The state is also tax-free, a great encouragement to anyone who wants to catch up on their shopping.

*Dartmouth, an Ivy League college in **Hanover**, is one of the state's most important educational landmarks. The area is renowned for its classic New England architecture. The area around Hanover is an excellent shopping region, with one-of-a-kind stores, antiques and authentic country stores. Nearby, Lake Sunapee has three working light-houses, and a rocky shore broken by stretches of sandy beaches, most notably the beach at Lake Sunapee State Park.*

*In the heart of the state is the "Lakes Region", with an exquisite combination of forests, rolling hills, mountains and lakes. Lake Squam, made famous as the location of the film, "On Golden Pond", and Lake Winnipesaukee, the state's largest lake, are named as reminders of the Indians who once paddled birchbark canoes there. Summer recreation includes golf, swimming, camping, hiking, biking and all manner of water sports, namely sailing, windsurfing, powerboating, cruising and even kayaking. **Wolfsboro**, the nation's oldest resort, is typical of the type of town that seems sleepy at first but proves itself to be quite sophisticated.*

*The "Merrimack Valley Region" takes much of it's character from it's cities, the largest of which are **Concord, Manchester** and **Nashua**. Concord, the state capital, has just over 30,000 people and retains a great deal of small town appeal. The city centers around the State House Plaza, where New Hampshire's most famous sons, Daniel Webster and Franklin Pierce, have statues serving as reminders of the importance of history to this state. The New Hampshire state legistlature is the 4th largest delibera-tive body in the world, with each of its 400 members answering to about 2,300 people.*

Manchester grew up around a mill which 100 years ago was the largest producer of cotton in the world, and is today experiencing a revitalization. Manchester is also home to the Currier Gallery of painting and sculpture, which is also the headquarters for the New Hampshire Symphony Orchestra and the Opera League. Nashua, as New Hampshire's second-largest city, is a center for high-tech business and industry. The city has it's own Center for the Arts, with two ballet companies and numerous art galleries. There are historic villages throughout the region, and a sense of "country" prevails.

*Embodying what is considered "typically New England", the "Monadnock Region" includes just 39 towns and villages, and is filled with three centuries of rich history and heritage. New England is here, in **Keene**, with the widest paved Main Street in the world, and stately brick buildings and the state college campus; in **Harrisville**, one of the most perfectly preserved mill towns in the Northeast; and in **Peterborough**, the model for Thornton Wilder's "Our Town", where the high-tech publishing industry is found amongst antique saltbox houses. **Dublin** is the home of traditional Northeast publications like "Yankee Magazine" and "The Old Farmers Almanac". Scale the 3,165 foot Grand Monadnock Mountain, the single-most climbed mountain in North America. The region has over 200 lakes and ponds which offer swimming, fishing, waterskiing, canoeing or sailing.*

The MOUNT WASHINGTON
HOTEL & RESORT

GOLF CLUB

Nestled among 18,000 magnificent acres of National Forest,
The Mount Washington Hotel offers outstanding service and a
wealth of activities - whether you stay a week, a day, or only
an hour . . . you're always welcome, anytime.

OUR ENDLESS ACTIVITIES INCLUDE:
• 27 holes of PGA rated Championship Golf • 18 hole practice putting
green • 12 clay tennis courts • indoor & outdoor heated pools • saunas
• jacuzzi • daily children's activities programs • equestrian center
• hiking • biking • fishing • scenic attractions • shopping

For information on our **GOLF PACKAGES** or other specials call:

1-800-258-0330
(603) 278-1000

THE MOUNT WASHINGTON HOTEL & RESORT, BRETTON WOODS, NEW HAMPSHIRE 03575

THE MOUNT WASHINGTON HOTEL GOLF CLUB
BRETTON WOODS, NH (On Rte. 302, between Bretton Woods and North Conway)
Telephone:(603)278-1000

Head Pro: Dean Webb - PGA   Architect: Donald Ross

18 Holes Par 71 6638 / 6154 / 5336 yds. Rating: 70.1
 9 Holes Par 35 3245 / 3020 / 2505 yds. Rating: 69 Slope: 120

One of America's most scenic courses, it has hosted four New Hampshire
Opens and is the permanent site of the New England PGA Pro-Am Festival.

$$	Resort	Golf Pkgs.	Public	Power Carts	Lessons	Lounge	Snack Bar	Meals	

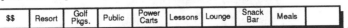

From the mountains to the sea, New Hampshire has 18 miles of Atlantic shoreline, with more than half set aside as public land. Three-hundred years of history and Yankee tradition abound, and you are invited to journey back to colonial times in meticulously-preserved homes and Revolutionary-era forts. Cruise to the off-shore islands or go on a whale watch to see these gentle giants up close. **Portsmouth**, the state's only port, still is a working boat dock, where salty fishermen bring home the day's catch. Portsmouth's winding streets are flanked by colonial row houses and grand mansions. Market Square is edged by stately brick buildings, shops and cafes, and Prescott Park has gorgeous gardens, fountains, a boat dock and fishing. Down the coast are towns like **Exeter**, with its quaint shops, and **Durham**, home of the University of New Hampshire, and **Dover**, the state's oldest continuous settlement. The area has a full calender of events, including jazz concerts under the stars and oceanside seafood festivals, theatre and dancing.

In the northeastern section of New Hampshire are the White Mountains, famous for their skiing and their views. Look out over spectacular mountain panoramas from bustling resort villages, tiny towns and unspoiled, virgin wilderness. Visit the highest peak in the Northeast, the 6,288-foot Mount Washington, and also the 768,000 acres White Mountain National Forest, dotted with crystal-clear lakes and streams, and abundant with wildlife. A hundred years ago, this area was known for its grand hotels and summer vacations done up in opulent style. Today, visitors come year-round for a more free-style getaway.

White Mountain
HOTEL AND RESORT

GOLF GETAWAY

Includes a deluxe room, breakfast off the menu, unlimited
golf per day and a shared cart for 18 holes. A 10% discount
will be offered on weekends prior to Memorial Day
Weekend and after Columbus Day.

*Nestled beneath Whitehorse and Cathedral Ledges, the White
Mountain Hotel and Resort is surrounded by the White Mountain
National Forest and is directly adjacent to Echo Lake State Park.*

*Our beautiful Albert Zikorus designed golf course is "one of the
most unique and singularly beautiful golf developments in
the country" as quoted by Golf Magazine.*

WHITE MOUNTAIN HOTEL AND RESORT
At Hale's Location
West Side Road, P.O. Box #1828
North Conway, New Hampshire
03860

1-800-533-6301
(603)356-7100

HALE'S
LOCATION
COUNTRY CLUB

THE HALE'S LOCATION GOLF & COUNTRY CLUB

NORTH CONWAY, NH (Off West Side Rd., between Glen & Conway)
Telephone:(603)356-2140

Manager: Kent Chaplin   Head Pro: Jonathan Rivers
Course Supt.: Robert Turcotte   Architect: Albert Zikorus

9 Holes   Par 36   2816 yds.

Surrounded by Echo Lake State Park and the
White Mountain National Forest, this course features rolling
greens and fairways, with breathtaking views from tee to green.

$$$	Resort	Golf Pkgs.	Public	Power Carts	Lessons	Lounge	Snack Bar	Meals	

Maine is recognized as one of the healthiest states in the nation, due in large part to it's clean air and Atlantic breezes. Maine is 320 miles long and 210 miles wide, with a total area of 33,215 square miles, or about as big as all the other New England states combined. It consists of 16 counties with 22 cities, 424 towns, 51 plantations and 416 non-organized townships. Maine boasts a total of 6,000 lakes and ponds, some 32,000 miles of rivers and streams, 17 million acres of farmland, 3,478 beautiful miles of coastline and 2,000 islands. Maine also claims America's first chartered city, **York**, which was proclaimed in 1641.

The State of Maine is the United States' largest producer of blueberries, and is renowned for it's shellfish, with a total catch of 1.7 billion pounds with a value of $130 million in 1990. Moose is the state animal, with many moose-watching sites located throughout the state.

Maine is home to author Stephen King, who sets many of his dark novels in rural Maine. As well, Kennebuckport is the summer home of former President George Bush, and was often the scene of high-level meetings during national crises.

The southern coast is often called the "southern gateway to Maine", and is an extremely popular tourist destination because it lies in such close proximity to more populous and southern American cities. Fewer than 100 miles of the Maine coastline is sandy beaches, and most of that is within this "South Coast" area. Most of the towns were settled during the 17th century, and many have preserved their local heritage through efforts of their own historical societies. The area is also a shoppers haven; outlet malls are abundant, and **South Portland** boasts the state's largest mall. **Freeport** is the home of L.L. Bean, the sporting goods outfitter, who have an extensive outlet in the town.

*#26 in America's 75 Best
Resort Courses, America's
5th Most Beautiful
and New England's
Top-Ranked Resort Course.*

GOLF DIGEST

*W*ith seven holes bordering Maine's rocky coast, the golf course at the **Samoset Resort** borders on the magnificent. And offers a challenge to every level of player, with a backdrop of the breakwater, lighthouses and the Atlantic. Add an ocean breeze, and you have a course that in scores of state PGA Championships and club competitions, has yeilded only two sub-par rounds from the blue tees.

While the front nine makes the most of its seaside location, always keeping the ocean in view, the back nine weaves leisurely through woods, ponds and gardens, delivering you, finally, back to the sea.

The **Samoset's** legendary signature hole, number seven, offers a spectacular view of the mile-long breakwater. A par five, dogleg left, it practically dares you to play over the ocean. (But golfer beware, the fickle winds have no mercy.)

Fortunately, our PGA staff is more thoughtful than the wind. They're ready to help you, and your game, with a clinic or private lesson. Count on them to assist you in staging a golf tournament or special event. Golf carts, equipment and accessories are readily available. And with our new practice facility, you can develop the finer points of your game.

(207) 594-2511
For Reservations

1-800-341-1650
Outside Maine Toll Free

S A M O S E T   R E S O R T - R O C K P O R T ,   M A I N E   0 4 8 5 6

SAMOSET RESORT GOLF CLUB

ROCKPORT, ME (on Rte. 1 between Bangor and Brunswick)
Telephone:(207)594-1431   Fax: (207)594-0722

Owner:Samoset Resort Investors
Head Pro: Bob O'Brian, PGA

Manager: Jim Ash
Course Supt.: Gregg Grenert, GSA

18 Holes   Par 70   6417/6010/5360 yds.

Rating: 69.3/67.2/69.1
Slope: 125/ 118/ 117

The Samoset golf course is open from April to November, New England weather permitting. The luxurious Samoset Resort is open year round.

$$	Resort	Golf Pkgs.	Public	Power Carts	Lessons	Lounge	Snack Bar	Meals	

Hugging the eastern border of New Hampshire is a region studded with lakes and streams, and timber forests that blanket the base of huge grey mountains. Powerful rivers, like the Kennebec and the Androscoggin push relentlessly to the sea, past cities like **Lewiston** and **Auburn**, twin cities located on the banks of the Androscoggin, and the state capital of **Augusta**, with over 1.2 million people, that straddles both banks of the Kennebec River. Augusta's capital dome, atop the State Capitol building, rises majestically above oaks and elms, and is visible for miles. The area is home to the bulk of Maine's pulp and paper industry, from the logging companies to small woodworking and paper products-manufacturers.

Back along the coast, to a point called the "Mid-Coast" region, you'll find a stretch of shoreline running north and east of **Brunswick**, to the mouth of the Penobscot River. Brunswick is the home city of Bowdoin College and the Maine State Music Theater. The nearby shipbuilding city of **Bath**, on the Kennebec River, is dominated economically by Bath Iron Works, a shipyard that has built many U.S. Navy vessels. **Boothbay Harbor** is a busy summertime resort and departure point for many scenic cruises and deep-sea fishing trawlers, which can be chartered. **Damariscotta** and **Newcastle** mark the beginning of the graceful Pemaquid region, where small fishing villages dot the headland. **Rockland** has a thriving commercial center and a bustling waterfront, and is site of the Maine Lobster Festival each August. **Camden** is where "mountains meet the sea", an elegant resort and shopping area, and home port to several of Maine's windjammer fleet.

KEBO VALLEY COUNTRY CLUB

BAR HARBOR, ME (On Eagle Lake Road, off Route 233)
Pro Shop: (207) 288-3000   Clubhouse: (207) 288-5000

Head Professional: Gregg Baker, USGA

18 Holes   Par 70   6102 yds.

The 8th oldest golf course in the U.S.A.
Discounts packages available with the nearby Bar Harbor Inn.

$$			Public	Power Carts	Lessons	Lounge	Snack Bar	Meals	

Spreading from Penobscot Bay, northeast along a scenic array of islands, harbors and headlands, is the "Down East/Acadia" region. The area's largest city is **Bangor**, a center of modern shopping, lodging and business, with open parks and wide, shady streets. As the lumber industry became more important and powerful in the early 1800s, Banger became a boom town because of it's central location between the forests and the cities. Bangor is now Maine's third-largest city, with a 31-foot tall statue of Paul Bunyon near the library to commemorate it's vivid logging history. **Bar Harbor**, on Mount Desert Island, is a commercial and recreation center, with many accomodations, restaurants and shops. A ferry takes passengers in Bar Harbor to and from Yarmouth, Nova Scotia.

The "Sunrise County" of Maine is the state's, and the nation's, easternmost border. The region is characterized by rocky beaches and rugged headlands of stark and timeless beauty. **Lubec** is the easternmost town in the United States, and is crowned by the red-and-white striped West Quoddy Head Lighthouse. This is blueberry area, with fresh-picked and pick-your-own crops scattered all over the place. As well, "Sunrise County" is a hotbed of Atlantic Salmon, and many other less rowdy fishing challenges. The region's oldest building is the 1770 Burnham Tavern in **Machias**, which is still a working tavern.

Northeastern Maine is a fertile, enormous area with potato farming, cattle and lumber the primary industries. One of the biggest attractions is Baxter State Park, a 200,000 acre tract of wilderness given to the state by a former governor, who stipulated that the land was "to be forever left in it's natural state". This is an area at the geological crosspoint between the dense forests of the Appalachians and the Eastern Canadian farmland, making for an exceptionally diverse vacation destination.

THE STRING OF PEARLS

Sugarloaf Golf Club

Truly Maine's finest year-round destination resort. From a full-service Inn to on-mountain condominuims, from barbeques to exquisite dining, and from the relaxing to the invigorating.
SUGARLOAF HAS IT ALL!

Enjoy championship golf on our course, carved out of the woods on the side of Maine's second highest mountain. It is without question, one of the most dazzling and demanding courses in New England and it takes full advantage of its location. The par-3 , eleventh hole features a cataclysmic drop over the Carrabassett River to a green well protected by two bunkers. It is one of the few 200-yard holes anywhere that enables you to tee off with an eight iron. With spectacular vistas and picturesque rivers, the expertly maintained layout makes great use of the natural slope.

1-800-THE-LOAF

SUGARLOAF IS LOCATED ON ROUTE 27 IN THE BEAUTIFUL CARRABASSETT VALLEY, 36 MILES NORTH OF FARMINGTON, MAINE , AND 40 MILES SOUTH OF WOBURN, QUEBEC.

sugarloaf/usa
The Maine Mountain Resort

SUGARLOAF GOLF CLUB

CARRABASSETT VALLEY, ME (36 miles north of Farmington)
Telephone: 1-800-THE-LOAF

Manager: John Diller Head Pro:Scott Hoisington
Course Supt.: Ed Michaud Architect: Robert Trent Jones, Jr.

18 Holes   Par 72   6922/6400/5324 yds.   Rating: 70.8/73.7   Slope: 137/136

The back nine features the "String of Pearls", six holes,
framed by the pristine whitewater of the Carrabassett River,
making them look as if they were perfect pearls on a necklace.

$$	Resort	Golf Pkgs.	Public	Power Carts	Lessons	Lounge	Snack Bar	Meals	

MARYLAND

RIVER RUN GOLF CLUB • BERLIN, MARYLAND ▲

Golf
Vacations

*It surprises many people to find out about **Ocean City**, Maryland. Long called the "White Marlin Capital of the World", Ocean City sports ten miles of clean, white beaches that sit right on the Atlantic Ocean. What surprises people most, however, is the number and variety of golf courses and packages in the area.*

Ocean City has built up its reputation as the "Nation's Number One Family Resort", with nearly 10,000 hotel and motel rooms, about 20,000 luxury condos and a host of cottages and apartments to choose from. There is never a problem with finding a place to stay, no matter what your budget. And most of these accommodations are recognizing the benefits of offering attractive packages to vacationing golfers, with unbelievable results.

Ocean City is fast becoming one of the major golf holiday destinations in America, with championship courses featuring hundreds of scenic holes, balmy summer breezes and panoramic views you won't believe until you see. The Town of Ocean City, also recognizing this relatively new wave of golfing in the area, opens its doors warmly during the golf season, and all year.

Golfer's Dream Come True

3 days unlimited golf, cart for first 18 holes daily. 9 championship courses with preferred tee times. 2 night's room, plus 2 breakfasts and 2 dinners in your choice of 5 restaurants. All taxes and surcharges included.

- Free club cleaning and storage
- Complimentary bag tag, tees & towel
- Indoor heated pool and whirlpool
- Libby's Restaurant & Lounge
- In-room microwave & refrigerator
- Golf widow & custom packages
- Rooms for social gathering

Many great packages throughout 1993
CALL NOW:
(410) 524-3000

Packages from: $**175.**⁰⁰

Weekdays March 1 - April 15, 1993

Comfort Inn

Comfort Inn Gold Coast
112th St. & Coastal Hwy. Ocean City, MD 21842

All prices are per person, based on double occupancy. Holidays and special events excluded. Travel Agency commissionable.

Since it's founding in 1875, this small fishing village has made a gradual transformation into one of the most popular vacation spots on the East Coast. Many people have made it a vacation "tradition", because once they visit they don't want to leave. Ocean City is Maryland's only seaside resort community, and offers much to see and do.

Ocean City is, of course, the "White Marlin Capital of the World", and earns that distinction by offering fishermen unparalleled angling opportunities. White Marlin is the fish Ocean City' famous for, but you can pit your skills against Blue Marlin, bluefish, tuna and wahoo. Watersports buffs can choose from any number of ocean-going aquatic activites, including sailing and parasailing, jet skiing, water skiing and windsurfing. Ocean City is further south than nearby Atlantic City, New Jersey, making the water just that much warmer.

*Ocean City's
Resort Golf Course*

L A N D I N G

EAGLE'S LANDING

OCEAN CITY, MD. (W. on Rte 50 from town, L. on Rte 611. L. on Eagle's Nest Rd.)
Telephone: (410)213-7277 or 800-2-TEE TIME

Owner: Ocean City Dept. of Recreation & Parks   Head Pro: Andy Loving
Architect: Dr. Michael Hurdzan   Course Supt.: Joseph Perry

18 holes   Par 72   7003 / 6306 / 5700 / 4896 yds.
Rating: 74.3 / 70.8 / 68.2 / 69.3   Slope: 126 / 121 / 115 / 115

A spectacular waterfront golf course featuring lush fairways and
contoured greens overlooking barrier islands and the Atlantic Ocean.

$$		Golf Pkgs.	Public	Power Carts	Lessons	Lounge	Snack Bar		Open All Year

**GOLF CLUB
& COMMUNITY**

RIVER RUN GOLF CLUB AND COMMUNITY

BERLIN, MD (On Beauchamp Rd., 8 miles W. of Ocean City)
Telephone: (410)641-7200   Toll Free 1-800-733-RRUN

Head Pro: Bob Baldassari - PGA   Course Designer: Gary Player
Course Supt.: Fred Heinlen

18 Holes   Par 71   6705 / 5949 / 5002 yds.

Just when you thought you'd played them all, along comes River Run
designed by world champion golfer, Gary Player. It takes full advantage
of spectacular landscape to surprise and delight you again and again.

$$	Resort	Golf Pkgs.	Public	Power Carts	Lessons	Lounge	Snack Bar	Meals	Open All Year

To many vacationers, however, Ocean City is a place to stretch out and lean back, and let the warm Atlantic breezes clear out the cobwebs. Ocean City beaches are perfect for building sandcastles, or for burying Dad up to his neck. The Boardwalk is the perfect place for a romantic stroll, and to watch the inspiring Atlantic sunsets.

Shops along the Boardwalk specialize in traditional Atlantic coast goodies, including cotton candy, french fries, mouth-watering fudge and saltwater taffy, an Ocean City delicacy. Ocean City's array of nightspots cater to any degree of nighttime fun, from throbbing discos and night clubs, to quiet pubs and cosy restaurants. There are, in fact, more than 160 restaurants in town, serving everything from French to Chinese to Italian and everything in-between. There's also exceptional Atlantic seafood caught fresh daily, including steamed crabs, lobster, oysters on the half-shall, and succulent steamed clams.

In the twilight days of summer, the Ocean City festival season begins. On the Labor Day weekend, the town puts on its annual Saltwater Festival, a celebration featuring food and continuous outdoor entertainment, arts and crafts, and top-name concerts. Later in the month, Ocean City presents Sunfest, the annual fall festival under four big-top tents on the beach. Sunfest provides an abundance of on-stage entertainment, and attracts about 300,000 people each year.

12500 Coastal Highway
Ocean City, MD 21842
For Reservations: 1-800-4-OC-GOLF
For Hotel: 1-800-227-5788

Our 19th hole has 12,000 gallons of 85° water year 'round.

Suites feature separate living room, bedroom and bathroom, full-size sleep sofa, wet bar, refrigerator/freezer, and an indoor heated pool! Double beds and efficiency suites are available. Spouse and group packages available.

Dates:	1/1-3/31	4/1-6/15	6/16-7/15	7/16-9/6	9/7-9/30	10/1-10/31	11/1-12/31
Sun-Thur							
STD Suite	33.50	42.50	60.50	71.50	51.50	36.50	33.50
EFF Suite	38.50	47.50	65.50	76.50	56.50	41.50	38.50
Fri-Sat							
STD Suite	38.50	50.50	66.50	79.50	64.50	47.50	38.50
EFF Suite	43.50	55.50	71.50	84.50	69.50	52.50	43.50

Includes complimentary golf towel and tees. Rates are per person, based on double occupancy and include continental breakfast, one round of golf per day. All rates shown above in U.S. dollars. Rates subject to change without notice. Surcharges may be added for some courses. Additional charges for Memorial Day and Labor day weekends will apply.

Your golden days of sun, sand, sea and golf gain an extra dimension of pleasure when your nights are pampered with all the comforts of home in your own Brighton Suite.

Complete with wet bar, refrigerator/freezer, two televisions with premium cable networks, two telephones and personal safe. Even a hair dryer and complimentary seasonal ammenities like plush beach towels.

All the comforts of home - for less than the cost of one room at comparable hotels.

The area outside Ocean City, while not as popular, makes for terrific day-trips when visiting Ocean City. The "Southern Eastern Shore", as it is known, is low, flat and sandy, and is covered with evergreens and fertile farmlands. It is also a region of tidal creeks, vast wetlands and wildlife refuges.

Sheraton
Fontainebleau Hotel

F or business or pleasure, come to Oceanfront luxury ... The Sheraton Fontainebleau Hotel. Enjoy the magic and the beauty that comes with the sunrise, the sunset, and the ocean breeze. Your imagination will run wild as you escape to where life's a bit more relaxed, more romantic, more exciting ... where Little Things Mean A Lot.

• Newly Remodeled Luxury Oceanfront Guest Rooms with Enlarged Bathrooms, Private Balconies, Refrigerator, Color TV with Free Cable & HBO with Remote Control, Complimentary USA Today, In-Room Coffee Maker & Automatic Sprinkler Protection • Non-Smoking Rooms Available • New Executive King Rooms Now Available • 2 Oceanfront Restaurants & Nighclub and Piano Bar • Happy Hour Daily & Live Entertainment Nightly • Poolbar, Beach Bar & Grill • Year-Round Indoor Heated Pool with Fully Equipped Health Spa, Jacuzzi, Sauna, Steam & Eucalyptus Rooms, Free Weights, Exercise Bikes and Training Beds • Hair & Nail Studio, Gift Shop, Jewelry Store & Game Room • 33,000 Square Foot Conference Center with 14 Meeting Rooms • 30 Miles from Salisbury Airport with Limo & Van Service • Kids Stay Free, Pets Allowed • Friendly Staff, Clean Wide Beach

GOLF PACKAGES

	2 Night Weekday *per person*	2 Night Weekend *per person*
10/24/92-4/22/93	$ 101.00	$ 131.00
4/23/93-6/8/93	$ 133.00	$ 168.00
6/9/93-7/22/93	$ 192.00	$ 222.00
7/23/93-8/21/93	$ 213.00	$ 232.00
8/22/93-9/5/93	$ 192.00	$ 222.00
9/6/93-10/23/93	$ 135.00	$ 172.00
10/24/93-4/21/94	$ 101.00	$ 131.00

includes 3 days/2 nights

• rates are per person, Double Occupancy • 2 Rounds of Golf with Cart • Club Cleaning and Storage • Meal Packages available upon request • 20% discount Dinner Menu Coupons • Tax Additional

1-800-638-2100

10100 Ocean Highway • Ocean City • MD • 21842
Phone: (410) 524-3535

The largest wildlife refuge in the area is the Blackwater Wildlife Refuge, which is the winter home of the Canada Goose. Nearby is Assateague Island, famous for its herds of wild ponies, which run free throughout the island's beaches, roadways and fields. The island also houses the Assateague Island National Seashore and Assateague State Park in Maryland, and the Chincoteague National Wildlife Refuge in neighboring Virginia.

THE BEACH CLUB GOLF LINKS

BERLIN, MD (On Deer Park Dr., 10 minutes from the beach in Ocean City)
Telephone: (410)641-4653(GOLF)   Toll Free: 1-800-435-9223

Head Pro: Hunt Crosby

18 Holes   Par 72   7020 / 6193 / 5167   Slope: 128 / 120 / 117

"Simply the Best." Stately, mature oaks and maples guard over 7000 yards of rolling fairways. Six imposing lakes dazzle the eye and challenge the skill of the player. Undulating greens, built to the strictest specifications and meticulously groomed.

$$	Resort	Golf Pkgs.	Public	Power Carts	Lessons	Lounge	Snack Bar	Meals	Open All Year

OCEAN CITY GOLF & YACHT CLUB

BERLIN, MD (On Country Club Dr., 7.5 miles S. of US Route 50, off Rte. 611)
Telephone: (410)641-1779   Toll Free: 1-800-442-3570

Head Pro: Dave Quelland

Bayside Course: 18 Holes Par 72 6211 yds.
Seaside Course: 18 Holes Par 73 6252 yds.

The perfect, easy to reach location and all the golf facilities
and amenities to turn a round of golf into a great experience!

$$	Resort	Golf Pkgs.	Public	Power Carts	Lessons	Lounge	Snack Bar	Meals	Open All Year

THE BAY CLUB

BERLIN, MD (On Libertytown Rd.)
Telephone: (410)641-4081   Toll Free: 1-800-BAY-CLUB

Head Pro: Denny Dennis

18 Holes Par 72 6956 / 6511 / 5609 yds.

The tees and greens are sited into the natural woodlands of the area. Adding to
the dynamic character of your golfing experience are acres of glistening lakes and
strategically placed sand traps, as well as an island green to get your attention.

$$	Resort	Golf Pkgs.	Public	Power Carts	Lessons	Lounge	Snack Bar	Meals	Open All Year

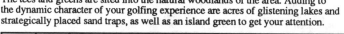

This is the native land of Maryland's "watermen", who are the tillers of the Chespeake Bay's annual seafood harvest. The "watermen" still use traditional equipment to trawl the water, and you can see them fishing from skipjacks, bugeyes and log canoes.

Salisbury is the regional center for transportation, education and travel, and is the largest city on the Eastern Shore. In **Cambridge**, in Wicomico County, is Annie Oakley's retirement residence. Oakley's house had an unusual roof, designed so Annie could sharpshoot from her upstairs window. From the town of **Wicomico** you can cross a river on a ferry that has been operated for nearly 300 years, and explore the sleepy town of **Whitehaven**, where it's said George Washington's grandmother lived. This area, and in particular the Choptank River, was the setting for James Michener's novel, "Chesapeake".

NUTTERS CROSSING GOLF CLUB

SALISBURY, MD (At US 13 By-Pass and Maryland Rte. 12, 2 miles from Salisbury)
Telephone: (301)860-GOLF (4653)

Owner/Developer: Thomas Ruark	General Manager: Robert Hussey
Head Pro: Willis Johnson III	Course Supt.: Charles Poole

18 Holes Par 70 6033 / 5700 / 4851 yds. Slope: 115

Ault, Clark and Associates have transformed a typically level Eastern Shore site into a beautifully lush rolling landscape, featuring over 50 sand bunkers, eight ponds and rolling greens built to USGA specifications.

$$		Golf Pkgs.	Public	Power Carts	Lessons	Lounge	Snack Bar	Meals	Open All Year	

"Chesapeake Country" has long been the major commercial fishing center of Maryland, with trawlers going down the Chesapeake Bay into the Atlantic Ocean to fish for seafood and commercial fish catches. The Nanticoke and Choptank Indians were the original inhabitants, and have been immortalized by the two rivers named in their honor. The first European settlement in the area, and in Maryland, is Kent Island, which was once inhabited by the Matapeake Ozininie Indians and established as a British trading post by William Claiborne in 1631.

This area is called "The Land of Pleasant Living", and blends the best of a colonial past with a uniquely scenic present. Calling itself the "land of the tidewater", the "Chesapeake Country" region is acres of scenic countryside and fertile farmlands, that offer corn, wheat and soybeans, and its Chesapeake Bay shoreline is constantly changing with the tides. Goose and duck hunting bring a major draw to the area, as the autumn brings thousands of migrating birds down the Atlantic Flyway.

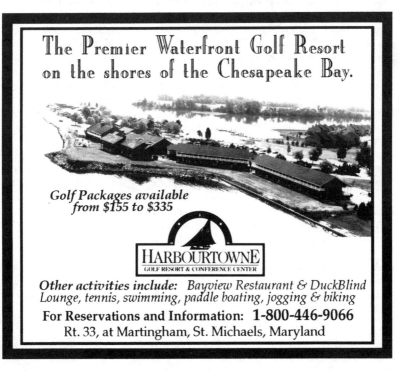

The Premier Waterfront Golf Resort on the shores of the Chesapeake Bay.

Golf Packages available from $155 to $335

HARBOURTOWNE
GOLF RESORT & CONFERENCE CENTER

Other activities include: Bayview Restaurant & DuckBlind Lounge, tennis, swimming, paddle boating, jogging & biking

For Reservations and Information: 1-800-446-9066
Rt. 33, at Martingham, St. Michaels, Maryland

Baltimore has been called "the downright most liveable major city in the U.S.", by "LIFE" Magazine, and they could be right. Still a thriving port off the Chesapeake Bay, Baltimore has a transformed Inner Harbor and downtown area with towering glass office towers mixed with the traditional Cape Cod-style homes. Baltimore's neighborhoods are the thing, which brings native-son Barry Levinson, the director of such movies as "Diner", "Avalon", "Tin Men" and "Toys", back home to shoot his films. Neighborhoods like Fell's Point, which is home to an 18th century square-rigged sailing ship and authentic colonial-era pubs that have been operating since the 1700s, and Federal Hill, which has a signal tower, a marine observatory and a battery for Union cannons, and is lined with one-to-two hundred year old rowhouses that have been faithfully restored, and others like Charles Village, Bolton Hill and Union Square, which date from the Victorian era.

Baltimore is a sporting town, with a major league baseball team, (the Baltimore "Orioles"), as well as minor league hockey and soccer teams, and is host to the Pimlico Race Course, home of the Preakness Stakes, the second jewel in thoroughbred horseracing's Triple Crown. Baltimore will also host the 1993 Baseball All-Star Game at their brand new Oriole Park.

The port of Baltimore houses the USS Constellation, the oldest U.S. warship afloat. The Maryland Historical Society is the guardian of the original manuscript of the Star Spangled Banner, by Francis Scott Key, at Fort McHenry. The homes of Babe Ruth, Edgar Allan Poe and other famous Baltimore residents are available to be viewed. The Baltimore Zoo, the Maryland Science Center and the World Trade Center, with the "Top of the World" restaurant, are all popular and fun attractions.

If shopping is your fun, then Baltimore is your place. A terrific place to browse is Antique Row, with artifacts from the medieval period to art deco. As well, there are fashion shops and boutiques, and the renowned art galleries of North Charles Street and the Baltimore Museum of Art.

Turf Valley
Hotel and Country Club

Located 20 Minutes From Baltimore's Harborplace and Less Than 60 Minutes From Washington, D.C.

Featuring
- **45 Holes Of Championship Golf**
- 173 Room Deluxe Hotel (including 13 suites)
- 30,000 Square Feet Of Meeting Space
- Lighted Driving Range
- Four Lighted Tennis Courts
- *Alexandra's* Fine Dining Restaurant
- Terrace On The Green Casual Restaurant
- Live Entertainment

Special Packages Available:
- Golf Package
- Golf School Package
- Weekend Package
- Meeting Package

For Reservations Call **800-666-TURF**

For More Information Call **(410) 465-1500**

Fax: (410) 465-9282

2700 Turf Valley Road   Ellicott City, MD 21042

In 1649 the port city of **Annapolis** was formed. On Chesapeake Bay south of the Baltimore area, Annapolis was the United States Capital for nine months, and the Old Senate Chamber of the Maryland State House was where General George Washington resigned as commander-in-chief of the Continental Armies, and began his path to become the first President of the United States. Three weeks after Washington's resignation, the Continental Congress ratified the Treaty of Paris and ended the war with Britain, signalling recognition of the new nation by the English.

Annapolis is Maryland's capital city, and is also the "sailing capital" of the United States. Everything in the city is within easy walking distance, with restaurant, shops and historic buildings all over the place. Annapolis calls itself a "museum without walls", because of the tremendous amount of historically significant architecture and locations there.

The countryside of Southern Maryland has changed little since the 1600s, when the first English colonists settled there. The land is very rural and antiquated, and is bounded by the Chesapeake Bay and Potomac River. However, their slogan of "So Much, So Close" is a reminder that Washington, D.C. is only a one hour drive away.

Many churches date back to the 1700s, illustrating the importance of religion to the new settlers. They also make for fascinating historic attractions, including St. Francis Xavier church in **Newtown**, the St. Ignatius Church at **Chapel Point**, and the Middletown Chapel, the oldest cruciform-designed church in Maryland. Nearby **St. Clements Island** was the landing site of the first Maryland colonists in 1634, and **St. Mary's** was England's fourth permanent settlement in America, and Maryland's first capital.

Visit the towering bald cypress trees at the Battle Creek Cypress Swamp Sanctuary near **Prince Frederick**, or hike the Calvert Cliffs, one of the richest deposits of marine fossils in the Eastern United States. Sailing and fishing are big pastimes, with many fish species native to the area, including white perch, pike, large mouth bass, flounder and crab. As well, there are 6 golf courses with a total of about 100 holes that roll along this beautiful landscape. Festivals in the area include the annual Air Expo at Patuxent Naval Air Station, as well as the St. Mary's County Oyster Festival in **Leonardtown**.

In 1791, Prince George's County, Maryland, donated some of its land to create Washington, D.C. This area of Maryland, surrounding the capital, is now the ideal place to stay when visiting the city.

A visit to **Washington** in the summer is an exceptional vacation idea because of the warm air and the abundance of famous things, (and people), to see. The first stop on any Washington tour is the White House, the Presidential residence and office at 1600 Pennsylvania Avenue. The Capital Building houses both the United States Congress and Senate, beneath an enormous dome topped by a recently-renovated statue. The Lincoln, Jefferson and Washington Memorials, are at opposite ends of the Tidal Basin of the Potomac River. The low, black wall of the Vietnam Veterans' Memorial is a somber tribute to the soldiers of America's tragic war. The tomb of former President John F. Kennedy is located a short drive across the Potomac at the Arlington National Cemetery in Arlington, Virginia, where an eternal flame burns in his

memory. The Smithsonian Institute is the nation's foremost museum and study center, housing exhibits ranging from Charles Lindburghs' plane, "The Spirit of St. Louis", to part of the set of the long-running TV show, "M*A*S*H".

The Maryland countryside surrounding Washington houses many Government agencies, most notably the National Security Agency and the U.S. Census Bureau. Andrews Air Force Base, home of the President's plane, Air Force One, is in Maryland. And who knows, you may even see President Clinton jogging the streets of Washington early in the morning.

Western Maryland is the link between America's Eastern Seaboard and its Central States. Bordering Virginia, West Virginia and Pennsylvania, the panhandle was used extensively by the Iroquois Indian tribe. Settlers used the National Road, running through a gap in the Appalachians, to expand America's boundaries.

The area has more than 75,000 acres of forest, parks, lakes and rivers, inviting tourists to hike, camp, fish and canoe through some of the finest white water in the East. You can ride through the mountains from **Cumberland** to **Frostburg** on the steam-powered Western Maryland Rairoad. The National Pike, the first transportation link from the eastern to western frontier, evolved into US Route 40. An annual festival with wagon train parades and local memorial events celebrates the history of the road each May.

Maryland sits at the apex of two distinct parts of the country; on one side is the oceanfront resort town of Ocean City, and on the other are the Appalachian Mountains. And within Maryland's unique boundaries lie some of the most exciting vacation spots in America. Maryland is a marvelous region around a tremendous national capital city, and is one of the best, undiscovered vacation spots anywhere.

Wisp Resort

The Wisp Resort Hotel and Conference Center gives you more reasons than seasons to plan your next vacation in Western Maryland.

Golf? Absolutely! The Golf Club at Wisp is **slope rated as the third most difficult in Maryland, maybe the world.** Well, probably not the world. Why aren't we the most difficult? Because we believe **golf should be fun!** I know that sounds crazy to some of you nuts. PGA Tournament? We're working on it. Rain? Well sometimes… but at the Wisp Resort that really isn't much of a problem. We have all kinds of things to do inside in case you don't want to smear yourself with bear grease and shed water like a duck. So, on the inside you can play **miniature golf**, eat, **swim**, eat, **play videos**, eat, **catch a movie on HBO**, eat, **visit the ten zillion antique stores** that are near by, eat…Speaking of eating, whether you prefer to catch a **pizza at Pizzazz**, have a **snack at the Sweet Street Cafe**, relax at the **23° Below Lounge**, feast at the **Bavarian Room**, or just socialize next to the pool,

WE HAVE IT ALL AT THE WISP

1-800-463-WISP

Star Route 2, Box #35, Deep Creek Lake
McHenry, Maryland 21541

GOLF CLUB AT WISP, THE

M^cHENRY, MD (Just off US 219 S. of I-68)
Telephone: (301)387-4911

18 Holes   Par 72   7122 / 6745 / 5666 yds.
        Rating: 74.1 / 72.5 / 72.5   Slope: 135 / 131 / 121

This championship course with tree lined fairways, at the base of the Wisp Ski Resort, rewards accuracy off the tee. Strategic fairway bunkers, five water hazards and large undulating greens make each hole unique and challenging.

$$	Resort	Golf Pkgs.	Public	Power Carts	Lessons	Lounge	Snack Bar	Meals	Open All Year

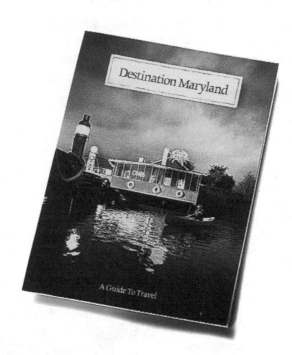

Go from the sublime to the ridiculous on a single tank of gas.

Mountains. Beaches. Big cities. Small towns.
The Bay. Maryland has it all, and all close by.
Call 1-800-862-7952 for your free guide.

Maryland
Live for the weekend ®

Maryland Department of Economic and Employment Development – Office of Tourism. William Donald Schaefer, Governor.

VIRGINIA

HANGING ROCK GOLF CLUB • SALEM, VIRGINIA ▲

Golf
Vacations

The State of Virginia proudly says that "Virginia is for lovers", and that includes golf lovers. Virginia is considered one of the "swing states", wherein it isn't really considered a Northern state because of its temperate climate, but its winters are a little too cool to be called a Southern state. It therefore falls into a unique category, and a unique position. Some of Virginia's prime attractions to the vacationing golfer are its extended golf season, and its central location to most Northern states and Eastern Canadian provinces. It doesn't take long, from the North or the South, to reach Virginia, the midway point on the Atlantic seaboard.

Virginia is also a state teeming with history. George Washington was born there, and Robert E. Lee grew up in Northern Virginia. The first permanent English settlement was founded in Virginia, and the Revolutionary War ended there. Virginia stretches inland a good distance, making the contrast of its landscape quite remarkable. From the pristine beaches of Virginia Beach, to the staggering heights and drops of the Blue Ridge Mountains, Virginia offers golfing vacations unparalleled.

Since the inception of the United States of America over two centuries ago, Northern Virginia has been a support for Washington, D.C., which runs between its boundary with Maryland. George Washington, Thomas Jefferson, James Monroe, Abraham Lincoln, Robert E. Lee, Jefferson Davis, Clara Barton and Walt Whitman, among many others, were brought to Northern Virginia by the great events of their times. Many fought there, all lived there, and all contributed immensely to the birth and sustenance of their new nation.

In Fairfax County, Virginia, which bounds Washington on the city's western edge, was where George Washington and George Mason gave voice to their angry frustration with the colonial government. It was in Mount Vernon that statesmen gathered to discuss the formation of a Constitutional Convention. At Gunston Hall, Mason wrote the Virginia Declaration of Rights, upon which the U.S. Bill of Rights was based.

Gunston Hall was also the home of George Mason, his wife and nine children, and is open to the public daily. The 1758 Georgian-style mansion boasts some of the most impressive woodwork in America. The Mount Vernon Plantation, ancestral home of George Washington, and first owned by his great-grandfather in 1674, was composed of five farms by the time Washington became President. His home, built between 1735 and 1787, is considered to have one of the best views of the Potomac River. Included in the artifacts on display is the bed on which Washington died.

*Nearby **Arlington** is best-known for the Arlington National Cemetary, which houses the internment of The Unknown Soldier, as well as the eternal flame of John F. Kennedy. Rows of white grave markers line the cemetery as far as the eye can see, marking the spots where the dead of many wars now lie. It is a somber, overwhelming and silently beautiful place, and is a fascinating place to stop on your way through the state.*

*The city of **Alexandria**, with its cobblestone walks and quaint historic townhomes, lends a genteel air to this part of Virginia. Founded in 1749 by Scottish merchants, Alexandria was already a flourishing seaport when Washington, D.C. was just being laid out. There are more than 1,000 preserved 18th and 19th century structures on view in the city, as well as exciting nightlife and delicious food.*

***Fredericksburg**, Virginia is much the same as it was when George Washington grew up there, on Ferry Farm. Fredericksburg is fifty miles south of Washington, but seems several hundred years further. The Rappahannock River runs through Stafford County and Fredericksburg, and the area was once a bustling colonial port. Captain John Smith discovered the region in 1608, and not much has really changed. The last major upheaval in Stafford County came in the years between 1862 and 1864, as Union and Confederate armies battled for this strategic ground on the main road to Richmond. In four major battles, over 17,000 died and 80,000 were wounded. Fredericksburg, caught in the middle, was devastated.*

Prosperity returned to the area after the war, and Victorian-style homes are prominently featured alongside colonial and Federal-style abodes. There are over 350 original 18th and 19th century buildings in Fredericksburg's 40-block National Historic District, and walking the streets of Stafford County and Fredericksburg is an experience that will certainly leave a timeless impression.

***Quantico** is the location of the F.B.I. training facility, as well as the Marine Corps Air-Ground Museum, with aviation and ground artifacts from 1940-45, housed in 1920s-era hangers. In **Dale City**, "Potomac Mills", one of the world's largest outlet malls, offers bargains without compare. Unique specialty shopping can be found in **Woodbridge** and **Occoquan**. The Washington-Dulles International Airport, named for the former Secretary of State John Foster Dulles, was built in 1962, and links the capital of the most powerful nation on Earth with the rest of the world. In 1976, Air France and British Airways began making regular trips to Dulles with their Concorde supersonic jetliner.*

GOLDEN HORSESHOE GOLD COURSE

WILLIAMSBURG, VA (50 mi. E. of Richmond, off I-64, follow signs to Williamsburg)
Telephone: (804)220-7696   Fax: (804)220-7798

Manager: John T. Hallowell   Head Pro: Del Snyder
Course Supt.: Rick Viancour   Architect: Robert Trent Jones, Sr.

18 Holes   Par 71   6700 / 6443 / 6179 / 5159 yds.

Opened in September 1963. Gently rolling hills with water hazards on 7 holes
and Bent grass greens. Ranked by *Golf Digest* as one of the 30 best resort courses.

$$$	Resort	Golf Pkgs.		Power Carts	Lessons	Lounge	Snack Bar	Meals	Open All Year

GOLDEN HORSESHOE GREEN COURSE

WILLIAMSBURG, VA (50 mi. E. of Richmond, off I-64, follow signs to Williamsburg)
Telephone: (804)220-7696   Fax: (804)220-7798

Manager: John T. Hallowell   Head Pro: Glen Byrnes
Course Supt.: Rick Viancour   Architect: Rees Jones

18 Holes   Par 72   7120 / 6722 / 6244 / 5350 yds.

Opened in October 1991. Abundant woodlands and natural terrain.
Water comes into play on 6 holes. This is a real "shot makers" course.
SEE COLONIAL WILLIAMSBURG AD - COLOR SECTION OF THIS BOOK.

$$$	Resort	Golf Pkgs.		Power Carts	Lessons	Lounge	Snack Bar	Meals	Open All Year

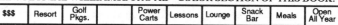

FORD'S COLONY COUNTRY CLUB

WILLIAMSBURG, VA (On Ford's Colony Drive)
Pro Shop: (804)258-4130   Toll Free: 1-800-548-2978

Head Pro: Scott Jones   Touring Pro: Fuzzy Zoeller
Course Supt.: Chuck Thompson   Architect: Dan Maples

Red/White: 18 Holes   Par 72   6755 yds.   Rating: 72.3   Slope: 126
Blue/Gold: 18 Holes   Par 71   6787 yds.   Rating: 72.3   Slope: 124

Ford's Colony, named one of Virginia's top 5 courses by *Virginia Golfer* magazine,
is the home of the Anheuser-Busch qualifier. It is now well on its way to the Ford's
commitment of 54 holes, establishing a major golf resort on the east coast.

$$$$	Resort	Golf Pkgs.	Public	Power Carts	Lessons	Lounge	Snack Bar	Meals	Open All Year

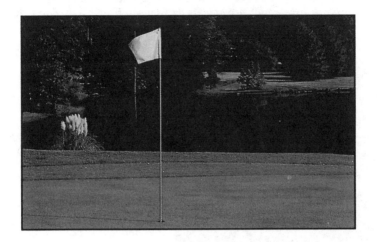

The area of Virginia, known as the "Tidewater/Hampton Roads" area, is renowned for its sandy beaches and abundance of resorts. Virginia Beach, long considered one of the most attractive surf-and-sand vacation spots on the East Coast, is the cornerstone of the resort industry along the coast of Virginia. Virginia Beach is considered the "largest pleasure beach in the world", according to the Guinness® Book of Records 1992, and a recent multi-million dollar revitalization project has made the Virginia Beach oceanfront and boardwalk even better.

Virginia Beach stretches 310 square miles, and is bounded by the Atlantic Ocean on one side and the Chesapeake Bay on the other. The climate is delightfully mild year-round, and offers golfers rare late-fall and early-spring golfing opportunities. The boardwalk, one of Virginia Beach's most popular attractions, is graced by soft-lit lampposts, teak benches and colorful flags. A romantic moonlit walk is par for the course.

*The Norfolk Naval Base, in nearby **Norfolk** along the James River between Virginia Beach and Williamsburg, is the world's largest naval base, and there you can find some of the grandest most powerful oceangoing vessels known to man. Also on site is the "MacArthur Memorial", a museum built in honor of the controversial military man, General Douglas MacArthur. Some incredible exhibits include the General's famous corncob pipe, the surrender documents of World War II, and MacArthur's tomb.*

QUALITY INN LAKE WRIGHT RESORT

NORFOLK, VA (Intersection of Rt. 13 and I-64)
Telephone: 1-800-228-5157

Owner: John R. Wright	Manager/Head Pro: Claude K. King - PGA
Course Supt.: Mike Spillar - GSA	Architect: Al Jamison

18 Holes   Par 71   6131 yds.

SEE OUR FULL PAGE AD OPPOSITE.

$	Resort	Golf Pkgs.	Public	Power Carts	Lessons	Lounge	Snack Bar	Meals	Open All Year

LAKE WRIGHT
Golf Course

THE ULTIMATE GOLF PACKAGE

- **3 DAYS OF UNLIMITED GOLF ON OUR 18-HOLE CHAMPIONSHIP COURSE**
- **2 NIGHTS IN A DELUXE ROOM AT THE LAKE WRIGHT RESORT, DOUBLE OCCUPANCY**
- **FULL AMERICAN BREAKFAST DAILY**
- **CLUB CLEANING & STORAGE NIGHTLY**

Other area courses available for an additional charge

FROM ONLY $99. PER PERSON

Available 9/7/92 - 5/27/93 and 9/5/93 - 5/26/94 Weekdays. Plus tax.
Weekends Only $149. Summer Packages Also Available.
Subject to availability. Advanced payment required.

LAKE WRIGHT RESORT FEATURES:
Central Location Minutes From Norfolk's Waterside Festival Marketplace,
Virginia Beach Oceanfront, Colonial Williamsburg, & Busch Gardens.
2 Putting Greens - Lighted Driving Range - Tennis Courts - Jogging Track
Swimming Pool - Main Course Restaurant - Tavern Off The Green Lounge

LAKE WRIGHT RESORT
AND CONVENTION CENTER

6280 Northampton Boulevard, Norfolk, VA 23502

CALL 1-800-228-5157 FOR RESERVATIONS

The city of **Norfolk** itself was destroyed by a British bombardment in 1776, and the only remaining building is the St. Paul's Church, which was built in 1739. The Chrysler Museum has an $80 million art collection that spans 5,000 years, and represents nearly every important period, style and artist. Thousands of items previously stored are now on display in a brand new wing.

Newport News, across the mouth of the James River from Norfolk, has been called the "place that launched a thousand ships", and is one of America's oldest ports. Newport News is also Virginia's fourth-largest city, and is often referred to as the "world's greatest harbor". The "Christopher Newport Park" and nearby Victory Arch pays homage to the founder of Newport News, the British captain who led three ships across the Atlantic in 1607 to ultimately land upriver in Jamestown. The Newport News was the birthplace of the modern navy, and its shipbuilding company is the largest private employer in Virginia. It is the only facility equipped to build the immense NIMITZ-class aircraft carriers.

Alongside Newport News is the Virginia Air and Space Center, a multi-million dollar facility which traces man's achievements in aviation and space from the earliest days of flight to the present. The NASA Langley Research Facility in **Hampton** is home to the original seven Mercury astronauts, and is used today to conduct extensive research for the Space Shuttle.

Virginia's Eastern Shore, a small finger of land extending from the southern tip of Maryland, separates the Atlantic Ocean from the Chesapeake Bay. The Eastern Shore is connected to the Virginia mainland by the 17.6-mile Chesapeake Bay Bridge-Tunnel, the world's longest bridge-tunnel complex. Swimming, fishing and beach fun are all part of the equation in this area, and the boating through the many inlets and channels would be an adventure not soon forgotten.

The easternmost town of Virginia, **Chincoteague**, is famous for pony penning, the wild pony roundup and auction held each July. For hundreds of years, the ponies have lived on the barrier island of **Assateague**, separated from Chincoteague Island by a small inlet. Today Assateague is a national wildlife refuge and a national seashore of incredible beauty. There is a wide variety of waterfowl on the island, and one of the most interesting is perhaps the Blue Heron.

Tangier Island, located in the middle of the Chesapeake Bay between the Eastern Shore and the mainland, was discovered in 1608 by Captain John Smith, and was settled in the late 17th century by Cornish fishermen. It can only be reached by charter boats, but the freshly-caught seafood makes a trip worthwhile.

Central Virginia runs along the state's border with North Carolina, and rests between the "Tidewater" region and the Blue Ridge Mountains. Perhaps most famous for Thomas Jefferson's home, "Monticello", this area reflects a proud, rich heritage that has been immaculately preserved.

*The city of **Richmond** has been the capital of Virginia for more than 200 years. Thomas Jefferson designed the state capital building, a majestic structure which sets the tone for the rest of the city, and the region. Richmond is brimming with historical attractions, including the Valentine Museum, the Edgar Allan Poe Museum, featuring memorablia and an enchanted garden dedicated to Richmond's premier literary citizen. A 400-passenger steamwheel Annabel Lee showboat, the Richmond's children's museum and a host of plantations that would make Scarlet O'Hara think twice about rebuilding Tara anywhere but here.*

The Petersburg National Battlefield and the city of Petersburg are the site of the longest military siege in U.S. history. Other attractions include Trapezium House, especially built to ward off evil spirits.

*The city of **Danville** describes a visit there as "picking a Victorian flower", because the range and abundance of Victorian homes are tremendous. "Millionaire's Row" is a collection of Main Street mansions which will stagger the senses as you study the incredible detail inherent in this style of home. The Sutherlin House, current home to the Danville Museum of Fine Arts and History, served as the Last Capital of the Confederacy. It was here that Jefferson Davis, a major in the Southern army, sought refuge, and where he received word of the end of the Civil War and surrender of the Confederates. Tobacco tours are available, and the faint smell of cured tobacco is in the air of this, the tobacco region of Virginia. The July 4 weekend is an event in Danville, with celebrations culminating in a colorful Hot Air Balloon Liftoff.*

A self-guided walking tour is available through the Appomattox Court House National Historical Park, which includes the McLean House, where Robert E. Lee formally surrendered to Ulysses S. Grant, bringing a formal end to the Civil War.

*Monticello is located in nearby **Charlottesville**, and offers a first-hand look at Thomas Jefferson's architectural genius. Ash Lawn-Highland, home of the fifth President, James Monroe, stands on a neighboring hill. The University of Virginia is in Charlottesville, and was founded by Jefferson.*

The southwestern tip of Virginia was America's western frontier until 1775, when Daniel Boone opened up the Wild West by forging the Wilderness Road through the

*Appalachian Mountains, and began the settlement of the rest of the United States. The Blue Ridge Mountains, the Allegheny Range and the Cumberland Mountains all dot the landscape and create breathtaking vistas from enormous mountain peaks. The Grayson Highlands State Park adjoins the Mt. Rogers National Recreation Site, which is the location of Virginia's highest point, at 5,729 feet. The southwestern region is thronged with parks, from the Hungry Mother near **Marion**, to Claytor Lake near **Dublin**, and the Natural Tunnel State, which sports an 850-foot long limestone tunnel, winding its way through the mountains.*

On the border with Kentucky, near the westernmost point of the state, are two awesome parks; Breaks Interstate Park, where a 1600-foot gorge has earned the named "Grand Canyon of the South", and Cumberland Gap National Historic Park, which includes Daniel Boone's famous pass to the West.

The Shenandoah Valley stretches for 200 miles through the Blue Ridge Mountains of the Appalachian Mountain Range, and marks Virginia's western boundary along the West Virginia state line. Meaning "daughter of the stars", Shenandoah is like nowhere else on Earth. Visitors are amazed by spectacular 102-foot rock towers and a stone bridge rising 215 feet above the land. The Valley is a mesh of farmland that seems to float away over the horizon. Eight vast limestone caverns overwhelm guests with a subterranean world of unbelievable crystal formations and rock erosions.

HANGING ROCK GOLF CLUB

SALEM, VA (On Red Lane)
Telephone:(703)389-7275

Head Pro: Billy McBride   Course Supt.: M. J. Benecke
Architect: Russell Breeden

18 Holes   Par 73   6828 / 6216 / 5669 / 4691

1st new public course in Southwest Virginia in 25 years.
Superb mountain location surrounded by natural beauty, streams, boulders
and virgin forest. One of the most challenging & exciting courses in the east.

$$	Resort	Golf Pkgs.	Public	Power Carts	Lessons	Lounge	Snack Bar	Meals	Open All Year

Guest Columnist   Julie Becker (Roanoke, VA)

VIRGINIA --- WESTERN STYLE

Daughter of the Stars - that's what the Indian word, "Shenandoah", means and as lovely as the word sounds rolling off the tongue, it only begins to describe the Shenandoah Valley, Blue Ridge Mountains and the southwest highlands of Virginia.

With the Blue Ridge Mountains on one side and the Alleghenys on the other, the Shenandoah Valley actually begins in Pennsylvania, and was first a major north/south route for the Indians. Then came the settlers, not the English from the Tidewater area, but the Scotch-Irish and Germans from Pennsylvania and the port of Philadelphia. Called Cohees, they must have been fiercely independent to settle and hold onto the rugged homesteads they carved out of the wilderness. The people today are just as independent, and the land is equally as beautiful and interesting.

Tidbits of information make the area come alive. Travelling north on I-81 between the boundary city of Bristol, Virginia/Tennessee, and Marion, Virginia is Abingdon, home of Virginia's state theater, "The Barter". From its depression-era start it has hosted many young actors now well-known. Although you can no longer trade a chicken for a ticket, you can still see some well-done theater. A tad north is Saltville, one of the Confederates' only sources of much-needed salt, and the site of several skirmishes. Wytheville, where I-81 and I-77 cross, has an historic Shot Tower dating back to the days of Indian battles on this western frontier. Molten lead was dropped from the top of the tower into the cold, clear waters of the New River, (called one of the oldest rivers in the western hemisphere). The lead balls that were formed were distributed to the frontierspeople and used to protect their families during the Indian wars. "The Long Way Home", the story of Laura Ingals Draper who was kidnapped by the Indians, then escaped and warned the settlers of an impending attack, is performed during the summer near Radford.

Salem, where Andrew Lewis is buried, is one of the oldest towns west of the Blue Ridge. With its southern-town obligatory Confederate monument and nationally-recognized private liberal arts college, it is now the home of a thriving antique center. Right next door, Roanoke is the "Star City of the South", a name bestowed as the result of a 1940s Merchant's Association Christmas advertising gimmick. The gimmick, a 196-foot high neon star sitting on top of a mountain in the city, still burns every night and can be seen for miles. Roanoke is also famous for its Historic Farmer's Market, the longest continuously operating farmer's market in the U.S. Originally a railroad town, it is home to the Virginia Museum of Transportation. Smith Mountain Lake, a 550-mile shoreline impoundment, is just east of here.

Lexington, north on I-81 and I-64, is the home of the Virginia Military Institute, the Washington and Lee University and the new Virginia Horse Center. Robert E. Lee is buried here and his horse, Traveller, is on display. Just west of town locals open a theater every summer in an abondoned lime quarry and kiln. Called "Limestone Theatre", its most famous presentation is "Stonewall Country", with original music. The Hall of Valor, celebrating the VMI Corps of Cadets participation in "the war of Northern aggression", is not far.

Continuing up the Valley, you will find the Cyrus McCormick Farm where the first mechanical reaper was designed, as well as Woodrow Wilson's birthplace. To the east just over the mountains lies Charlottesville, Thomas Jefferson's home, and as the roads wind north and east, wonderful rolling panoramas with nuggets of history and friendly, independent people are around every corner.

Roanoke is the Shenandoah Valley's largest city, and the Roanoke Valley is a breathtaking sight at any time of the year. Stage coaches used to roll through this land on their way out West, and today Roanoke is still at the crossroads of the two Americas. Situated on the Blue Ridge Parkway, which runs through the Shenandoah and connects with the Skyline Drive further north, offers visitors to Roanoke an interesting combination of new world and old mountain culture.

Roanoke's Farmer's Market is among the oldest markets in the nation, dating back over a hundred years. Alongside the Market is Roanoke's Center In The Square, an entertainment, museum and restaurant complex which is the pride of downtown Roanoke. The city is the birthplace of Booker T. Washington, a black man who rose from slavery to become a prominent educator and statesman. Nearby Lexington is the burial place of Confederate Civil War General Robert E. Lee.

A visit to Roanoke would not be complete without seeing the world-famous Mill Mountain star, a 196-foot tall star that shines brightly over the city. Roanoke also offers some of the most intriguing and challenging golf in the Shenandoah Valley.

Staunton was the birthplace of Woodrow Wilson, the 28th President, and the Woodrow Wilson Birthplace is furnished with many personal possessions including Wilson's inaugural Pierce-Arrow automobile. In Mount Solon, history of a different flavor comes alive with America's longest continuous held sporting event, the Mount Solon Jousting Tournament Held in August, the Tournament features jousters competing in this medieval sport. As well, the Mount Solon Natural Chimneys are rock towers that border the jousting meadow.

Waynesboro is famous for "hospitality in the Valley", and has built a reputation on courtesy, sincerity and warmth which is shown to all their visitors. Located at the intersection of the Blue Ridge Parkway and the Skyline Drive, Waynesboro offers golfing amidst mountains and meadows, as well as fishing, hiking and other mountain activities. Shopping in downtown Waynesboro is a cross between Factory Outlets and smaller, more intimate shops.

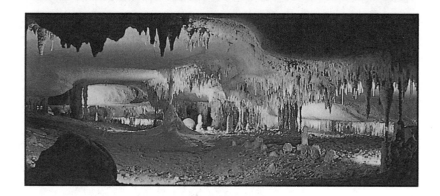

The Luray Caverns, north of Staunton and Waynesboro on the Skyline Drive, are immense caves discovered in 1878 by Andrew Campbell and Benton Stebbins, who followed winding passageways from one incredible room to the next. Today, millions of people have visited these caverns, with its wishing pond and the Great Stalacpipe Organ, a unique instrument that combines a man-made pipe organ with tiny hammers that strike stalagtites from the ceiling, creating accurate symphonic sound. This is the largest and most popular cavern in the United States. Be sure to notice the "fried eggs" formations if you visit.

Caverns Country Club Resort

CAVERNS COUNTRY CLUB RESORT

LURAY, VA (Airport exit from US 211, 1 Mi. W. of Luray)
Telephone: (703)743-7111

Owner: Luray Caverns
Course Supt.: Michael Ketchum

Head Pro: Breck Johnson
Architect: Mal Purdy

18 Holes   Par 72   6452 yds.

Gently rolling fairways with large trees and bent grass greens.
Magnificent setting. World famous Luray Caverns are nearby.

$$	Resort	Golf Pkgs.	Public	Power Carts			Snack Bar		Open All Year

SHENANDOAH

Bryce

An 18 hole - 6024 yards par 71 Championship course, built along the beautiful mountains in the Shenandoah Valley.

Part of the Bryce Family Resort, this course is open all year.

(703) 856-2121

Lunch and dinner are served daily. The dining rooms are rather rustic and informal, a friendly, bustling spot with colonial spindle chairs and bare wooden flooring.

Golf Packages are available through the Hotel Strasburg and golfers have a choice of play at these two fine area courses:

hotel STRASBURG

In the northwest corner of Virginia at the top of the George Washington National Forest, is the oldest settlement in the Shenandoah Valley . . . the Town of Strasburg.

It is here, in this untouched historic town, near the Skyline Drive that this Queen Anne Victorian property, recently upgraded is deserving of much attention.

The four story white clapboard, black shuttered, rectangular building is situated on a main corner in the center of town. It was built in 1895 as a hospital, took on its present role as a place of dining and lodging in 1915, and now serves as a working display for the Strasburg Emporium antiques. ...

(703) 465-9191 1-800-348-8327
(US Toll Free)

GOLF

VALLEY

SHENANDOAH VALLEY
G • O • L • F  C • L • U • B

This 27 hole Championship course is rated *one of Virginia's top 20 golf courses*. Complete with Clubhouse and Tee Room, Shenandoah Valley Golf Club can compliment any golf outing with a full and varied menu in their beautiful banquet facility.

(703) 636-2641

For more information on GOLF PACKAGES contact:

...All the formidable antique furnishings throughout the common and guest rooms are for sale. The guest rooms are on the second and third floors, and in the adjacent colonial Taylor House. Each room has a list of the furnishings for sale and a description and history of the pieces.

Many of the rooms have television and some have jacuzzis, including the four in Taylor House. The latter have large sitting rooms, beautifully decorated bedrooms and views of the stunning Shenandoah mountains.

 201 Holliday Street
Strasburg, Virginia 22657

(703) 465-9191 1-800-348-8327
(US Toll Free)

PACKAGES

*The town of **Strasburg** has one of Virginia's largest collections of antiques, as well as a museum and an abundance of Civil War history. The land was first settled by Indians, and then defended by Stonewall Jackson and his men during the bloody war. Strasburg offers fine accommodation and wonderful cuisine.*

Winchester, in the northern tip of the state, was once a Shawnee Indian campground, and was later settled by Pennsylvania Quakers in 1732. Originally named Frederick Town after the father of George III of England, the city was eventually renamed Winchester in honor of the ancient English capital. When he was 16, George Washington was employed by Lord Fairfax to help survey lands in the region, and by 1755, at the age of 23, Washington was a colonel in the Virginia militia and was responsible for the building of Ft. Loudoun, which is today a Winchester museum. In 1758, Washington was elected by the people of Frederick County to serve in the House of Burgesses, his first political office. During the Civil War, Winchester changed hands 72 times, with five major battles fought in the area. General Stonewall Jackson was stationed in Winchester on orders from General Lee, due to its strategic location.

BRYCE RESORT

BAYSE, VA (On Hwy. 263 W., from exit 273 off I-81)
Telephone: (703)856-2121

Head Pro: Greg Bowman   Course Supt.: Roger Schmitt
Architect: Ed Ault

18 Holes   Par 71   6024 yds.

Built along the beautiful mountains in the Shenandoah Valley.
Tight fairways cross water on 10 holes. Power carts are manditory.
SEE OUR AD ON PAGE 251.

$$	Resort	Golf Pkgs.		Power Carts	Lessons	Lounge	Snack Bar	Meals	Open All Year

SHENANDOAH VALLEY GOLF CLUB

FRONT ROYAL, VA (On Rte. 658, off Rte 661)
Clubhouse: (703)635-3588   **Golf Shop: (703)636-2641**

Head Pro: Mike Ahrnsbrak - PGA   Course Supt.: Peter Schmidt - GSA

27 Holes: Red Course   9 Holes   Par 36   3087 yds
           White Course   9 Holes   Par 35   2976 yds.
           Blue Course   9 Holes   Par 36   2523 yds.

Rated top 20 in Virginia. A very scenic course with lots of trees.
SEE OUR AD ON PAGE 250.

$$		Golf Pkgs.	Public	Power Carts	Lessons	Lounge	Snack Bar	Meals	Open All Year

JUST ONE MILE EAST OF INTERSTATE 81 ON ROUTE 50

AT THE TOP OF VIRGINIA

• Delicious Foods • Choice Beverages
• Excellent Service • Warm Hospitality

Nestled at the top of the historic and picturesque Shenandoah Valley with 150 acres of gently rolling hills, tree lined fairways and fast sloping greens. Six beautiful lakes, well placed traps and bunkers add to the competitive and scenic layout.

CALL FOR WEEKDAY GREEN FEES & CART SPECIALS

(703)662-4319

1400 Millwood Pike, Winchester, Virginia 22602

CARPER'S VALLEY GOLF CLUB

WINCHESTER, VA (On Millwood Pike, Rte. 50, exit 313 off I-81)
Clubhouse: (703)662-1287   Pro Shop: (703)662-4319

Owner/Manager: Richard Dick   Head Pro: Rick Miller - PGA
Course Supt.: Bill Racey   Architect: Ed Ault

18 Holes Par 70 6135 / 6025 / 5100 yds.
      Rating: 69.1 / 68.6 / 70.7 Slope: 111 / 115 / 119

Whether you're a scratch golfer or tee-up just for the fun and relaxation the game provides, you are sure to find this course both challenging and enjoyable.

$$		Golf Pkgs.	Public	Power Carts	Lessons	Lounge	Snack Bar	Meals	Open All Year	

In the Heart of the Shenandoah Valley
in the Midst of the Blue Ridge Mountains

The SHENVALEE

Visit SHENVALEE and discover enjoyable, relaxing golf in the beautiful and historical Shenandoah Valley. Set in the midst of the picturesque Blue Ridge Mountains of Virginia, it offers all you need for a memorable golf vacation.

True to its history, SHENVALEE's beautifully maintained and uniquely designed 27 hole PGA course first opened to the public in 1927. Its front nine was built by a large force of men wielding picks and shovels and using horse-drawn wagons to transport dirt. The back nine holes were added in 1963.

Here hospitality is a way of life. Fine dining in an elegant restaurant with delicious food and warm ambiance, a quiet drink in the "Sand Trap Tavern" and graciously appointed rooms - poolside or overlooking the golf course.

- EXCELLENT GOLF PACKAGES -

Two day to seven day packages are very reasonable and special mid-week packages are even less.

FOR MORE INFORMATION CONTACT:

THE SHENVALEE GOLF RESORT

P.O. Box 430, New Market, Virginia 22844
Tel: (703) 740-3181 • Fax: (703) 740-8931

THE SHENVALEE GOLF RESORT

NEW MARKET, VA (Follow signs from exit 264 at I-81)
Telephone: (703)740-3181   Fax: (703)740-8931

General Manager: Edy Orebaugh

Old Course:	9 Holes	Par 36	2828 yds.
Creek Course:	9 Holes	Par 36	2857 yds.
Miller Creek:	9 Holes	Par 36	2779 yds.

In the Heart of the Shenandoah Valley in the midst of the Blue Ridge Mountains. Unique in design and beautifully maintained.

$$	Resort	Golf Pkgs.	Public	Power Carts	Lessons	Lounge	Snack Bar	Meals	Open All Year

Sheraton Inn Harrisonburg

The hospitality people of **ITT**

OFFERS
UNLIMITED 3 DAY GOLF PACKAGE

Weekday Package **$215.00** per person*
Weekend Package **$220.00** per person*
(*Based on double occupancy)

Including:
- **Two Nights Lodging • Two Dinners • Two Breakfasts**
- **Hors d'Oeuvres • Three Days Unlimited Golf**
- **Golf Cart (for 1st. eighteen holes each day)**

Located only minutes away, nestled in the Shenandoah Valley in the shadows of the Blue Ridge & Massanutten Mountains are 6500 yards of gently rolling fairways that present a challenge to the seasoned golfer and offer an enjoyable experience to the weekend player.

Large tees and greens compliment this 18 hole par 72 championship course.
An additional nine holes are available for your enjoyment.

Following golf . . . .
- Indoor/Outdoor Heated Swimming Pools • Jacuzzi
- Sauna • Hiking • Caverns • Fishing • Horseback Riding
- Antique Malls & Outlet Shopping (only minutes away)

- ADVANCE RESERVATIONS ARE RECOMMENDED -

For more information contact:
ALICE L. REICHARD
Tel: (703) 433-2521 Fax: (703) 434-0253

1400 East Market St. Harrisonburg, Virginia 22801

It's common knowledge that "Virginia Is For Lovers", and whether you love history, scenery or a great round of golf, Virginia is the vacation destination for you. From the original landing site of Christopher Newport and the colony of Jamestown, to the year-round excitement of Virginia Beach and the Shenandoah Valley, Virginia provides an exceptional vacation atmosphere.

WEST VIRGINIA

SPEIDEL GOLF COURSE AT OGLEBAY • WHEELING, WEST VIRGINIA ▲

Golf
Vacations

West Virginia is bounded by five states along its unusual border. This uniqueness of shape has helped give West Virginia many faces. Beginning on the East at the convergance of the Potomac and Shenandoah Rivers, and heading west over mountains, forest and farmlands to the Ohio River along its Western border, West Virginia's landscape offers a little bit of everything. The styles of golf in West Virginia vary with the topography, and are nearly limitless.

Historically, West Virginia is probably best known as the setting of the 1880's feud between the Hatfield and McCoy families of Logan County, West Virginia and Pike County, Kentucky. No one really knows how it began, but it was possibly linked to the dawn of a new industrial age and the subsequent scramble for land, timber and mineral rights. The feud drew attention from around the world, and labelled the area as backward. Although sensationalist newspapers stated there were over one hundred slayings, when the feud ended in the early 1890's, only twelve people had been killed.

In 1742, German emigrant John Peter Salley noted "a great plenty of coals" along the Coal River in Boone County. The nineteenth century introduction of coal mining into the five southwestern counties made the most sweeping changes which characterize "Coal Country" as it is known today.

Before railroads were brought to the area in the late 1800's, coal could not profitably be mined or transported to market. With the 1880 arrival of the Norfolk & Western rail line, and subsequent rail lines in the next decade, valuable mining opportunities could be realized from the incredible coal stems of West Virginia. Since coal was first mined in the state, over 4.1 billion tons have been produced.

The major coal production centers of Southwestern West Virginia began as single-family farmland, and had little contact with the outside world. With the advent of full-scale coal production, it was neccessary to import thousands of laborers, including blacks from the South and also European immigrants. This created a cultural mix and diversity completely foreign to these remote Appalachian communities. Because there were few settlements in the area, mining companies built company towns adjacent to their mines. Rent for housing was deducted from the miners' paychecks, as well as food, clothing and other supplies purchased at the coal company's store.

"Coal Country" was the scene of many turbulent conflicts between miners, coal companies and the government during the 1920s. In the Battle of Matewan, in May of 1920, coal company detectives and miners died in a showdown over the right to join the United Mine Workers of America. A year later, the murder of the Matewan Chief of Police and miners' advocate Sid Hatfield at the McDowell County Courthouse touched off a series of tragic events which led to the Battle of Blair Mountain. This rebellion of 10,000 armed miners against coal company officials was the largest insurrection in the United States since the Civil War, and was ended by the introduction of federal troops.

The West Virginia of today is a marked contrast to the gritty mining operations of the last century. While still a principal commodity, coal production does not have the same demand as it once did. With the downturn in coal production, however, has come a new wave of tourism, with visitors discovering West Virginia's bountiful and beautiful regions.

The "Eastern Gateway" is located along the easternmost finger of the state. In Colonial America, the "Gateway" served as a retreat for the aristocracy, who found it a quick step from Virginia and Maryland. Today, it serves as a getaway from the stress of life.

Berkeley Castle, built in 1875 near the Potomac River, is a Victorian monster meant to dominate the landscape in the romantic tradition of the late-19th century. Overlooking Berkeley Springs, the castle features a large ballroom, a wide carved staircase, tower room and a collection of antiques. The Berkeley Castle is still open for public tours, and is in hot demand as a wedding site.

The mineral waters at **Berkeley Springs** once drew Indians from Canada to the Carolinas, who came to witness the miraculous healing powers of the Springs. As America's first spa, the Springs and bath became popular with the colonial elite, such as George Washington and Lord Fairfax. In the 19th century, summering in Berkeley Springs meant matchmaking, end of season balls, duels and daily promenades through the town. Today, the warm, healing waters are open all year in the Berkeley Springs State Park's spa and Roman baths. The "Eastern Gateway" has gained fame as a retreat offering natural cures and renewed health, with modern health spas and mineral baths side by side.

Cycling is recommended if you want to see the countryside. You can bike through historic towns and unspoiled terrain, with some challenging mountain biking if you're up to it. Boating and hiking are also popular outdoor activities, as is golf, with several terrific courses throughout the area.

This region is known for its wealth of historic homes and country retreats, and most have been preserved splendidly. West Virginia takes great pride in its historical preservation efforts, and there are many National Historic Parks and restored towns and villages from various time periods throughout the state. Many historic homes have been converted into comfortable bed and breakfasts, whose owners invite travellers to stay and experience some country charm and historic atmosphere.

CACAPON RESORT STATE PARK GOLF COURSE
BERKLEY SPRINGS, WV (On U.S. Rte. 522)
Telephone: (304)258-1022

Manager: Phil Dawson
Course Supt.: Carl Kreyenbuhl

Head Pro:Charles Fields
Architect: Robert Trent Jones

18 Holes Par 72   6940 yds.

Seventy-two sand traps provide ample opportunity to "go to the beach" and the 4th and 8th holes share a unique 100-yard wide green. The rolling terrain at the foot of the Cacapon Mountains is ideal for this championship course.

$$	Resort	Golf Pkgs.	Public	Power Carts	Lessons	Lounge	Snack Bar	Meals	Open All Year

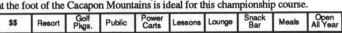

The "Potomac Highlands" is a collection of 13 mountain counties, and is the largest single natural scenic and recreation area in the Eastern United States. Legend says that, in 1748, hunter George Casey Harness scrambled to the top of Cabin Mountain, gazed in awe at the valley below and shouted, "Behold, the Land of Canaan!" The "Potomac Highlands" is a land preserved in untouched magnificence, beckoning vacationers of all interests to visit.

Within the Highlands boundaries rise more than one hundred of West Virginia's highest mountain peaks, including Spruce Knob, towering at 4,860 feet. Surrounding them lie thousands upon thousands of acres of wilderness. There are two national forests, a national recreational area, four designated wilderness zones, and no fewer than 11 state parks and forests. This is the land of exceptional mountain golf, with several courses and resorts offering many diverse and challenging holes for all skill levels.

The diversity of the Highlands takes a visitor from soaring mountaintops to windswept plains and lush, fertile valleys. Wild orchids grow in the Cranberry Glades, and a primeval forest stands tall beside the tumbling roar of Blackwater Falls. Nearby, the city of **Elkins** provides creature comforts with a hearty mountain charm and West Virginia hospitality.

The Droop Mountain Battefield in Pocahontas County, is the site of the state's largest Civil War Engagement and Re-enactment, and is one of many historic battefields open to the public.

The region is riddled with beautiful and mysterious caverns, some of which are prepared for walk-in tours. Seneca Caverns feature guided tours from April to October, while the Smoke Hole Caverns are open year-round.

Resort & Conference Center
A WEST VIRGINIA STATE PARK

CANAAN VALLEY RESORT

DAVIS, WV (On Hwy. 32, south of Davis and north of Harman)
Telephone:(304)866-4121   or: 800-225-5982

Owner: West Virginia State Parks   Head Pro: Bud Harold
Architect: Godfrey Cornish

18 Holes   Par 72   6436 yds.

Breathtaking vistas and gentle rolling terrain. Cool summertime temperatures and low humidity, coupled with excellent playing conditions on this carefully manicured course makes for the ultimate golfing experience.

$$	Resort	Golf Pkgs.	Public	Power Carts	Lessons	Lounge	Snack Bar	Meals	Open All Year

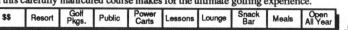

"Mountaineer Country", bounded along the north by Pennsylvania and on the east by Maryland, is the home to research and development in West Virginia, where high tech meets the ways of the old world. From the region's earliest days in the mid-1700s, "Mountaineer Country" has meant adventure and solitude. That seclusion is what has today brought technological thinkers and academics to the area.

*At **Philippi** on June 3, 1861, the six-pound guns of the Union Army approached from one end of town. The Confederates fled to the other end, and before the day was out, the two sides met in combat, marking the first important land battle of the Civil War. This event is relived at Philippi's "Blue and Gray Reunion", held annually.*

Also in Philippi is the largest two lane covered bridge still in use on a federal highway. The bridge was heavily desired by both sides during the Civil War, and changed hands dozens of times. It is now being restored to its original configuration and appearance.

*In the town of **Grafton** on May 10, 1908, the first Mother's Day service was held at the St. Andrew's Methodist Church. Built in 1873, the church stands today as the International Mother's Day Shrine, and is open for tours.*

*During the warmer months, festivals abound in the "Mountaineer Country". The Labor Day weekend's West Virginia Italian Heritage Festival at **Clarksburg** is recognized as one of the top 100 attractions in North America, with the flavor and feel of Italy flowing from everywhere in town. The Preston County Buckwheat Festival is held in the Fall, and features "buckwheat cakes, pork sausage and fixin's". The Mountaineer Balloon Festival at **Morgantown** has grown each year, drawing balloonists from around the world to come soar the stunning Mountaineer landscape in mid-Autumn. The Mason-Dixon Festival at the Morgantown Riverfront Park celebrates the end of the Civil War along the famous North-South dividing line, which runs along the Southern Pennsylvania border with Maryland and West Virginia.*

As West Virginia's heartland, the "Mountain Lake" region is well-named. Sparkling water amidst towering mountains accent this lush landscape. The "Mountain Lake" area maintains a quiet, tranquil atmosphere while providing everything a vacationer could possibly need.

*The West Virginia Wildlife Center near **Buckhannon** is a unique wildlife sanctuary, where species native to the area roam free, and where sick and orphaned animals go to get well again before being released into the wild. The sanctuary keeps people at a distance from the wildlife, allowing an intriguing look into the natural, wild habitat of species like bears, wolves and elk.*

HAWTHORNE VALLEY
GOLF COURSE

SNOWSHOE MOUNTAIN RESORT

Discover a true mountain golf getaway at Snowshoe, West Virginia. Nestled in the great Alleghenies, golfers can now experience fine golf in the cool mountain climate of West Virginia. Snowshoe's Hawthorne Valley golf course, designed by the legendary Gary Player, utilizes over 7000 yards to take you over rushing mountain streams and through the lush woodland foothills of Snowshoe Mountain Resort.

Special Golf Vacation Packages have been designed especially for you to take advantage of this new course.

Golf Vacation Packages
The Classic..................................$199. per person*
Two nights lodging, two rounds of golf, golf cart, two breakfasts, complimentary use of practice range, golf gift, yardage book, daily golf clinic, meet the Pro reception, guaranteed tee times.

The Golfer's Getaway.................$158. per person*
Two nights lodging, two rounds of golf, golf cart, range balls, golf gift, guaranteed tee times.

*Double Occupancy, Two night minimum.

During your stay at Snowshoe, you and your family can enjoy a game of tennis, go mountain biking, horseback riding, hiking, fishing, dine in the many fine restaurants or take in the natural beauty that the area offers. There is something for everyone at Snowshoe.

Call today to plan your next golf vacation in the mountains of West Virginia. (304) 572-5252.

HAWTHORNE VALLEY GOLF COURSE
SNOWSHOE MOUNTAIN RESORT
PO Box 10 • Snowshoe, West Virginia • 26209

The "Mountain Lake" region is renowned for its crafts and antiques. Artisans from around the state come to display their wares at Jackson's Mill, built in 1808 and the historic boyhood home of Civil War General "Stonewall" Jackson, home to the Stonewall Jackson Heritage Arts and Crafts Jubilee held over the Labor Day weekend.

The area hosts festivals throughout the year, including the famed Strawberry Festival held in Buckhannon each May. Here you can get strawberries served any way you can imagine. The Braxton County Fairs and Festival Celebration in Sutton, runs in late July and a highlight is the Fireman's Rodeo, with ladder throwing, hose laying and a bucket brigade competition.

When explorers and pioneers first crossed westward over the Blue Ridge Mountains in search of a better life, they found a land that was stunningly beautiful, but untamed and wild. Today, this land known as the "New River/Greenbrier Valley" has been transformed into a rugged but comfortable wilderness.

Over one-third of West Virginia's 40 parks are in this area, and there is a long tradition of preserving the wildness of the land. As early as 1925, some of West Virginia's leaders saw the need for preservation and protection of the state's natural beauty, and their foresight can be appreciated today.

Below the mountains of the "New River/Greenbrier Valley" region are many subterranean diversions. Organ Cave, near **Ronceverte**, was a natural store of saltpeter, one of the ingredients in gunpowder, and as such was a principal target during the Civil War. General Robert E. Lee's men are reported to have made much of their ammunition in this cave. Lost World in **Lewisburg** is comprised of a main cavern approximately 1000 feet long, with several waterfalls and numerous terraced, pedestal-like stalagmites.

The town of Lewisburg was host to a short but vivid Civil War battle. While lasting only an hour during the predawn of a May morning in 1862, the battle has retained a lasting impact on the people of this community. Carnegie Hall in Lewisburg was a gift from Andrew Carnegie, and now serves as a non-profit educational center. The State Fair of West Virginia held in Lewisburg during August attracts many visitors from all over.

Southern West Virginia is 'FORE'...

GOLFERS

Escape . . . to the cool, lush green mountains of the Southern West Virginia Highlands.

Challenge yourself on a different, gently rolling course each day.

GREAT MEETING FACILITIES TOO!

Easily accessible via I-77 & I-79

For More Information . . .

Southern West Virginia Convention & Visitor's Bureau
P. O. Box 1799 • Beckley, WV 25802
(Inside WV) 304-252-2244

1-800-VISIT WV

YOU WON'T HAVE TO DRIVE FAR!

Nine Local Golf Courses

- Grandview Country Club
- Hawks Nest
- Twin Falls
- Willow Wood
- Beaver Creek
- White Oak Country Club
- Glade Springs Resort
- Lakeview Golf Course
- Pipestem State Park

330 Yard Driving Range On Site!
PGA Pro-Lessons Available
May Through October

Beckley Hotel Offers

- 200 Rooms-Indoor Pool and Jacuzzi
- Conference and Banquet Facility for 1,000
- The Carriage House Family Restaurant
- The Brass Lantern-for intimate dining
- Free HBO, TBS, ESPN, CNN, TNT, Cable TV
- AAA, AARP, CAA, CARP Corporate and Government Rates, and Special Packages

- Groups and Individuals
- Motorcoaches Welcome
- On-Site Mini-Mall
- PGA Pro Golf Driving Range
- On Site Sanitary Disposal For RV/Motorcoach
- On Site Kennel/Pets Welcome

BECKLEY HOTEL

For Reservations or Information, Call 1-800-274-6010
Beckley, West Virginia • Exit 44, Off I-64/I-77

Beckley, *located at the crossroads of I-77 and I-64, is emerging as one of the newest and brightest spots for golf in the state. Traditionally a coal town, and nestled in the heart of "Coal Country" in the southern part of West Virginia, Beckley is attracting golfers from around the world to play some of the wonderful courses. Local business people and visitor bureau officials are actively pursuing Beckley as a new "Golf Mecca", and reasonably so; the climate is moderate and tempered from the early spring through the late fall. Unlike some locations north of Beckley, the area can sustain a golfing season for about eight to nine months. And with its central location Beckley is close to just about anywhere.*

The sister cities of **Huntington** *and* **Charleston** *are surrounded by low lying hills and straddle the Kanawha River. Both are popular convention sites and are the business hub of West Virginia. As the state capital, Charleston is a vibrant mix between its history and its progress. The State Cultural Center in Charleston offers a beginning look at the history of the state, and of the "Metro Valley" region in particular. Downtown Charleston is a cross section of modern highrises, Victorian and Art Deco architecture. Trolleys take visitors on a 25-cent ride from Old Charleston Village through the East End historical district, and its wealth of massive, charming homes, to the lawns and buildings of the State Captial Complex. At night, small bars and glittering nightclubs offer musical entertainment ranging from blues and jazz fusion, to rock, pop and traditional country.*

Huntington is a university town and one of the nation's inland ports, renowned for its neighborly attitude and its unique role as the melting pot of northern, southern and midwestern cultures. The boundaries of Huntington stretch from city to rolling hills. The West Virginia Bell, docked in Huntington and South Charleston, offers dinner cruises on the Kanawha River. Huntington is also the starting point for the famous New River Train excursion. The train carries railroad buffs through the "Metro Valley" and New River Gorge, pulled along by vintage steam engines. Huntington is where the connection of the C&O Railroad was made in 1868, linking the Wild West with the civilized East.

The "Mid-Ohio Valley" has been called West Virginia's "Western Frontier", and is bounded by the mighty Ohio River along its western border. This was once America's frontier, and was the gateway west, to adventure and the unknown. Today it is a land of romantic getaways and historical fascination.

This is a gentle landscape, where streams meander lazily westward and the land spreads out before you. This is more Midwestern in its landscape, and much flatter than the rest of West Virginia.

This is a place where romantic adventures and escapes are par for the course. Hotels in the region offer special packages for lovers, and area landmarks are geared to the true romantics. Harmon Blennerhassett, an Irish immigrant, built a beautiful mansion for his bride, Margaret, on an island in the "Mid-Ohio Valley" in 1796. That was the first of many romantic, Victorian buildings built in the area. In **Parkersburg**, the Blennerhassett Hotel was completed in 1889, and survived many years of neglect after the oil boom of the Midwest ended to today become a breathtaking, luxurious hotel.

Parkersburg is also the home of a beautiful 1926 theater, an Egyptian Renaissance structure that was set to be demolished but was restored in May of 1989, and now hosts film festivals and live theater. The Middleton Doll Factory nearby allows visitors to see artisans create dolls, from start to finish.

GLADE SPRINGS RESORT

DANIELS, WV (At intersection of I-64 & I-77 near Beckley WV)
Telephone: (304)763-2000   Toll Free: 1-800-634-5233

Manager: Don Parris   Head Pro: Steve Hazelwood
Course Supt.: Rodney Noel   Architect: George Cobb

18 Holes   Par 72   6176 yds.

An all suite resort featuring golf, tennis, horseback riding,
swimming, fishing, hiking, with rafting and skiing only minutes away.
Meeting space available for groups of 10 - 500.

$$$	Resort	Golf Pkgs.	Public	Power Carts	Lessons	Lounge	Snack Bar	Meals	Open All Year
✓	✓	✓	✓	✓	✓	✓	✓	✓	✓

TWIN FALLS RESORT STATE PARK

MULLENS, WV (5.5 mi. from Maben, off W.V. Rte 97, left at Bear Hole Rd.)
Telephone: (304)294-4000

Manager:A. Scott Durham, Supt.   Head Pro: Joe Comer
Architects: Geoffrey Cornish/George Cobb

18 Holes Par 71 5977 yds. Rating: 70.1

Bent grass greens and bluegrass fairways
set amidst a beautiful state park. Accomodations
available at Twin Falls Lodge, Cottages, and Campground.

$	Resort	Golf Pkgs.	Public	Power Carts	Lessons		Snack Bar	Meals	Open All Year

PIPESTEM RESORT STATE PARK GOLF COURSE

PIPESTEM, WV (On Rte. 20 between Hinton and Princeton)
Telephone: (304)466-1800

Manager: Tourism & Parks   Head Pro: Bill Robertson
Course Supt.: Larry Ball   Architect: Geoffrey Cornish

18 Holes Par 72 6131 yds.

This championship course offers a commanding view
of the Bluestone River Gorge from the 17th hole.
This scenic course will be the site of the 1993 West Virginia Open.

$	Resort	Golf Pkgs.	Public	Power Carts	Lessons	Lounge	Snack Bar	Meals	Open All Year

*If you love golf but hate to compete for space,
we have the perfect plan for you.
Our Golf Packages are available April 1st. to
October 31st. Packages include three 18-hole
championship courses for the exclusive use of
our guests. Unlimited use of the practice
range. Preferred starting times. A
professional golf clinic. Even daily cleaning
and storage of your clubs. When you add
spacious accommodations, plus breakfast
and a six-course dinner daily, one thing
is certain; you shouldn't have any
reservations about making one.
Call 1-800-624-6070 or (304) 536-1110
or see your travel agent.*

*White Sulphur Springs, West Virginia 24986
A CSX Resort*

Parkland is everywhere. At the northern tip are the 1400 acres of the Tomlinson Run State Park near New Manchester, with 33 acres of water. The 700 acre Brooke Hills Park near Wellsburg has outdoor sports in every season, and summer stock theater. Grand Vue Park near Moundsville has the country club setting West Virginia parks are famous for, with charming rental cabins available.

Wheeling, along the Ohio River, is the birthplace of the State of West Virginia. Independence Hall has the restored historic courtroom wherein the structure of the 35th state was hammered out. Wheeling is also home to the Oglebay Municipal Park and Oglebay Resort, which is the flagship to America's municipal park system. The park was a gift to the city from industrialist Col. Earl Oglebay, and is one of the largest resorts in the United States. Oglebay's sister park, Wheeling Park, offers four-season fun including adult and teen activity centers and a popular giant waterslide.

Speidel in Golf Digest's 75 best public golf courses

Golf Oglebay

Enjoy some of the best golf you've ever played this Summer at one of America's finest Resorts.

Package good thru Oct. 28 Sunday thru Thursday

Oglebay Golf Package

$85 Per Person Per Night
Double Occupancy in Wilson Lodge

Call for reservations and tee times

800-633-9975
in USA 800-624-6988

includes **36 Holes Daily**
- **18 holes daily on Speidel Robert Trent Jones designed course and 18 holes on Crispin**
- **Unlimited Par-3**
- **$10 Food Coupon**

Oglebay

Wheeling   West Virginia   26003

West Virginia touches so many places, and has absorbed so many different ways of life that it is truly a diverse vacation spot. From its colorful history as a coal producer and site of the Hatfield-McCoy feud, to the vibrancy of Wheeling, Charleston, Huntington and its other urban centers, the state of West Virginia has retained its reputation as a first-class holiday getaway.

SPEIDEL GOLF COURSE

WHEELING, WV (At Oglebay, on Interstate 70, off I-79 south of Pittsburgh)
Canada: 1-800-633-9975   U.S.A.: 1-800-624-6988

Head Pro: Karen Waialae   Course Supt.: Ed Murphy
Architect: Robert Trent Jones

18 Holes   Par 71   7000 yds.

Ranked by *Golf Digest* as one of America's best public golf
courses. Multiple tee placements for all levels of play. A beautiful course.

$$	Resort	Golf Pkgs.	Public	Power Carts	Lessons	Lounge	Snack Bar	Meals	

CRISPIN GOLF COURSE

WHEELING, WV (At Oglebay, on Interstate 70, off I-79 south of Pittsburgh)
Telephone: (304)243-4090   Canada: 1-800-633-9975
                              U.S.A.: 1-800-624-6988

Head Pro: Karen Waialae   Architect: Robert Beiry

18 Holes   Par 71   5670 yds.

This natural course traverses the beautiful West Virginia
hills and offers the golfer ever changing views of Oglebay.

$$	Resort	Golf Pkgs.	Public	Power Carts	Lessons	Lounge	Snack Bar	Meals	Open All Year

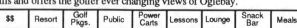

The legend and heritage surrounding *"Lakeview"*, the original, 18 - hole championship golf course, is reason enough for professionals, beginners and spectators alike to journey to Morgantown, West Virginia.

Now added is the lure of *Lakeview's* new *"Mountainview"* golf course and a multi-million dollar Fitness and Sports Complex .

With a gracious lobby, distinctive activity centers, 187 spacious, well-appointed rooms, and 79 luxurious 2-bedroom condominiums the difference and style of *Lakeview* is very evident.

Two unique restaurants . . . "Reflections-on-the-Lake" and "The Grille" offer atmosphere, service and cuisine second to none.

FOR MORE INFORMATION AND RESERVATIONS CALL:

800-624-8300 (Toll Free)

The Easiest
Drive in Golf . . .

Located 75 miles south of Pittsburgh, the drive to Lakeview on Interstate 68 or US Rt. 40 is all inter-state highway. Many people think it is one of the easiest and most beautiful drives in the Eastern U.S.

Route 6, Box 88A
Morgantown, WV 26505
(304) 594-1111
800-624-8300

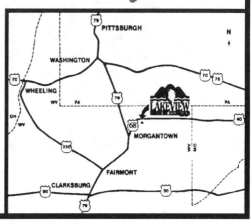

FOUR VALUABLE GOLF TIPS:

1) Canaan Valley   3) Pipestem
2) Cacapon   4) Twin Falls

...Or the best tip of all —

West Virginia Resort State Parks!

Enjoy the luxury of resort accommodations, championship courses, incredible scenery and an array of activities and entertainment that's suited for the entire family.

Our custom designed golf packages make West Virginia Resort State Parks the best value going in the mid-Atlantic.

Phone 1 800 CALL WVA and make your reservations today!

TENNESSEE

PICKWICK LANDING STATE PARK G.C. • PICKWICK DAM, TENNESSEE ▲

Golf
Vacations

Loosely classified as one of the "swing states", Tennessee is probably best known for its music and its whiskey. Beale Street, in Memphis, is called "the birthplace of the blues", where a man named W. C. Handy struck a mournful chord and touched off a musical revolution.

Tennessee's musical mythology carries down the streets of Memphis to Graceland, which was home to Elvis Presley from the late 1950s until his death in 1977, and is maintained by "The King's" estate as a museum. Elvis is buried there, (if you, in fact, believe he's dead!), and much of his life is on display, including his tour bus and his private jet, the "Lisa Marie". Elvis' first recording studio, Sun Records, is also in Memphis, and was responsible for launching innumerable other famous careers including Jerry Lee Lewis, Roy Orbison and Johnny Cash.

Memphis grew up along the mighty Mississippi River, and this proud heritage is remembered at the incredible "Mud Island", a 50-acre park of culture and history about the "Father of Waters". The spectacular River Walk is a detailed, flowing scale model of the Mississippi, tracing its route from Minnesota to the Gulf of Mexico. Memphis is also home to first-rate museums and galleries, and Overton Park is one of the nation's finest zoos.

One of the darkest days in Memphis' history came in 1968 at the Lorraine Motel, with the assassination of Civil Rights leader Dr. Martin Luther King, Jr. To remember this tragedy, the motel has been converted into America's first National Civil Rights Center. Author Alex Hailey's hometown of **Henning** *is located close by, which served as the setting for his epic novel, "Roots".* **Jackson**, *northeast of Memphis, was the home of Casey Jones, the ill-fated engineer who rode "Old 382" into legend.*

Reelfoot Lake, near Tennessee' western boundary with Missouri, was created by a series of earthquakes, and is one of the nation's finest fish hatcheries. Reelfoot is also the winter home of the American bald eagle. The state's largest park, Natchez Trail, covers more than 43,000 acres along the shores of the Tennessee River.

The "Heartland" of Tennessee is a land of gently rolling hills and bluegrass meadows surrounded by the towering Highland Rim of the Appalachians. The Tennessee Walking Horse breed was developed in this agricultural region, and the breeding and training of champion horses is a major industry.

PARIS LANDING STATE PARK GOLF COURSE

BUCHANAN, TN (On US 79)
Telephone: (901)644-1332

Owner: State of Tennessee   Head Pro: Keith Hickman

18 Holes Par 72 6479 yds.

This very contoured course is cut out of a hardwood forest with several holes bordering on Kentucky Lake. The signature hole is number 4, a 182-yd. par 3, with a beautiful vista overlooking the lake. Bent grass greens.

$		Golf Pkgs.	Public	Power Carts	Lessons		Snack Bar	Meals	Open All Year
$		Golf Pkgs.	Public	Power Carts	Lessons		Snack Bar	Meals	Open All Year

PICKWICK LANDING STATE PARK GOLF COURSE

PICKWICK DAM, TN (On State Hwy. 57)
Telephone: (901)689-3149

Owner: State of Tennessee   Head Pro: Reg Scott

18 Holes Par 72 6401 yds.

This course features hybrid bermuda greens and fairways. There are several challenging dogleg holes, the No. 1 handicap hole being number 2, a 371-yd. par 4, with a difficult second shot to the green.

$		Golf Pkgs.	Public	Power Carts	Lessons		Snack Bar	Meals	Open All Year
$		Golf Pkgs.	Public	Power Carts	Lessons		Snack Bar	Meals	Open All Year

The lush rolling countryside opens up onto **Nashville**, the "Country Music Capital of the World". Nashville is home to the Grand Ole Opry®, which is where country music grew up. The Opry® has been entertaining folks from far and wide for more than 60 years, with Opry® shows scheduled every Friday and Saturday throughout the year, with matinees added from April to October. The Grand Ole Opry® Radio Show continues to be the longest-running radio show in history.

Opryland® is America's only musical showpark, which depicts the history of this brand of music, as well as a variety of other styles including pop, rock, bluegrass, showtunes, etc., and offers many rides, like the brand new "Chaos". There are also museums on site honoring Roy Acuff and Minnie Pearl.

The Grand Ole Opry® and Opryland® are part of the Opryland USA® complex, which includes the Opryland Hotel, a full-service, standard-setting hotel set on 4 1/2 acres, with an indoor pool, tropical gardens, restaurants, shops and an 18-hole Scottish-style golf course.

As well as the "Country Music Capital", Nashville is the state's political capital, and one of its most impressive pieces of architecture is the State Capitol Building. Designed by William Strickland in 1859, it is a classic example of Greek Revivalist architecture, and is viewed as Strickland's masterpiece. Another of Nashville's distinctive buildings is the Parthenon, which is the only exact-sized replica of the ancient, original Greek temple. It is due in large part to these two pieces that Nashville has earned its distinction as the "Athens of the South".

Another noteworthy piece of Nashville's charm is the Broadway Dinner Train, which is a living testament to a bygone era of luxury passenger trains. A sumptuous meal is served aboard elegantly restored dining cars, while the train follows a route from downtown Nashville to **Old Hickory**, covering a distance of about 35 miles. The route was part of the Tennessee Central Railway, which was completed in 1904 and sold in 1986 to the Nashville and Eastern Railroad.

SPRINGHOUSE GOLF CLUB

NASHVILLE, TN (1-1/2 mi. from Opryland Hotel with shuttle service every 1/2 hr.)
Telephone: (615)871-7759   Fax: (615)871-5906

Director of Golf: Chuck Eade
Course Supt.: Andrew Brennan

Head Pro: Neil Collins
Architect: Larry Nelson

18 Holes   Par 72   5788 yds.

Scottish Links layout bordered by the Cumberland River and a 100-ft. limestone
bluff. The course plays from 5000 to over 7000 yards from five different set of tees.
Accommodations available at Opryland Hotel.

$$$	Resort	Golf Pkgs.	Public	Power Carts	Lessons	Lounge	Snack Bar	Meals	Open All Year

The Jack Daniels Distillery is located in nearby Lynchburg, and is one of only two places in the world where genuine Tennessee sour mash whiskey is made. In Columbia, visit the home of former President James K. Polk in a town noted for its antebellum architecture.

Rising like a giant wall spanning the width of the state, the Cumberland Plateau forms the western boundary of the vast Tennessee Valley. While the heavily-forested plateau is quite flat, it is laced with mountain streams that have cut massive gorges into the sandstone, and mighty waterfalls tumble over rock cliffs into canyons below.

HENRY HORTON STATE PARK GOLF COURSE

CHAPEL HILL, TN (Exit #46 from I-65 S. and follow the signs)
Telephone: (615)364-2319

Owner: State of Tennessee   Head Pro: Kerry Blanton

18 Holes   Par 72   6580 yds.

This course features large bent grass greens and hybrid bermuda fairways gently contoured and cut through hardwood forests. Hole #18 is one of the longest in Tennessee - a full 615 yards from the championship tees.

$		Golf Pkgs.	Public	Power Carts	Lessons		Snack Bar	Meals	Open All Year
$			Public						Open All Year

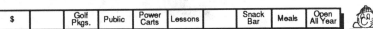

MONTGOMERY BELL STATE PARK GOLF COURSE

BURNS, TN (On Hwy. 47, take I-40 W. from Nashville, 40 Miles, follow the signs)
Telephone: (615)797-2578

Owner: State of Tennessee   Head Pro: Darryl Hartsfield
Architect: Gary Rodger Baird

18 Holes   Par 72   6065 yds.

Be sure to play this course in the spring for the best view of the myriads of dogwood trees all over the course. Large, contured bent grass greens are surrounded by mounds. Hybrid Bermuda fairways.

$		Golf Pkgs.	Public	Power Carts	Lessons		Snack Bar	Meals	Open All Year
$			Public						Open All Year

The pure beauty of the Cumberlands is preserved in state parks and wilderness areas throughout the area. Fall Creek Falls State Park is named for the highest waterfall in the Eastern United States, and there you can challenge the rapids of some of the toughest white water streams in the country, or take a peaceful canoe trip down the Sequatchie River.

Chattanooga is a city famous for it's Civil War battefields, it's Lookout Mountain attractions and it's long attachment to the railroads. The city winds out along the Moccasin Bend of the Tennessee River at the foot of Lookout Mountain, and on a clear day you can see seven states from Rock City Gardens, the famous attraction where millions of years of geological activity is etched into stunning rock formations. It was railroads that made Chattanooga an important objective during the Civil War, and today, Chickamauga - Chattanooga is the oldest, largest and most visited National Military Park in the United States.

FALL CREEK FALLS STATE PARK GOLF COURSE

PIKEVILLE, TN (State Hwy. #30)
Telephone: (615)881-5706

Owner: State of Tennessee
Architect: Joe Lee

Head Pro: Billy Maxwell

18 Holes   Par 72   6378 yds.

This course has northern bluegrass fairways and bent grass greens and features many dogleg holes synonymous with a Joe Lee design.

$		Golf Pkgs.	Public	Power Carts	Lessons		Snack Bar	Meals	Open All Year	

The Cherokee Indians called it Shaconage, the "Place of the Blue Smoke"; today, we know it as the Great Smoky Mountains National Park, and at 500,000 acres it protects the largest virgin forest remaining in the United States. Millions of visitors each year come to stand high atop the breathtaking summits, and to walk silently through millenia-old forests or fish for trout in rushing streams.

Gatlinburg is on the edge of the park, and has grown from a quaint mountain village to a major resort area. With over 300 shops and an imaginative array of wares, Gatlinburg may be the largest concentration of craftspeople in the South. Attractions in Gatlinburg include the Elvis Hall of Fame, with many personal items from "The King", as well as Gatlinburg's Mysterious Mansion, a house patterned after an 18th century mansion featuring false panels, sinking floors and a bevy of animated creatures.

BENT CREEK GOLF RESORT

GATLINBURG, TN. (On Hwy. 321, 11 Mi. N. of Gatlinburg)
Telephone: (615)436-2875   US Toll Free: 1-800-251-9336

Owner/Mgr.: James A. Calkin Jr.   Head Pro: Mark Wallace
Course Supt.: Don Clabo   Architect: Gary Player

18 Holes   Par 72   6084 yds.

Golf course is set in the picturesque
Greenbriar Valley 15 minutes away from Gatlinburg.

$$	Resort	Golf Pkgs.	Public	Power Carts	Lessons	Lounge	Snack Bar	Meals	Open All Year

Pigeon Forge is nestled in the Smokies, and makes for a terrific stop on any trip. The "First Lady" of Pigeon Forge is Dolly Parton, who lives there and has opened a theme park called "Dollywood", which hosts exhibits and rides year-round.

Knoxville is the urban gateway to the Smokies, and traces its roots back to a solitary fort built on the Tennessee frontier. James White's Fort still stands in the shadow of modern skyscrapers. Bustling Knoxville is home to the University of Tennessee, and headquarters of the Tennessee Valley Authority, the nation's largest public utility. The region was carved by people following Daniel Boone west through the famous Cumberland Gap, which is now a National Historic Park. The Lost Sea, in Sweetwater, is described as the largest underground lake in the world, and walking tours are available through a cave or by glass-bottomed boat.

Along Tennessee's eastern border with North Carolina, the first settlements outside the original 13 colonies were founded by Daniel Boone and his compatriots. Near **Limestone**, you can visit the birthplace of another of America's folk heroes, Davy Crockett. Stroll along the brick sidewalks of charming **Jonesborough**, which is Tennessee's oldest town. **Greenville** was the birthplace of Andrew Johnson, America's 17th President, and a National Historic Site has been set aside in his honor. The Cherokee National Forest encompasses over 600,000 acres in 10 Tennessee counties, and are open for hiking, camping, hunting and fishing.

Tennessee was the gateway for Daniel Boone to conquer the West, through the Cumberland Gap, and was the birthplace of the blues. Its boundary encompasses part of the Great Smoky Mountains, and borders the Mississippi River. Tennessee was the place where Elvis Presley first picked up a guitar and sang, "That's Alright Mama", and, years later, where he was laid to rest. It's heritage as the home of country music is legendary and uncontested, all of which serve to make Tennessee a first-rate holiday destination.

GRAYSBURG HILLS GOLF COURSE

CHUKEY, TN (12 Mi. N/E of Greeneville, on State Rte. 93)
Telephone: (615)234-8061

Owner/Mgr.: Fred Stewart   Architect: Rees Jones

18 Holes   Par 72   6804 yds.

One of the top public golf facilities in Tennessee.
A quiet setting surrounds this challenging yet enjoyable golf course
with it's 60 sand bunkers and strategically located water hazards.
Golf packages available with Garden Plaza Hotel. SEE AD ON FACING PAGE.

$$		Golf Pkgs.	Public	Power Carts	Lessons	Lounge	Snack Bar		Open All Year

Graysburg Hills

"A GOLFERS MOUNTAIN PARADISE"

Enjoy a beautiful 6744 yard Rees Jones designed golf course with open fairways, large greens, and a scenic mountain backdrop.

Stay at the Garden Plaza, Johnson City, Northeast Tennessee's newest full service hotel featuring spacious rooms, indoor/outdoor pool and Ezra's Restaurant and Lounge.

Also enjoy many different attractions including state parks, caverns, shopping, restaurants, and near by Gatlinburg ,Tennessee. All of this, without the crowds of some golf resorts, for only

$58⁰⁰

GOLF PACKAGE INCLUDES:
• One nights lodging • One day unlimited golf
(with cart for first 18 holes)
(Price per person double occupancy)

Garden Plaza Hotel

For more information
or reservations call:

(615)929-2000

211 MOCKINGBIRD LANE • JOHNSON CITY, TENNESSEE 37604

Tennessee State Parks
Winter Green
Golf Vacation Packages

For more information call individual park:

Fall Creek Falls State Park
Route 3   Pikeville, TN 37367
(615) 881-5706

Paris Landing State Park
Route 1   Buchanan, TN 38222
(901) 644-7359

Henry Horton State Park
US 31A, Route 1
Chapel Hill, TN 37034
(615) 364-2222

Montgomery Bell State Park
US 70, P.O. Box 39
Burns, TN 37029
(615) 797-3101

Pickwick Landing State Park
State Highway 57
P.O. Box 15
Pickwick Dam, TN 38565
(901) 689-3135

STATE PARKS

NORTH CAROLINA

COMPLIMENTS OF PINEHURST AREA CVB • NORTH CAROLINA ▲

Golf Vacations

North Carolina is the self-proclaimed "Golf State, U.S.A.", and it is a title it's earned in areas like Pinehurst, Fayetteville, Wilmington and the Cape Fear Coast. Everywhere is tuned in to golf and to making a golf holiday as pleasurable as it can possibly be. From accommodation packages with hotels and some of the best-known, top-name courses, to community support in the form of golfer discounts and incentives to visit, North Carolina's eye is firmly on the vacationing golfer.

The Southwest Mountains of North Carolina provide some of the most challenging and exciting golf in the state. The Cherokee Indians called the mountains the "Great Blue Hills of God", and they mark the meeting place between the Blue Ridge Mountains and the Great Smoky Mountains. The Great Smoky Mountains National Park is a 514,000 acre landscape that is the most popular national park in America. More than 100 species of trees, and 1500 species of flowering plants thrive in this mountain sanctuary, protected from man and the ravages of progress.

The area is home to the Biltmore Estate, the largest private home in the United States. Built in 1895 by George W. Vanderbilt, this 250-room French Renaissance chateau offers self-guided tours both up and downstairs, as well as through the Estate winery, the gardens and the grounds of this 12,000 acre property. The Estate is furnished with countless millions of dollars worth of antiques, including the ivory chess set used by Napoleon during his exile on the island of Saint Helena.

North Carolina's Distinguished Golf Resort

High Hampton is a distinguished resort on 1400 scenic acres at 3600 ft. in the southern Blue Ridge Mtns. at Cashiers, North Carolina. Rates are modest and include three meals daily.

High Hampton's 18-hole, par 71 private course with bent grass greens is located adjacent to the Inn. It was designed by George W. Cobb, internationally famous golf architect. Mr. Cobb, who designed more than 350 courses, complimented High Hampton by saying: "I have yet to see a course – designed by me or by others – with greater natural beauty or one more enjoyable to play."

In addition to the scenic 18-hole course with its spectacular views of the mountains and lakes, High Hampton has an excellent practice range and two practice putting greens. The hitting area of the practice range is covered for protection from the occasional rains.

Free golf greens fees in April and November when staying at the Inn.

A Mountain Golf Resort
Your Entire Family Can Enjoy

On our private 1400-acre estate is an 18-hole, par 71 golf course with bent grass greens. Also tennis, sailing, fishing, nature and wildflower trails. Children's program. American Plan. Gracious hospitality. Also available: private vacation homes with daily maid service.

In the National Register of Historic Places

High Hampton Inn & Country Club

PO Box 338, Dept. 227 ◊ Cashiers, NC 28717-0338
1-800-334-2551 ext. 227 ◊ (704) 743-2411

The mountain city of Asheville has an immaculate collection of early 20th century architecture, including structures of national significance. The city skyline is a showcase for Art Deco, with a good portion of it's buildings sporting this tell-tale design. Author Thomas Wolfe's boyhood home is in Asheville, a home he would call "Dixieland" in his later work. The home is preserved at the Thomas Wolfe Memorial State Historical Site.

Nearby Chimney Rock is a 1,200 foot-high natural stone tower at least 500 million years old that stands in solitary vigil over miles of forest. On a clear day, it is said you can see 75 miles from the peak. At the turn of the century, Dr. Lucius Morse came to the mountains seeking a more favorable climate, and was so intrigued by the giant granite monolith over Hickory Nut Grove that he bought 64 acres of Chimney Rock Mountain. It was his dream to preserve its beauty and heritage while developing a natural scenic attraction. Today, the Park is more than 1000 acres including Chimney Rock itself, Hickory Nut Falls and a Nature Center, making Dr. Morse's dream an enjoyable reality.

*Haywood County, which includes **Maggie Valley** and **Waynesville**, was settled by pioneers over 200 years ago, but more recent settlers have come from the north and the south the retire in the area's temperate climate. Over forty percent of the county is protected land, and it has more wild plants and trees than any one place in the world. The Maggie Valley and Waynesville Resorts are located in this area, which is often called the "Gateway to the Great Smokies".*

Maggie Valley Resort
& Country Club

Breathtaking scenery surrounds this challenging course located in the Great Smoky and Blue Ridge Mountains. Headquarters of the Professional Golf Schools of America. Outstanding cuisine and atmosphere.

$$	Resort
Golf Pkgs.	Public
Power Carts	Lessons
Lounge	Snack Bar
Meals	Open All Year

Manager: Russ Smith   Head Pro: Ted Staats
Course Supt.: Mike Stamey   Architects: Wilmer Brimmer, William Prevost

Maggie Valley, NC (6 Mi. S. of I-40, ½ Mi. from intersection of 276 & 19)
704-926-1616 ext. 16   US Toll Free: 800-438-3861 ext 16

You Gotta Golf Maggie!

Four season resort. 18-hole championship golf course. Scenically beautiful, naturally challenging, the front nine is on the valley floor, the back nine goes up through the mountains. The elevation gradually changes from 2,600 feet at the third hole to 3,500 feet on the 13th. There is water play on 13 of the 18 holes. Fairways are wide. Four times the site of the North Carolina Open Golf Tournament, Maggie's course brings players back to play it again, and again.

The mountain background (the Blue Ridge and the Great Smokies) provides both scenic beauty and climate control, protecting Maggie from extremes in temperature.

Golf facilities are complete: full-service pro shop, locker room, golf lessons, practice putting green, and driving range.

Delicious food. Delightful entertainment. Charming fully appointed guest rooms. 35,000 sq. ft. of spectacular gardens. Oversized swimming pool. Tennis courts.

Year 'Round Golf Packages and Special Holiday Packages
800-438-3861 ext. 16

The Nantahala National Forest, part of the Great Smoky Mountains National Park, was explored in 1540 by Spanish conquistador Hernando DeSoto, and was establsihed by the Federal Government in 1920 as a National Forest, encompassing more than 500,000 acres and featuring dramatic sheer cliffs from 400 to 750 feet high.

In 1846, the mountain people of North Carolina were faced with starvation and famine because there was no way to bring food into the rugged countryside. In 1880, due in large measure to this tragedy, the original Western North Carolina Railroad track was completed from **Piedmont** to Asheville, with extensions following to Waynesville and **Murphy** the next two years. The Great Smoky Mountains Railway now runs tours along these lines, to help recapture a bygone time.

Waynesville Country Club Inn

WAYNESVILLE COUNTRY CLUB INN

WAYNESVILLE, NC. (I-40 to exit 20, to W. Waynesville exit, turn L. follow signs)
Telephone: (704)456-3551

Owner/Mgr.: Reimar K. Steffen
Course Supt.: Caney Kilby

Head Pro: Duane Page
Architects: John Drake/Tom Jackson

18 Holes   Par 70   6050 yds.

Also another 9 holes. Bent grass greens and scenic views over rolling fairways, through brooks and streams. Good golf, good friends, good times.

$$	Resort	Golf Pkgs.	Public	Power Carts	Lessons	Lounge	Snack Bar	Meals	Open All Year

Travelling north through the Blue Ridge Mountains, you can pick up the beautiful, scenic Blue Ridge Parkway, a 250-mile stretch of highway that winds through the mountain crest from the Great Smokies to Virginia. The highway is especially designed for scenic travel, and the speed limit never exceeds 45 mph.

These are some of the oldest mountains in the world, older than both the Andes and the Alps. They have been softened over the milleniums into gently rolling peaks, but are still quite an amazing spectacle. Many State Parks dot the Blue Ridge Mountains, including the Stone Mountain State Park, with an area of 13,411 acres, Doughton Park, which is the largest recreation area on the Blue Ridge Parkway, the New River State

Park, which encompasses 700 acres near **Jefferson**, where the New River winds its way among the Appalachian Mountains to become the second oldest river in the world, after the Nile, and Mount Jefferson State Park, which is 489 acres of undeveloped land.

This area is also home to the Ashe County Frescoes, some of the most interesting examples of frescoe painting in the United States. Painted by Ben Long, who studied under a Florentine master, the frescoes are found at two quaint 19th-century churches, the Holy Trinity Church in **Glendale Springs**, and Saint Mary's Episcopal Church in **West Jefferson**.

ETOWAH VALLEY
COUNTRY CLUB & GOLF LODGE

ETOWAH VALLEY C.C. & GOLF LODGE

HENDERSONVILLE, NC (On Hwy. 64, west of I-26)
Telephone: (704)891-7022   US Toll Free: 1-800-451-8174

Owners/Mgrs.: John & Frank Todd

9 Holes Par 35 3392 yds.   9 Holes Par 36 3488 yds.
9 Holes Par 35 3193 yds.

It's all here, georgeous mountains, great climate and a beautiful golf course just waiting to be conquered. Lush fairways bend, fold and roll to perfectly manicured bent grass greens. It's mountain golf at its best.

$$	Resort	Golf Pkgs.	Public	Power Carts	Lessons	Lounge	Snack Bar	Meals	Open All Year

The North Wilksboro Speedway is host each year to the Gwyn Staley Memorial Auto Race, as well as the Wilkes 400 Grand National Stock Car Race. Historic **North Wilksboro** tours are run by authentically-costumed guides, who lead you on visits to Tory Oak, the restored Robert Cleveland log home built about 1770, and the Old Wilkes Jails,(where Tom Dula, (of "The Ballad of Tom Dooley"), was held before he was hanged.

The town of **Valle Crucis** has the Mast General Store, which was built in 1883, but more notably is home-base of Noah Llama Treks, Inc., which use llamas to bring hikers into the rugged high country. Only a limited number of llama treks are available each year.

The town of **Blowing Rock**, North Carolina is named for the Blowing Rock, which is a rock formation that uses air currents from the Johns River Gorge below to return objects once they've been tossed from a high cliff. Legend says that an Indian brave once fell from this rock, but thanks to the prayers of an Indian princess, he was safely carried up by the air currents.

The Tweetsie Railroad is also in Blowing Rock, where narrow-gauge steam engines carry passengers through mountain passes and a frontier village, with the ride open during the warmer months of the year.

Fort Defiance, built in 1789 by Revolutionary War General William Lenoir, is located in **Happy Valley**, outside of **Patterson**, and is the site of a former frontier fort. The site has a restored home that contains more original furnishings than any other such restoration in North Carolina.

SPRINGDALE COUNTRY CLUB

CANTON, NC. (Hwy. 110 S. from Canton to US 276, S. 6 Mi.)
Telephone: (704)235-8451

Owner/Mgr.: G. Fredrick Tingle   Course Supt.: Bob Feser
Architect: Joe Holmes

18 Holes   Par 72   6812 yds.

A creek meanders through the hilly front and flat back of
this golf course. Excellent accommodations, good food, with
unique golf packages, including a personal cart for each twosome.

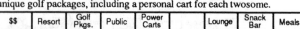

$$	Resort	Golf Pkgs.	Public	Power Carts		Lounge	Snack Bar	Meals	Open All Year

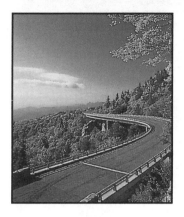

South of Blowing Rock, a section of the Blue Ridge Parkway called the Linn Cove Viaduct has become a major attraction. A feat of modern engineering, the highway winds around Grandfather Mountain without ever appearing to touch anything more solid than the air it extends into. A hiking trail below the highway allows visitors to see how this "floating" highway is suspended.

Grandfather Mountain itself is a major attraction, with a mile-high swinging bridge connecting two rocky peaks for pedestrian travel. You have a good chance of seeing bears, cougars, deer and eagles in the area.

Linville Falls and the Linville Gorge Wilderness Park offer visitors 7600 acres of a primitive natural environment surrounding the fast-flowing Linville River. Linville Falls cascades hundreds of feet into a rugged gorge, and the Linville Caverns have well-lit, well-marked passageways along an ancient underground river.

*From **Jacob's Ridge** on North Carolina Route 181 on summer evenings, when the conditions are just right, you may be able to see the mysterious colored lights floating up from Brown Mountain in the east.*

Roan Mountain, in the Pisgah National Forest, is the world's largest natural garden of crimson-purple rhododendron, with their peak blooming time in mid-June. Mount Mitchell is the highest peak in the Eastern United States, and, at 6684 feet, you can see as far away as the Great Smoky Mountains.

*Heading east out of the Appalachian Range, you journey into the Foothills regions of North Carolina. Asheboro, in the Northern Foothills, has the world's largest habitat zoo, containing a 1,300-acre recreation of the major continents of the Earth where animals can be viewed in their natural environment. The Richard Petty Museum in **Randleman** offers a different kind of wildlife, paying tribute to the famed race car driver with several of his cars on display, as well as a video presentation highlighting his career, and a collection of his 30 years-worth of trophies.*

HEMLOCK GOLF CLUB

WALNUT COVE, NC. (On Power Dam Rd., off Hwy. 89, 3 Mi. N. of Walnut Cove)
Telephone: (919)591-7934

Owners/Mgrs.: Keith & Kadren Robertson
Course Supt.: Keith Robertson

Head Pro: Tommy Zigler
Architect: Orell Robertson

18 Holes   Par 70   5482 yds.

This course, adjacent to the Dan River, has well kept greens, and is very hilly with nice views.

$			Public	Power Carts	Lessons		Snack Bar		Open All Year	

High Point is home to the North Carolina Shakespeare Festival, which draws on talent from around the world to perform. Korners Folly in **Kernersville** is an unusual 22-room house that was built on seven levels, with a top floor that was converted in 1897 to become the nation's first "Little Theater".

The Alamance Battleground State Historic Site in **Burlington** is the place where, in 1771, backcountry farmers called the "Regulators" took on the colonial milita of Royal Governor William Tyron. Burlington is also the home of the Burlington City Park Carousel, a 1906 Dentzel merry-go-round that has been lovingly restored to its original condition, with a hand-carved menangerie of forty-six realistic animals, including pigs, ostriches, cats and horses. A major outlet mall is also in Burlington, with over 100 stores and services offering bargain and off-prices.

The major city in the Southern portion of the Foothills region is **Charlotte**, which is the largest city in the state with an impressive skyline, but with a hospitality not in keeping with a traditional large city.

The Charlotte Motor Speedway boasts the second-largest live audience in the nation during their thrilling "World 660 "Race, as well as five NASCAR races. Charlotte's National Basketball League franchise, the Charlotte "Hornets", play to packed houses all season long.

The first branch of the United States Mint outside of Washington was established in Charlotte in the early 1800s, to handle all the gold that was being discovered in the nearby Reed Gold Mine. The state's largest museum of science and technology, "Discovery Place", is also located in Charlotte.

Near **Harrisburg**, the "Memory Lane Museum" is dedicated to the 1950s, with everything from antique autos, classic and "muscle" cars, and an authentic "Wurlitzer" jukebox. The Peterson Doll & Miniature Museum in High Point curates the South's largest collection of dolls, with nearly 100, some dating back as far as the 15th century.

Architect Dan Maples transformed a Pinehurst quarry into a spectacular golf course aptly named "The Pit". Here a unique golf experience awaits golfers looking for a different challenge.

HOLLY INN
The Past, Gracefully Recaptured.

Amid the majestic loblolly pines of North Carolina's Sandhills region, sits a charming New England-style village built before the turn of the century by wealthy Bostonian James Tufts.

Tufts brought famed architect Law Olmsted to design the small resort village, and recruited Scotsman Donald Ross to design the now famous golf courses.

At the heart of the new village, in 1895, Tufts built the Holly Inn, a five-storey country inn, resembling the ones he had long enjoyed on Cape Cod. For over 90 years celebrities, presidents, sports & golfing legends, and many other guests from around the world have travelled to Pinehurst to enjoy the graceful style and restful hospitality of the Holly Inn.

Today, completely restored and placed on the National Register of Historic Sites, the Holly Inn is still operated with a dedication to service reminiscent of days gone by.

The Holly Inn is pleases to announce the availability of golf packages at many of the Pinehurst area's finest golf courses, including but not limited to:

✦ **The Pit**   ✦ **Longleaf**
✦ **Pinewild Country Club**
✦ **Talamore**   ✦ **The Legacy**

all within a few minutes drive of the Inn.

For more Information or Reservations contact your Travel Agent, or call:

1-800-682-6901
(in North Carolina)

1-800-533-0041
(outside North Carolina)
Cherokee Road, Box 2300, Pinehurst, NC 28374

*Old Salem, in **Winston-Salem**, is an 18th century Moravian congregational town founded in 1766, with a treasury of well-kept old buildings, many restored and opened as exhibits. Most buildings in town have been in continuous use since the 1700s. The Stroh Brewery, also in Winston-Salem, is the largest plant under one roof in North Carolina, brewing over four million barrels of beer annually.*

*The Southern Foothills area is tobacco country, and **Concord**, outside Charlotte, is home to the Phillip Morris USA Cabarrus Manufacturing Center, a 1.8 million square foot plant with tours available to see how cigarettes are made. The Hanging Rock State Park, also in the area, is a 5862-acre tract featuring Hanging Rock, a jutting outcropping of rough granite.*

McAdenville is North Carolina's "Christmas Town", where each December more than 200 trees are strung with thousands of brightly-colored light. Nearby, the Belmont Abbey Cathedral is part of a Benedictine Monastery and was once the only Abbey Cathedral in the United States. The bricks used to construct the Gothic-style cathedral were baked by the monks from Gaston County clay found on the site during its construction between 1891 and 1894.

*Coming out of the Foothills and into the lush, green fields of the Heartland Area, you will find some of the oldest and most prestigious golf in the world. The **Pinehurst-Southern Pines** area courses have hosted royalty, celebrities and the privileged few since 1898, after James Walker Tufts fueled the Pinehurst legend. Tufts, a philanthropist from Boston, came to the area and envisioned a resort community which would take*

BEACON RIDGE COUNTRY CLUB

WEST END, NC (On Longleaf Drive)
Telephone: (919)673-2950

Head Pro: Tony Thacker   Architect: Gene Hamm

18 Holes   Par 72   6511 yds.   Rating: 70.6

Trees, sand, water and distance combine to test the skills of
the most seasoned players while club players are still offered a
fair and delightful opportunity to capitalize on well-struck golf shots.

$$	Resort	Golf Pkgs.	Public	Power Carts	Lessons	Lounge	Snack Bar	Meals	Open All Year

The Area's Premier Public Golf Club

LEGACY GOLF LINKS

ABERDEEN, NC (On US Hwy. 15-501 S., off Us #1 S.)
Telephone: (919)944-8825   Fax: (919)944-9416

Owner: Club Development Associates   Head Pro: Danny Barrett
Course Supt.: Peter Dejak   Architect: Jack Nicklaus II

18 Holes   Par 72   6477 yds.

Golden Bear design. Fully appointed clubhouse, golf shop, club
and shoe valet service, day lockers. Legacy's level of maintenance
is consistant with the most prestigious private clubs in the area.

$$$	Resort	Golf Pkgs.	Public	Power Carts	Lessons	Lounge	Snack Bar	Meals	Open All Year

advantage of the warm climate and soft landscape. He employed Frederick Law Olmsted, the architectural firm responsible for the construction of Central Park in New York City, and in seven months the Pinehurst Village stood among the slender pines and rolling sandhills of North Carolina.

Golf at Pinehurst began in 1897, when a local dairyman complained to Tufts that a guest at the hotel had been hitting a little white ball around and often hitting the dairyman's cows. A year later, Tufts saw to it that Pinehurst had its own nine-hole golf course.

Donald Ross was commissioned by James Tufts to organize the golf at Pinehurst, which effectively launched Ross' 48 year, 600-course design and maintenance career in the United States. Donald Ross spent the rest of his life in Pinehurst and built the first four Pinehurst courses. In 1961, Ellis Maples added a fifth course, with all courses designed to begin and end at the club house, which has today become the Pinehurst Country Club.

DEERCROFT GOLF & COUNTRY CLUB

WAGRAM, NC (Hwy. 15 - 501, 18 miles south of Pinehurst)
Clubhouse: (919)369-0111   Pro Shop: (919)369-3107

Manager: John Landrum   Head Pro: Kelly Allard - PGA
Course Supt.: Mark McInnin - GSA   Architect: Gardner Girley

18 Holes   Par 72   6200 yds.

Host of two PGA Qualifiers, Senior Tour Qualifier, and
voted in the top fifty golf courses in North Carolina 4 years running.

$$$	Resort	Golf Pkgs.	Public	Power Carts	Lessons	Lounge	Snack Bar	Meals	Open All Year

FOXFIRE RESORT & COUNTRY CLUB

PINEHURST, NC. (On Hoffman Rd.)
Telephone: (919)295-4563

Head Pro: Tom Graber   Architect: Gene Hamm

East Course: 18 Holes   Par 72   6851 yds.
                    Rating: Men's - 72.4, Ladies' - 70.3
West Course: 18 Holes   Par 72   6741 yds.
                    Rating: Men's - 72.4, Ladies' - 70.3

$$	Resort	Golf Pkgs.	Public	Power Carts	Lessons	Lounge	Snack Bar	Meals	Open All Year

THE MAGNOLIA INN

Established 1896

Step back into the 1890's with us.

"Finest dining in Pinehurst."
GOLF DIGEST

SPECIALTY GOLF PACKAGES

3 DAYS / 2 NIGHTS INCLUDES BREAKFAST & DINNER

from **$196.00** (Off-Season)
per person / double occ.

from **$300.00** (In-Season)
per person / double occ.

Includes rounds of golf at Pinehurst Country Club's #1, #3, #4, #5 and #6 golf courses equivalent to the number of nights stay at the inn. Normal Pinehurst Country Club surcharges to play #2 and #7 golf courses will be added.

- or -

from **$160.00** (Off-Season)
per person / double occ.

from **$240.00** (In-Season)
per person / double occ.

Includes rounds of golf equivalent to the number of nights stay at the Inn, at any of the following courses: The Pit, Long Leaf, Foxfire, Deercroft, Legacy, Talamore, Mid-Pines, Southern Pines C. C., Whispering Pines C. C., Seven Lakes C. C., Woodlake C. C., and Whispering Woods.

♦ ♦ ♦

' Let us assist you in arranging your Pinehurst Golfing Holiday. One call to our Toll Free Number and your only chore from that point on will be to get to the practice tee prior to your starting time.'

Ned & Jan Darby
(Owners/Innkeepers)

For Reservations & Information Call:
(919)295-6900 or Toll Free: 1-800-526-5562

Corner of Magnolia & Chinquapin
P.O. Box 818, Pinehurst, North Carolina 28374

THE TALAMORE LLAMA EXPERIENCE

The centuries-old tradition of using llamas to help humans carry packs has been expanded to the sport and pleasure of golf. These gentle, hardy animals can carry two bags of clubs with ease and sure-footedness. Their soft padded feet are kind to the delicate surfaces of a golf course. Known for their friendly and quiet manners, llamas make the perfect caddy. They carry the bags and complain not about the weight nor the golfers swing.

Talamore's internationally publicized Llama caddies are the only known llamas in use on a golf course east of Denver, Colorado. They were purchased from Lars A. Garrison of Stamford, Vermont, and are of Bolivian origin & fourth and fifth generation American breeding.

They have been featured in more than 170 ASSOCIATED PRESS newspapers. USA TODAY, and STARS & STRIPES in Europe; CNN and HEADLINE NEWS in the U.S. , and overseas in Melbourne, Australia and in Europe; on local TV stations throughout the U.S.; on radio talk shows in 14 cities in the U.S. and in Melbourne; GOLF DIGEST, GOLF SPORTS in Germany, DISNEY, TIME and DIVERSION magazines.

GENERAL LLAMA FACTS

- Llamas make excellent pets and are excellent wool producers.
- They can carry up to one-quarter their weight and can be trained to pull a cart.
- They are easy to raise and can be handled by almost anyone. One acre is enough to raise 3 or 4
- They are ruminant, like cows, goats & sheep, and browse or eat hay and get an additional pound of low protein grain per day. THEY LOVE FRESH GRASS & WEEDS.
- They are classified as farm animals and their droppings are almost odorless and make excellent fertilizer they can be trained to go in designated areas.
- They are members of the camel family: live 15 to 20 years: and weight 250 to 450 pounds. They are very quiet and communicate by making small humming sounds.
- Tales of spitting are true, but the act is normally limited toward other llamas
- Llamas are adaptable to most climates: and there are about 40,000 in the United States

THE DELUXE LLAMA CADDY PACKAGE

includes
a complimentary shirt and hat, the Llama assistant
who helps with the yardage and club selection.

The cost is $100.00 per player
(plus the appropriate green fee)

For the LLAMA Experience call:

800-LLAMA-92
- TALAMORE GOLF AND TRAVEL -

THE PINEHURST AREA

❏ *Travel Arrangements*
❏ *Accommodations*
❏ *Tee Times*
❏ *Meeting Facilities*
❏ *Golf Schools*

Custom Golf Packages to the World's Golf Capital. Enjoy world-class golf on dozens of courses designed by some of America's top golf course architects.

TALAMORE
GOLF & TRAVEL

Call to make your plans or for a free color brochure.

1-800-552-6292

TALAMORE
AT · PINEHURST

TALAMORE AT PINEHURST

SOUTHERN PINES, NC (On Midland Rd.)
Telephone: (919)692-5884   Fax: (919)692-4421

Gen. Mgr: John Musto   Head Pro: John McDougald
Course Supt.: Chandler Masters   Architect: Rees Jones

18 Holes   Par 71   6720 / 6293 / 5748 / 4903 yds.
          Rating: 72.9 / 70.8 / 67.9 / 69.0   Slope: 142 /134 /126 /125

GOLF WEEK named Talamore as one of the top 50 courses in North Carolina.
GOLF DIGEST named Talamore the best new public golf course in the South.

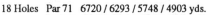

$$$		Golf Pkgs.	Public	Power Carts	Lessons		Snack Bar		Open All Year

A quiet, comfortable room, special VIP treatment, fine dining and entertainment, and access to Pinehurst area's many fine public courses are yours when you select the Days Inn. Located on U.S. 1 South in Southern Pines.

Golf Packages Include:
☆ Lodging ☆ Daily Green Fees
☆ Daily Full Breakfast and 1 Dinner Per Person
☆ Taxes and Gratuities

Guest Services Include:
Color cable TV with HBO and ESPN, poolside bar / terrace, swimming pool, Dining in Brandy's Restaurant and Gathering Place, live entertainment in J. Albert's Lounge

(919)692-7581 • 1-800-325-2525
1420 U.S. Highway. 1 South, Southern Pines, North Carolina 28387

WHISPERING WOODS GOLF CLUB

WHISPERING PINES, NC (On Cardinal Circle, off Airport Rd)
Telephone: (919)949-4653

Manager: Tommy Albin   Head Pro: James Maples - PGA
Course Supt.: Mark Sellars   Architect: Ellis Maples

18 Holes   Par 70   5111 / 6144 / 6177 yds.

Home of the"ELLIS MAPLES CUP". With varying
degrees of elevation changes this course is a challenge to all golfers.

$$	Resort	Golf Pkgs.	Public	Power Carts	Lessons	Lounge	Snack Bar	Meals	Open All Year

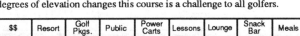

PALOMINO MOTEL

OFFERING YEAR-ROUND GOLF PACKAGES

"Over 15 Years of Experience Booking Golf Packages"

GOLF:
- 20 golf courses located in Pinehurst / Sandhills area
- All tee times booked in advance
- Only minutes away from driving range and putting green at Quail Ridge Golf Course

LODGING:
- Spacious town homes overlooking Quail Ridge Golf Course
- 92 new and remodeled rooms spread over 17 acres
- Satellite TV, direct dial telephones and individual temperature controls

RECREATION:
- Hospitality suite featuring big screen TV and wet bar
- Fully computerized indoor golf simulator playing at Pinehurst #2
- Fitness center, sauna, spa and outdoor swimming pool
- Fishing lake and picnic area

"Come and Experience Southern Hospitality at its Finest"

1-800-641-6060
24 HOUR RESERVATION LINE

P.O. Box #777, US I-15 - 501 Bypass South, Sanford, N C 27331-0777

QUAIL RIDGE GOLF COURSE

SANFORD, NC (On US 1, just past US 15 - 501 exit)
Clubhouse: 1-800-344-6276   Pro Shop: (919)776-6623

Owners: Bill & Jim Parrish   Architect: Ellis Maples

18 Holes   Par 72   6300 yds.

Longleaf Pines set off the rolling fairways and offer a
beautiful backdrop to the Bent Grass greens and Bermuda fairways.

$$		Golf Pkgs.	Public	Power Carts	Lessons	Lounge	Snack Bar	Meals	Open All Year

Pinehurst's famed "No.2" course quickly became the course of choice to discriminating golfers, and the resort blossomed as the sport and relaxation center of the East Coast. Today, Pinehurst and all it area courses thrive with the growing popularity of golf holidays, as well as the emergence of many luxury lifestyle properties and neighborhoods around the courses.

The PGA/World Golf Hall of Fame is located in Pinehurst, which holds momentos such as clubs from golfing heads of state, portraits of those inducted into the "Golfing Hall of Fame", and a collection of antique clubs which date back to the 1600s.

Pinehurst's climate averages a minimum of 51 °F between March and November, with an average of 267 sunny to partly-sunny days during the year, making it one of the most ideal places to play and stay. And with over two dozen golf courses within 20 miles of the Pinehurst/Southern Pines area, you could stay forever and always find something new.

Fayetteville Has Everything From The Green Berets To Putting Greens.

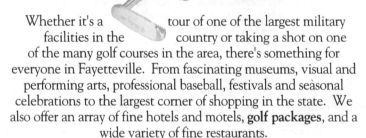

Whether it's a tour of one of the largest military facilities in the country or taking a shot on one of the many golf courses in the area, there's something for everyone in Fayetteville. From fascinating museums, visual and performing arts, professional baseball, festivals and seasonal celebrations to the largest corner of shopping in the state. We also offer an array of fine hotels and motels, **golf packages**, and a wide variety of fine restaurants.

Spend some time in Fayetteville on your next vacation...after all, the fun's always greener on our side.

FAYETTEVILLE AREA CONVENTION AND VISITORS BUREAU
Call or write and get "the real story" on vacationing in Fayetteville.
515 Ramsey Street, Fayetteville, NC 28301, (919) 483-5311 or tToll Free: 1-800-255-8217

Of the more than forty towns, cities, villages and counties in the United States named after the Marquis de Lafayette, a hero of the American Revolutionary War, *Fayetteville*, North Carolina is the only one he ever visited.

The Marquis was a Frenchman who came to Fayetteville in 1825, and the local settlers, descendants of Highland Scots who had populated the lush Cape Fear Riverbanks showed him the sights. In 1865, Union General William Sherman and the Union Army considered levelling Fayetteville, but instead only destroyed a Confederate arsenal and the local newspaper office.

In 1914, the young George Herman Ruth came to Fayetteville, and hit his first professional home run while playing for a minor league baseball team. His fans in Fayetteville nicknamed him "Babe of the Woods", which was eventually shortened to "Babe" Ruth.

In 1918, a military base was commissioned near Fayetteville, and after first housing only 5,000 men, grew during the Second World War to almost 100,000. Fort Bragg, and neighbor Pope Air Force Base, are today one of the largest military complexes in the world. The base is an attraction which draws everyone from war heroes to Presidents.

Anybody visiting Fayetteville is encouraged to visit the Fayetteville Area Convention and Visitors Bureau, who have mapped out several self-guided and organized tours that are custom-tailored for anyone's interest. Trips to areas of historical significance within the Fayetteville limits, and those within an hour's drive have been included.

Fayetteville went through a renaissance in the 1980s, with much of the spotlight placed on historical and cultural heritage and preservation. Both the population and the business base have grown considerably within the past decade, and the city of Fayetteville in strongly and eagerly encouraging continued growth.

Fort Bragg and the Pope Air Force Base have had arguably the biggest impact on the area, bringing in more than $3 billion annually to the city's economy, and becoming the single largest employer in both Fayetteville and Cumberland County. The population of the base on any given day exceeds 130,000 men, women and children, (families of the Armed Forces personnel). There are more than 300 miles of roads throughout the bases, covering over 200 square miles. Most roads are open to the public, and visitors are invited to take a self-guided tour with 15 stops through Fort Bragg. Pope Air Force Base is usually closed to the public for security reasons. A tour of the base can be arranged with permission from the Air Force PAO Office, or the Fayetteville CVB.

Fort Bragg has several of the most elite military units on its grounds, including the 18th Airborne Corps, the 82nd Airborne Division, the Special Forces, (known as the Green Berets), and the Rapid Deployment Command. Pope is home to the 317th Tactical Airlift Wing and its fleet of C-130 Hercules transport planes, which carry troops, supplies and equipment wherever they're needed. It is also apparently true that the mega-top-secret, hush-hush "Delta Force" anti-terrorist squad is located at Bragg, but nobody will confirm or deny its existence.

STAY-N-PLAY at the
BEST in FAYETTEVILLE

GOLF PACKAGES INCLUDE:
- Deluxe overnight accommodations. Each room features in-room coffee service, remote control color television with free HBO, CNN, & ESPN, AM/FM clock radio and seperate seating area.
- Continental breakfast in our full service restaurant
- Daily green and cart fees for 18 holes • Preferred tee times
- Courtyard with Gazebo and outdoor pool
- Indoor whirlpool and exercise room • Cozy lounge

PARTICIPATING COURSES:

COURSE	ARCHITECT	YARDS	GREENS	MILES FROM HOTEL
Baywood	S. Gooden	6763	Bent	15
Carolina Lakes	R. Ruleorwitz	6377	Bent	17
Cypress Lakes	L.B. Floyd	7240	Bent	15
*Deercroft	G. Didley	6745	Bent	35
Gates Four C.C.	W. Byrd	7011	Bent	10
Keith Hills C.C.	E. Maples	6660	Bermuda	30
King's Grant	J. Holmes	6750	Bent	9
Lakewood C.C.	R.T. Burney	6708	Bent	33
*Legacy Golf Links	J. Nicklaus II	6989	Bent	31
Pirates Ridge	H. Stegal	6000	Bermuda	13
*The Pit	D. Maples	6600	Bent	37
*Woodlake C.C.	E. & D. Maples	7045	Bent	25

* Surcharge at these courses

COURTYARD by Marriott
is easily accessible from major Interstates and is located adjacent to outlet malls, restaurants and movie theaters.

CALL OUR SALES DEPARTMENT
FOR RESERVATIONS

(919)487-5557

4192 Sycamore Dairy Road, Fayetteville, North Carolina 28303

The John F. Kennedy Special Warfare Museum at Fort Bragg contains examples of unconventional weapons, from punji stakes from Vietnam, to German and Japanese armaments and Soviet rocket launchers. Across the street is the First Special Operations Command and the Hall of Heroes, where Special Forces exhibits and unit awards are on display. A monument presented by John Wayne to the Special Forces for their help during the filming of "The Green Beret", stands nearby on the grounds of the JFK Chapel. Parts of that film were shot on location at Fort Bragg.

The 82nd Airborne Division Museum houses more than 3,000 artifacts, including weapons, grenades, uniforms, helmets, gliders, planes and parachutes, and a popular attraction is the Golden Knights parachute team. They perform almost daily, 300 times per year, free-falling to Earth in death-defying aerobatics. The Golden Knights have received more awards than any other parachute team in history.

The Pope Air Force Base allows visitors to drive alongside an airstrip to get a close-up look at some massive planes, like the C-130, the C-141 and occasionally the 6-storey C-5A, the world's largest plane. Takeoffs and landings are going on all the time at the base, which also houses a $17 million flight simulator.

The city of Fayetteville has fifty-nine structures listed on the National Register of Historic Places, one of them being the Market House, located in the heart of downtown. Called "the most photographed building in the Carolinas", the Market House was built in 1832 and was spared from destruction by General Sherman in 1865, because it is said he admired it's unique Spanish-Moorish design.

KING'S GRANT GOLF & COUNTRY CLUB

FAYETTEVILLE, NC (On Hwy. 401 N., 1/2 mi. past Methodist College on the left.)
Direct Tee Times: (919)630-1114   Fax: (919)630-2122

General Manager: John M. Rose, Jr.   Head Pro: Robert Wilson
Course Supt.: Peter Horn   Architect: Jim Holmes

18 Holes   Par 72   5863 yds.

Not overpowering in distance, but accuracy is important. A shot maker's course with water on holes 10 to 18. Varying elevation and terrain with bent grass greens.

$$$		Golf Pkgs.	Public	Power Carts	Lessons		Snack Bar		Open All Year
		✓	✓	✓	✓		✓		✓

KEITH HILLS COUNTRY CLUB

BUIES CREEK, NC. (I-95 S. to Hwy 421, 10 Mi. W. to Buies Creek)
Telephone: (919)893-5051

Manager: Cad Upchurch   Course Supt.: John Williams
Architect: Ellis Maples

18 Holes   Par 72   6600 yds.

Keith Hills is consistently rated in North Carolina's top 30 golf courses.

$$		Golf Pkgs.	Public	Power Carts			Snack Bar		Open All Year

*For fans of Civil War history, Fayetteville and the area surrounding it is a great place to visit. The last major Confederate offensive, an attempt to stop Sherman from meeting up with General Grant in Virginia, was fought at the Bentonville Battlefield near Newton Grove in March, 1865. Averasboro Battleground, situated between **Wade** and **Erwin** outside Fayetteville, was a gory battle with casualties rivalling Gettysburg. Farmers are still discovering artifacts when plowing their fields nearby.*

Fayetteville has become known quite extensively for its exquisite golf. More than 40 courses are scattered within a 40-mile radius of the city, and it was in Fayetteville in 1728 that the country's first golf ball was hit, by a Scotsman named Alex MacGrain. Golf is a year-round attraction in Fayetteville because of the temperate climate and well-kept fairways. Accommodations in the area gear themselves ideally to golf, with most offering packages with local courses.

GOLF & COUNTRY CLUB

GATES FOUR GOLF & COUNTRY CLUB

FAYETTEVILLE, NC (Off Hwy. 59 north from I-95 exit 41)
Clubhouse: (919)425-2178   Pro Shop: (919)425-2176

Owner: J. P. Riddle   Manager: Miriam Roberts
Head Pro: Alan Billings - PGA   Course Supt.: Rick Greenwade

18 Holes   Par 72   6544 yds.

Built in 1967 by Willard Bird, this championship course is a
magnificent setting of gentle rolling fairways with large bent grass greens.

$$		Golf Pkgs.	Public	Power Carts	Lessons	Lounge	Snack Bar	Meals	Open All Year	

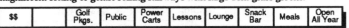

The Challenge of Golf ...Not **Your Budget**

The golfer's perfect situation; pit your skills against challenging greens right in *Holiday Inn Bordeaux's* backyard. Your Package is complete with green fees & cart for 18 holes. To get your day stared right, we've included a complete breakfast, and there's more. You get the best of nine championship courses, plus comfortable accommodations central to shopping and all major attractions.

Kings Grant Golf & C.C.	18 Holes	6200 yds.	Par 72
Baywood Golf Course	18 Holes	6800 yds.	Par 72
Cypress Lakes	18 Holes	7240 yds.	Par 72
Gates Four Golf & C.C.	18 Holes	7011 yds.	Par 72
Keith Hills C.C.	18 Holes	6660 yds.	Par 72
Carolina Lakes	18 Holes	6400 yds.	Par 70
Scothurst C.C.	18 Holes	7000 yds.	Par 72
Wood Lake C.C.	18 Holes	7003 yds.	Par 72
Pine Burr Golf Course	18 Holes	6100 yds.	Par 72

$80.00*

2 Days of Golf / 1 Night Stay
* (per person / double occupancy)

✦ easy access to all golf courses ✦ preferred tee times
✦ daily green fees and cart for 18 holes ✦ full breakfast
✦ full service hotel with: *Wellington's Fine Dining, Cafe Bordeaux, Bowties Night Club, Sportz Cue and Spirits,* outdoor pool, close to Cross Creek Mall and other shopping, close to Fort Bragg and Pope Airforce Base

1-800-325-0211

Tel: (919) 323-0111   Fax: (919) 484-9444

1707 Owen Drive, Fayetteville, North Carolina 28304

Radisson
PRINCE CHARLES HOTEL FAYETTEVILLE

450 Hay Street, Fayetteville North Carolina 28301

(919)433-4444 • 1-800-333-3333

Tee up with the Prince and play courses designed by the royalty of golf... Floyd, Maples, Nicklaus.

Every foursome should experience our Royal Golf Package and unwind in a hotel that reflects the tradition of the masters.

GOLF PACKAGES

, • Store your bags in a two-room suite with wet bar, refrigerator, ice maker, and coffee maker
• Swing into action with a complimentary deluxe breakfast
• Daily green and cart fees for 18 holes
• Preferred tee times
• Follow through with a complimentary Health Club visit
• Score a birdie in Chloe's, our full service restaurant
• Putt out in Babe's Lounge with a complimentary drink of your choice

HISTORIC HOTELS *of* AMERICA

National Trust for Historic Preservation

RODEWAY INN

FABULOUS CAROLINA SANDHILLS GOLF AVAILABLE AT ECONOMICAL RATES.

Package Includes:

✦ Green Fees ✦ 18 Holes per day Electric Cart Fee (single rider surcharge payable at golf course) ✦ Deluxe Double Occupancy Accommodations ✦ Remote Control TV, Cable, HBO, ESPN, CNN ✦ Outdoor Pool ✦ Free Local Calls ✦ Ground Floor Rooms

Prime Time Restaurant & Lounge on property

For availability, rates and reservations call:

(919)485-51161

2507 Gillespie Street, Fayetteville, North Carolina 28306

FAYETTEVILLE'S ORIGINAL GOLF PACKAGE

Fabulous Carolina golf and warm Southern hospitality will ensure you of a pleasant, relaxing golf holiday at the Quality Inn Ambassador or the Econo Lodge I-95. It is pure golfers delight on superb courses designed in championship tradition combined with year-round moderate climate of the Sandhills.

HERE'S WHAT YOU GET:
- Unlimited golf on any of the 12 championship courses including Cypress Lakes
- 18 Holes per day electric cart fee
- Preferred starting times
- A full hot breakfast
- Deluxe double occupancy accommodations including HBO, ESPN & CNN.
- Non-Golfer per person $26.73
- All Rates Based on Per Person Double Occupancy
- Rates Include Tax
- No Discounts Applicable
- No Rain Checks
- Unlimited Golf on One Course Per Day

Golf	Nights	Breakfast	Total
1	1	1	$53.55
2	2	2	$107.10
3	2	2	$133.91
3	3	3	$160.64
4	3	3	$187.46
4	4	4	$214.19
5	4	4	$241.01
5	5	5	$267.75

'1990 ECONO LODGE OF THE YEAR'
'1992 GOLD HOSPITALITY AWARD'
I-95 EXIT 49
P.O. Box 65177
Fayetteville, NC 28306
(919) 433-2009 - FAX

AMBASSADOR
I-95 BUS & 301 S
P.O. Box 64166
Fayetteville, NC 28306
(919) 485-8682 - FAX

cypress lakes
GOLFCOURSE
"HOME OF THE FLOYDS"

We offer a unique golfing
and lifestyle experience for those
who value privacy and unspoiled natural beauty

1-800-446-0650
CALL FOR RESERVATIONS

THE QUALITY CHOICE

Fayetteville is in the heart of Southern hospitality, and more than 100 festivals, fairs and events take place which have helped make Fayetteville's warmth and good nature a welcome destination, and have earned it the nickname, "Festiville".

Some of the most popular events include the Dogwood Festival, a 10-day celebration culminating with the Fort Bragg/Pope Air Force Base Open House, which attracts nearly 100,000 people annually. Sunday-on-the-Square, another popular festival, is held the first Sunday in May and attracts nearly 20,000 people with live entertainment, craftspeople and dancing, as well as much more.

CYPRESS LAKES GOLF COURSE

HOPE MILLS, NC. (Off I-95 Exit 41, follow signs)
Telephone: (919)483-0359   Fax: (919)483-2542

Owner: Al Prewitt   Manager: Tom Prewitt
Head Pro: Ken Robertson - PGA   Course Supt.: Arden Smith
Architect: L.B. Floyd

18 Holes   Par 72   6640 yds.

Home of the "Floyds".... Ray Floyd - 1986 US Open Champ, sister Marlene - Touring Pro, and dad L.B. Cypress Lakes has earned its right as one of the region's finest courses, with lush Bermuda fairways and bent grass greens.

$$		Golf Pkgs.	Public	Power Carts	Lessons	Lounge	Snack Bar	Meals	Open All Year

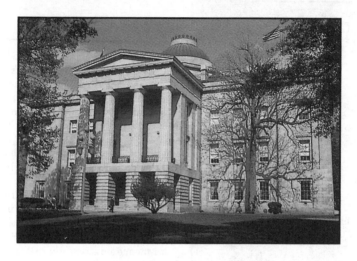

Raleigh has been the state capital since 1788, and his home to the North Carolina Museum of History, the Museum of Natural Sciences and the State Legislative and Capitol buildings. The State Legislative Building is a five-domed marble structure that occupies an entire city block and is the only state building in the country devoted entirely to the Legislative branch of government. The State Capitol is a Greek Revival building which was completed in 1840, and the Capital Area Visitors Bureau is located next door.

Historic **Oakwood** is street after street of turret towers, gabled roofs and columned porches, and is thought to be one of the nation's finest examples of Victorian architecture. Christ Episcopal Church, constructed in 1848, is considered one of the most notable Greek Revival buildings in the South.

North of Oakwood is **Mordecai Park**, where you can see the birthplace of former President Andrew Johnson, as well as the Iredell-Badger Law Office which was established in 1810, an authentic 1842 working kitchen, and the Mordecai House, a Greek Revival building which has been home to five generations of the same family.

Northwest of Raleigh, in nearby **Durham** *is the first public university in the nation, the University of North Carolina, which is over 200 years old. Duke University is also in Durham, which is one of the most prestigious and beautiful institutions in the United States. Duke Chapel is a Gothic structure patterned after England's Canterbury Cathedral, with a carillon, 210-foot Bell Tower, and Flentrop organ.* **Hillsborough**, *near Durham, was the State Capital during the Revolutionary War.*

Hamlet was once a major hub of the railroad, with forty-two trains stopping there daily at it's peak point. The Hamlet-Wilmington rail line is the longest straight stretch of track in the United States.

In *Laurinburg*, the Indian Museum of the Carolinas emphasizes the art, archaeology and anthropology of Native Americans, and houses one of the largest libraries of Native books in the Native American Library.

Kenley is home to the Tobacco Museum of North Carolina, with tobacco equipment, a video presentation and, in summer months, a tour of a working tobacco farm. In *Brogden*, the town marks the birthplace of actress Ava Gardner with the Ava Gardner Museum, which has the world's largest collection of memorabilia from her forty films and her life.

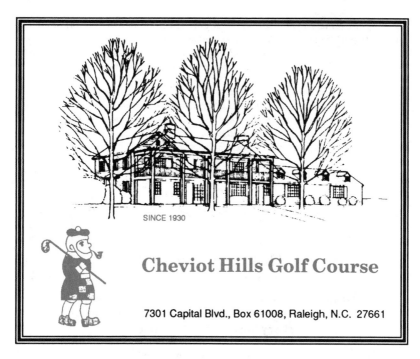
CHEVIOT HILLS GOLF COURSE

RALEIGH, NC. (On US 1 N. of Raleigh, 1 Mi. N. of Plantation Inn,)
Telephone: (919)876-9920

Owner: Bill Edwards   Head Pro: J. Percy Card
Course Supt.: J. Ray Autry   Architect: Gene Hamm

18 Holes   Par 71   6500 yds.

Interesting, scenic course requiring many different shots over rolling countryside similar to Cheviot Hills in Scotland (after which it was named). Bent grass greens.

$			Public	Power Carts	Lessons		Snack Bar		Open All Year

North Carolina enjoys its position as one of the Atlantic Coastal states, and it's seaside shores take full advantage of their prime location. The Northern Coast stretches down from Virginia, and is sheltered by a long , narrow line of islands that make for a splendid choice of beachfront scenery.

The Wright Brothers took mankind's first powered flight in **Kitty Hawk**, along the Northern Coast, and the Wright Brothers National Memorial is erected in their honor, including a reconstructed hanger and shop similar to the ones used by Wilbur and Orville for their December 17, 1903 flight into the pages of history.

Nags Head Wood is one of the best examples of a mid-Atlantic maritime forest. This national landmark contains 640 acres of protected wetlands, dunes and hardwood forest. **Nags Head** is also home to Rear View Mirror, an automotive entertainment center and museum. There are over 60 antique and classic cars, including one-of-a-kind, prototypes and famous film and television vehicles.

New Bern • North Carolina

DAYS INN NEW BERN GOLF PACKAGES

✦ Double Occupancy Room
　　✦ Continental Breakfast
　　　　✦ Green Fee and Cart Rental

Weekday Rates (Monday -Thursday)
3 Days/3 Nights **$142.00** per person*
4 Days/4 Nights **$179.00** per person*
Weekend Rates **$175.00** per person*
(* Prices subject to change. Does not include 9% N.C. sales tax.)

Your choice of four superb golf courses:
• The Emerald Club (formerly Greenbrier) • Carolina Pines
• Fairfield Harbor • River Bend

New Bern Days Inn is conveniently located near beaches, boating, USMC Cherry Point and Camp LeJeune. Tyron Palace and the Historical Area are only two blocks away. Walking tour is available.

We offer 110 tastefully decorated units, cable TV, swimming pool and feature luxurious dining in our restaurant and lounge "THE FISH MARKET BAR & GRILL" serving excellent seafood, steaks and live Maine lobster.

1-800-325-2525
(Reservations)
(919) 636-0150
(Hotel Direct)

925 BROAD STREET, NEW BERN, NORTH CAROLINA 28560

Across from historic Roanoke Island is the Bodie Island Lighthouse, with black and white bands wrapping around it. The lighthouse is part of the Cape Hatteras National Seashore, the country's first national seashore, which runs for 75 miles down the Outer Banks islands of **Bodie, Hatteras and Ocracoke**, covering a distance of over 30,000 acres.

Nearby **Manteo's** waterfront is home berth for a ship built from a design of the original 16th-century ship that brought colonists to America. The ship is part of the Elizabeth II State Historic Site. Ocracoke was once a base for pirates, such as Edward Teach, better known as Blackbeard, and whose ship was captured nearby. Some say that Blackbeard's famous treasure in still buried nearby.

The barrier islands of the Southern Coast are accessable only by boat, and are not inhabited. The Cape Lookout Light Station, at **Cape Lookout**, was built in 1859 and is still operational. These barrier islands stretch up the coast 58 miles to the Ocracoke Inlet and are part of the National Park System of the Outer Banks.

Beaufort, settled in 1710, was once the state's largest seaport. The town was attacked by pirates in 1747, and was a watering hole for the wealthy. Beaufort's shady, peaceful Old Burying Grounds date back to 1731, and are listed on the National Register of Historic Places.

New Bern was settled in 1710 by Palatine Germans and Swiss. More than 150 landmarks in New Bern are on the National Register of Historic Places. New Bern was once the North Carolina State Capital, and the Tryon Palace Restoration and Garden Complex will take you back to the time when a king ruled the land, and through a revolution that brought the concept of democracy and freedom to the people. Both royal and state governors lived in the Tryon Palace with their families, and conducted official business and entertained, as well.

EMERALD GOLF CLUB, THE

NEW BERN, NC. (Hwy. 70 W. to Glenburnie Rd. exit, L. one block, turn R.)
Telephone: (919)633-4440

Owner/Mgr.: David S. Woodruff
Course Supt.: Jim Lanier

Dir. of Golf: Jerry Briele
Architect: Rees Jones

18 Holes   Par 72   6900 yds.

Voted by *Golf Week Magazine* one of the top 50 development courses in the Southeast. FORMERLY GREENBRIER GOLF CLUB.

$$$	Resort	Golf Pkgs.	Public	Power Carts	Lessons	Lounge	Snack Bar		Open All Year

On his Southern tour in 1791, President George Washington was wined and dined in the Tryon Palace. A restoration project was done to replicate the time of William Tryon, the Governor of North Carolina during the Revolutionary War.

Before the Civil War, North Carolina was the nation's leading producer of wine. America's first cultivated grape, the Muscadine, originated there. Today, the Duplin Wine Cellars in **Rose Hill** make more than 120,000 gallons of wine, including a North Carolina champagne made from a 200-year-old recipe.

The Cape Fear Coast extends along the most southerly of North Carolina's Southern Coast, and is a world of sports, history, island beaches and incredible natural beauty. The historic port of **Wilmington** is home to the New Hanover County Museum, which is dedicated to preserving and analyzing the rich history of the Lower Cape Fear, and contains 400 pieces from the former Blockade Runner Museum.

Wilmington is one of the fastest-growing East Coast deep-water ports, entering the pages of history before the Revolutionary War and was the last Atlantic port open to Blockade Runners during the Civil War. Today, it has one of the largest districts listed in the National Register of Historic Places.

Beau Rivage Plantation

BEAU RIVAGE PLANTATION

WILMINGTON, NC (On. Hwy. #421, 7 Mi. S. of Wilmington)
Telephone: (919)392-9021   Toll Free: 1-800-628-7080

Owners: Eddie & Peggy Lewis   Head Pro: Tom Willock
Course Supt.: David Carriker

18 Holes   Par 72   6166 yds.

Natural rolling hills with bent grass greens and
paved cart paths. Beau Rivage offers on-site deluxe
accommodations with private balcony and a view of the course.

$$	Resort	Golf Pkgs.	Public	Power Carts	Lessons	Lounge	Snack Bar	Meals	Open All Year

PORTERS NECK PLANTATION
AND COUNTRY CLUB

PORTERS NECK PLANTATION & COUNTRY CLUB

WILMINGTON, NC (On Porters Neck Road. 10 Minutes from Wrightsville Beach)
Telephone: (919)686-1177   Sales Info: 1-800-423-5695

President: John A. Elmore II   Head Pro: Matt Peebles - PGA
Course Supt.: Robert Nance III

18 Holes   Par 72   6323 yds.

Designed by *Golf Digest's* #1 designer Tom Fazio,
this course is already being talked about as one of the best in the Carolina's.

$$$		Golf Pkgs.	Public	Power Carts	Lessons	Lounge	Snack Bar	Meals	Open All Year	
$$$		Golf Pkgs.	Public	Power Carts	Lessons	Lounge	Snack Bar	Meals	Open All Year	

Wrightsville Beach is a small island community that is frequented year after year by families who came and enjoyed themselves completely. Wrightsville Beach sports miles of pure white beaches for quiet walks, protected areas for swimming in sparkling water, fishing from the surf, piers for boats, sailing, diving, surfing and water skiing.

Carolina Beach has a fun Boardwalk with water slides and rides, and the Carolina Beach State Park is one of the most biologically diverse parks in North Carolina. This area is part of a small region of the world where the Venus Fly Trap grows naturally.

LOCKWOOD GOLF LINKS

HOLDEN BEACH, NC (Hwy. 17 to Hwy. 130 to Holden Beach, follow the signs)
Telephone: (919)842-5666   US Toll Free: 1-800-443-7891

Owner/Manager: Ernest Hewett
Course Supt.: Chuck Brendlen

Head Pro: Bobby Blackwell - PGA
Architect: Willard C. Byrd

18 Holes   Par 72   6801 yds.

Breathtaking Lockwood Folly River and Intracoastal Waterway views are just part of the reason this course is counted among the most scenic on the coast. Tree-lined, nonparallel fairways afford a sense of seclusion and openness.

$$$	Resort	Golf Pkgs.	Public	Power Carts	Lessons	Lounge	Snack Bar	Meals	Open All Year

THE CAPE GOLF & RACQUET CLUB

WILMINGTON, NC (On Hwy. 421 S., 8 Mi. S. of Wilmington)
Telephone: (919)799-3110   Fax: (919)791-2534

Owner: Thomas Wright   Manager/Head Pro: Margaret Freeman - LPGA
Course Supt.: Randy Edwards   Architect: Gene Hamm

18 Holes   Par 72   6200 yds.

Features a double green on holes 15 & 17. Bermuda greens and
fairways highlighted by twenty four lakes, ponds, and salt water marshes.

$$$	Resort	Golf Pkgs.	Public	Power Carts	Lessons	Lounge	Snack Bar	Meals	Open All Year

ACCEPT THE CHALLENGE!

P.B. Dye Has Laid Down The Gauntlet...

Eighteen holes of exhilerating play along the Intracoastal Waterway at St. James Plantation in Southport North Carolina.

Dye routed this course through marshes and forests leaving behind a collection of pot bunkers, bulkheads, multi-level fairways and greens. Making par on some of these holes would be just cause for a...Medieval celebration.

The Gauntlet

THE GAUNTLET GOLF & COUNTRY CLUB

SOUTHPORT, NC (20 minutes N. of Myrtle Beach on Hwy. 211)
Telephone: (919)253-3008   or: 1-800-247-4806

Architect: P.B. Dye

18 Holes   Par 72   6489 yds.

The Gauntlet features all the trademarks
that have made Dye courses so famous. Private club
service including caddies and club cleaning at daily fee prices.

$$$		Golf Pkgs.	Public	Power Carts	Lessons	Lounge	Snack Bar	Meals	Open All Year	

OAK ISLAND GOLF & COUNTRY CLUB
LONG BEACH, NC. (I-95 and I-40 to 17 S. to 133, 1/2 Mi. to Club entrance)
Telephone: (919)278-5275

General Manager: Tom Elder   Head Pro: Tom Elder
Course Supt.: Bill Lewis   Architect: George Cobb

18 Holes   Par 72   6608 yds.

This championship golf course is located steps away from the Atlantic Ocean.
It ambles through live and water oaks. The ocean breeze is a constant factor.

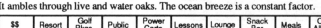

$$	Resort	Golf Pkgs.	Public	Power Carts	Lessons	Lounge	Snack Bar	Meals	Open All Year

Bald Head Island is like visiting a sub-tropical island, with the tallest building being Old Baldy, North Carolina's oldest lighthouse, built in 1817 and made from hand-hewn stone. Over 180 species of birds have discovered this island, and there are 800 acres of maritime forest, as well as the largest expanse of salt marsh and tidal creek in the state, and a dune ridge that rises as high as 55 feet above sea level, and 14 miles of wide, beautiful and uncrowded beaches.

*Historical **Southport By The Sea** is a quaint fishing village built in 1754, where you'll find a "whittlers' bench" on the waterfront, where fishermen still go to swap tales.*

North Carolina can be considered the first of the true "Southern" states one would reach from the north, and is plum with traditional Southern hospitality and a welcoming warmth that lasts the whole visit. Golfers flock to the state for its ideal playing weather nearly year round, and to the vibrant history of golf in North Carolina. There really seems no better time to experience this golfers' paradise than now, so take advantage of the terrific play-and-stay packages and get ready to see why North Carolina is really "Golf State, U.S.A."

ALPHABETICAL INDEX
BY FACILITY

INDEX

INDEX

ALPHABETICAL INDEX
BY STATE / PROVINCE & CITY